APOLLINARIANISM

APOLLINARIANISM

AN ESSAY ON THE CHRISTOLOGY OF THE EARLY CHURCH

BY

CHARLES E. RAVEN, D.D.

Sometime Fellow and Lecturer in Theology
Emmanuel College, Cambridge

Wipf & Stock
PUBLISHERS
Eugene, Oregon

Wipf and Stock Publishers
199 W 8th Ave, Suite 3
Eugene, OR 97401

Apollinarianism
An Essay on the Christology of the Early Church
By Raven, Charles E.

ISBN: 1-59244-955-7
Publication date 10/18/2004
Previously published by Cambridge University Press, 1923

TO

MY WIFE

PREFACE

"APOLLINARIANISM is the prevalent heresy of to-day: why don't you make a study of it?" That advice given to me by one of the most revered of my teachers fifteen years ago fixed my desire to investigate the teaching of the great Greek heresiarch; and a year later I submitted a thesis upon him for a Cambridge Fellowship. Professor Gwatkin whose learning, enthusiasm and generosity were an inspiration and remain an ver-honoured memory to generations of students, encouraged me to continue the subject; and it has occupied much of my time since those days. The war prevented the completion of the work, and the long interruption has compelled me to revise the whole material and re-examine the conclusions that I had formed.

Those conclusions will certainly be regarded by orthodox critics as dictated by "modernist" prejudice. In view of this it is well to state plainly that when the task was begun I was myself an Apollinarian in the sense that I accepted belief in the impersonal humanity of our Lord. It was only as the investigation continued that the evidence forced me to the conviction that Apollinarianism both in its ancient and its modern form was untenable and the acceptance of Professor Bethune-Baker's verdict that "Paul of Samosata had behind him a genuine historical tradition to which in our reconstruction of doctrine we must return."

My obligations are three-fold: first to my teachers and colleagues at Cambridge and in particular to Mr

J. H. A. Hart, to Professor Gwatkin and to Professor Bethune-Baker, the last of whom has been always ready to give me the assistance of his wide knowledge of patristics and his keen and candid criticism: secondly to the writers who have studied the same field and especially to Dr Hans Lietzmann of Bonn without whose invaluable edition of the works of Apollinarius this essay could hardly have been undertaken: and finally to the friends who have made the production of it possible, to the Syndics and to the staff of the University Press, to Mr and Mrs Sherwood, beneath whose roof much of it was written and whose help in other directions has been invaluable, to Mr Uvedale Lambert who has read it all in proof, to my sister who has compiled the index, and to her for whose sake the study was first begun and in whose comradeship it has now been finished.

C.E.R.

July 1923.

CONTENTS

CHAPTER I

THE BEGINNINGS OF CHRISTOLOGY

CHRISTIANITY is fundamentally an experience of communion with God in Christ and of fellowship in Him, an experience which led His disciples from the first to claim that Jesus was for them and for mankind God and Lord[1]. It is primarily a matter of the spirit, not of the brain-cells. Yet from the first it was inevitable that the Christian missionary in vindicating the faith that was in him should undertake to interpret it, and however simple the categories in which he did so the result is after some sort a Christology. "How can these things be?" was the natural question of every intelligent hearer; and if it was to be answered the reply must be adapted to the needs and peculiarities of the enquirer. Few pictures of early Christendom are more wildly inaccurate than that which imagines the Apostles as starting upon their work equipped with a precise system of theological dogma, a complete and consistent tradition containing in itself the rudiments of all later developments. If we can free ourselves from the besetting tendency to read back into the past the formularies and conventions established by centuries of patient experiment, we shall recognise that these results were reached by a process of evolution. They are the survivals from a multitude of conjectures framed in the

[1] It was speedily crystallised into membership in a society: but even Battifol admits that the unity of Christians is "based directly and solely on faith in Christ and His supernatural life in us" (*Primitive Catholicism*, p. 64).

face of existing difficulties and in the light of a variety of rival religions and philosophies. The Christian evangelist did not shut himself up in his study and receive there a perfect solution of all his problems: he met his would-be convert in the rough-and-tumble of argument, striving to convince him that what at first seemed a mockery and a stumbling-block was in fact congruous with the ideas and satisfying to the needs of humanity. Prophet or lawgiver, sage or wonder-worker, demon or demigod, in all of these classes he attempted at one time or another to classify his Lord, borrowing from the minds of his neighbours analogies by which to explain Him to them.

It is possible that in so doing Christians fell at once into error. Christ had declared that "no man knoweth the Father save the Son and he to whom the Son willeth to reveal Him": and one of the greatest of His followers had endorsed the claim and warned his fellows that while "no man hath seen God at any time," yet "he that hath seen the Son hath seen the Father." If the early Church had realised the full meaning of such words, she would perhaps have been less ready to interpret Christ in terms of previous and non-Christian conceptions of God and would have escaped the errors which sprang from her employment of the Hellenic Absolute, Changeless and Infinite, as her definition of deity. She would have concentrated her attention upon Jesus as did the Fourth Evangelist and, accepting the revelation in Him as the key to the mystery, have been initiated through Him and Him alone into the knowledge of the Godhead as Love and Light and Life. To do so, however, would have been to raise up insurmountable barriers against the spreading of the gospel.

Only by accepting contemporary opinions and employing recognised ideas and language could the Christian secure a common ground for the discussion of his faith. He had to become all things to all men if he were to win them; and when in consequence he was tempted rather to read into Jesus a pagan notion of the divine than to explore the nature of God and man as seen in Him, such a concession to past beliefs was a necessary step in the evolution of Christianity if all aspects of truth were to be united and all the kingdoms of the earth enrolled in the service of God and of His Christ. Grievous as have been the mistakes into which she was led, pathetic as are her wanderings in blind alleys and side paths, we need not lament that the Church was challenged from the first to make her faith plain, nor that her doctors were swift to take up the task. That there was a general agreement on a few facts of history and on the quality of a common experience corroborative of and explicable by those facts is plain enough. The New Testament itself demonstrates how variously the revelation could be interpreted and how individual and empirical were the moral and theological deductions from it. The central message was simple: cultus and organisation, creed and philosophy, grew slowly and with countless ramifications[1]. Only time could prove which branches bore leaves for the healing of the

[1] Their fixation probably occurred in this order; certainly the development of the ordered society was much more rapid than that of doctrine: ecclesiology was settled before theology. The evolution of Catholicism on its institutional side lies beyond the scope of this book: and what is stated here refers only to the growth of Christology. It is noteworthy that Battifol whose *Primitive Catholicism* is the most learned and detailed answer to Söhm, Harnack and A. Sabatier, says nothing on our subject and very little on any doctrine except that of the Church.

nations. For many a vigorous bough, then as now, suddenly revealed the corruption latent at its heart: many were cut down, some impatiently and perhaps prematurely: others, equally rotten, were saved and nursed back into a show of vitality. So the seed which Jesus had sown germinated and expanded into a tree. Bergson's famous description[1] of the progress of life, often thwarted and checked, often side-tracked and frustrated, yet ever rallying from a setback, and ever discovering new paths by which to accomplish its end and to subjugate matter to its sway, is a faithful picture of the march of the Spirit as seen in the history of Christian doctrine. And there could be no other way.

So it was that, having no authoritative statement of their beliefs ready to hand and indeed knowing no earthly guide which could supply what was needed, the infant Church set to work to formulate her faith in such terms as should harmonise it with the particular preconceptions, outlook and temperament of her converts. Each nationality, almost each individual, has at first a peculiar solution to offer. The prophetic tradition of the Jews and their familiarity with the inspired saints of the Old Testament, which expressed themselves in the humanistic ideas of the Ebionites; the esoteric imaginings of Eastern theosophists which are so crudely materialised and misrepresented by the orthodox opponents of Gnosticism; the legal precision of the Latins which appears in the terse phrases of the old Roman creed; the philosophic genius of the Greeks which soon raised them to the position of the recognised theologians of Christendom; these are the chief forms in which the early "liberty of prophesying" revealed itself. The long

[1] *Creative Evolution*, pp. 267–8.

catalogue of heretical sects, that "viper brood of Satan and Simon Magus his firstborn," gives us an idea of the fertility of invention lavished upon the subject. In every new field of human enquiry there must always be a period of groping, wherein the wildest and most grotesque fancies are tolerated through lack of any systematic knowledge of the points at issue or any recognised process of exact investigation. The present position of the study of psychic phenomena supplies a parallel to that of Christian theology in the second century. No one clearly knew what was the scope of legitimate enquiry: no one could readily separate genuine deduction from plausible guesswork: no one could foresee which of the many temples erected in honour of the Nazarene was founded upon the rock. Parthians and Medes and Elamites, strangers from Rome, Jews and proselytes, all had striven to tell in their own tongues this wonderful work of God; and the result was much more like Babel than Pentecost.

This state of chaos is by no means faithfully mirrored in the literary remains of the time; for with few exceptions those alone have survived which commended themselves to the orthodox of later centuries. And the superficial student of doctrine may easily obtain a wholly false impression. For to him the Church of the Synagogue, the sects of Ophites, of Valentinus and Basilides, Marcion and the Montanists, the authors of the apocryphal gospels and of the Clementine literature are mere shadows to be classified and docketed and dismissed as unimportant. Looking back upon the period, he sees little except the triumphant succession of the Greek Apologists and imagines their work to be the expression of the *communis sensus fidelium*. In reality, of course, such a picture is purely fictitious. A contemporary would have seen a number of isolated pioneers gathering knots of disciples around them in their own neighbourhood, in some cases in communion with the churches of their own province, in others forming schismatic congregations of their own. Amid the welter of speculation he would have found it difficult to forecast what would be the lines of future development or even to discover which of these varying sects represented the true faith most adequately. For although the majority of Christians were no doubt uninfluenced by experiments in doctrine and united rather by membership in the Church than by agreement in reasoned belief, this was due rather to a lack of interest in theology than to the possession of fixed formularies or definite knowledge. Even at Rome where the desire for order and uniformity early showed itself, a study of the pontificates of Victor or of Callistus ought to warn us against assuming any large fixity of dogma. And the failure of Hippolytus proves that as yet there was no general recognition of the Logos-theology which he championed and which for the catholicism of the East was alone to survive out of all the tangle of the time.

To justify this picture of the evolution of formulated doctrine in the second century we need only refer to the works of its greatest figure, the link between East and West, Irenaeus. Alarmed by the variety and novelty of the speculations which were threatening to conceal or drain dry the main channel by diverting its flow into a hundred wandering rivulets, the great bishop set himself to examine these experiments in irrigation and to test their power to supply the water of Life. Did they derive from the true source? Did they transmit the true current? Were the fruits produced under their influence worthy of the Lord's garden? He had no elaborate apparatus for his work. But he knew what Christ meant to him; and he had a simple rule by which the conditions essential for the Christian experience were summarised, and the Bible and especially the Gospels which he recognised as normative, and the memory of his teachers in the faith and above all the authority of his position as an official representative of an organised and world-wide community. In other respects, too, he was a learned man, though inferior in intellectual power and speculative ability to the great Gnostics whom he attacked. But he had commonsense and that instinct for truth which is an accompaniment of saintliness and counts for far more than brilliant brains or vivid imagination. And so, though much of his work is blundering and confused, and much, if judged by later standards, is defective to the verge of heterodoxy, no Christian of his time has a surer grasp of fundamentals, or more faithfully expresses the convictions of believers, or more often anticipates in phrases of startling insight the conclusions of succeeding ages[1]. Yet, for all his appeal to authority, he too is a pioneer so far as theology is concerned[2]; and it is his hold upon Christ, not the

[1] Christology does not loom large in his thought, and is nowhere clearly worked out. *Haer.* iii. especially 19, and v. 1, contain his ideas. Adam was made of flesh and soul and capable of receiving Spirit, that is, perfection and unity with God. His fall destroyed this possibility. Christ is man united with God, flesh, soul and Spirit. He thus restored to man the possibility of perfection, spiritual life or adoption.

[2] The bulk of his argument is ecclesiastical, and he is more successful in denouncing the presumption of the Gnostics than in expounding an answer to their problems. Whether he was also a pioneer in ecclesiology is a question into which it would be irrelevant to enter here: cf., amongst others, Harnack, *H.D.* II. 67–71; Battifol, *Primitive Catholicism*, pp. 198–217.

existence of a precise and elaborate tradition, that guides him on his way.

It is neither possible nor for us necessary to describe the various interpretations of the fact of Christ propounded in that period of untrammelled conjecture. They were driven from the Church and their authors are in most cases mere names. How much Christendom has been impoverished by their wholesale rejection we can only estimate from our knowledge of the repeated attempts from age to age to restate their positions, and from our experience of the limitations of the Greek theology which was their successful rival. But deplore their loss as we may, it is evident that for the Western world at that time the Greeks preserved and explained the fundamentals of Christianity far more appropriately than Ebionites or Gnostics. Their presentation showed itself capable of winning men to Christ, of perpetuating the fact of salvation in Him, and of developing into a philosophy adequate to the conscience and intellect of the churches of the Empire. From their influence upon later generations and their relationship to Apollinarius it is important for us to consider their characteristic tenets and the work of the great thinkers who are his spiritual forefathers.

When the earliest Christians were trying to translate the content of their belief into language intelligible to Gentile audiences, the first requisite was a formula which should express the relationship of the Godhead manifest in Jesus to that of the Supreme Being whom He had called Father. Their choice was somewhat limited: for to speak of Him as God was insufficient and misleading, while to adopt His own title of Son would suggest the popular polytheism and the gross fables of Olympus. Messiah or Christ soon became a name rather than a description: "prophet" failed to do justice to His Godhead; "aeon" to His Manhood. The initial advantage of His Greek converts was largely due to the fact that for them alone a term existed which was not only singularly appropriate in itself but had already been employed to interpret the religion of Israel to the students of the philosophy of Hellenism. This was, of course, the term "Word" or Logos.

The Memra or Word of the Lord was familiar to every reader of the Old Testament, and in the later Wisdom literature had been practically personified as the intermediary between God and man, the agent of the divine self-revelation in the world. Philo had already made frequent use of it in his attempt to commend Judaism in the guise of a religious philosophy to the Greeks of Alexandria; and though, when speaking strictly, he treats it only as a function or attribute of the one God, he frequently uses language which taken alone would imply that the Word was a personal being distinct from and the cosmic representative of Jehovah[1]. For like most later Jews he found himself forced both by the growth of reverence and by the general tendency towards deism to introduce the conception of a mediating power or powers between the world and the remote, changeless and undefinable deity. The "thrones, dominations, princedoms, virtues, powers" of the Rabbis were conveniently summed up in the Logos of

[1] For a full treatment of Philo's usage cf. Soulier, *La doctrine du Logos chez Philo d'Alessandrie*, and, more recently, Lebreton, *Origines du dogme de la Trinité*, pp. 183–205. There are in Philo three passages in which the Logos is called God, θεός or δεύτερος θεός, *De Somn.* i. 229; *Leg. alleg.* iii. 207; and a fragment on Genesis in Eusebius, *Praepar. Evang.* vii. 13.

the Hellenists; and it is not surprising that the Fourth Evangelist, writing in Greek for an universal church, should apply the same term to the pre-existent divine being who became flesh and dwelt among us, or that the "Word" should speedily be adopted into the dogmatic of the early Church.

Indeed, the motives which influenced Philo would make "Logos" equally serviceable to Christians in their very similar task. For, besides being a translation of Memra in the sense of the Spoken Word of God, it also bears the meaning of the rational principle in man and the universe, and thus is brought into harmony with the fundamental tenets of Greek philosophy in general and with the phraseology of the most important contemporary sect in particular. The belief that the reason or intelligence, which separates man from the irrational animals, is also the element in his nature whereby he can mount from the delusions of the phenomenal to the knowledge of the actual and eternal, is accepted in practice by all thinkers and is the theme of Plato's highest rhapsodies. But in Stoicism the term Logos was itself employed to describe the sum of those forces by whose agency the order of the whole and of its parts is maintained, in whose laws is found the ultimate authority for nature and for man, and which is at once the source and the ground of all existence: it thus bore for Stoicism a meaning almost coextensive with that which it bore for Judaism[1]: so far as such materialists could use the thought of God, He was to them the

[1] The question of the relationship of Stoicism to Judaism is one of great interest, but lies outside our scope. Whatever the debt of Stoic ethics to the Law or of the Wisdom literature to Hellenism, the conceptions of the Word of the Lord in Ezekiel and of the Logos in Heracleitus are clearly independent.

Logos. If even their experts could so rise above the limits of the physical theory which they had borrowed from Heracleitus as to write hymns so full of the sense of divine personality as that of Cleanthes, we may be sure that the populace for whom a diffused Stoicism was the substitute for religion would never have thought of the Life-force as impersonal, and when they heard Christians speaking of a divine Word of God would have felt that the message had a familiar ring.

The term Logos, then, was common ground to Jews, Greeks and Christians, and it is not surprising to find that the earliest Christian philosophy was largely constructed simply by combining the various ideas thus brought together. This is what happened, for instance, in the case of Justin. In the Dialogue with Trypho, in which naturally the Jewish strain of meaning is prevalent, he dwells at length upon those passages in the Old Testament and the Wisdom literature which can be used to prove that the Logos was then recognised as the firstborn of God, as co-operating with Him in the work of creation, and as His messenger and representative in revelation. He quotes, for example, the verse which afterwards became the subject of such burning controversy: "The Lord created me as the beginning (or first principle) of His ways[1]," as well as "Let us make man in our image[2]" and "The Lord rained down fire from the Lord[3]." In the Apologies, on the other hand, we as naturally find the Greek strain dominant. He takes up the Stoic conception of the macrocosm and the microcosm, and dwells upon the homologous pre-

[1] *Proverbs*, viii. 22 (LXX), quoted in *Dial.* 61 and 129.
[2] *Genesis*, i. 26, in *Dial.* 62.
[3] *Genesis*, xix. 24, in *Dial.* 129.

sence of the Logos in the universe and the "seeds of Logos" in individual men, assigning to this immanent Logos not only the inspired utterances of the prophets[1] but also all the glimpses of truth and righteousness in the philosophers, lawgivers and poets of the pagan world[2], since the whole human race has received a share of His power[3]. Finally, in both works he adds the specifically Christian claim that this Logos of which men possess a divine spark has appeared in perfect fulness in Christ[4], that this Logos, who has revealed Himself in such divers ways to patriarchs and saints, has been born of a virgin to fulfil His Father's purpose[5]. As regards His nature Justin expressly states that Christ was "body and Logos and soul" (ψυχή)—that is, that the Logos in Him took the place of the highest element, the λογικόν, in us[6]. That his whole theology is simply a development of the ideas suggested by the past usage of the word "Logos" is further seen most clearly from Justin's attitude towards God the Father. Very little mention of Him is made at all and we feel that He is no essential part of the author's scheme. Although in one or two passages His goodness and mercy are quoted in a casual phrase[7], He is a mere lay-figure, a dim, far-away, nameless, unknowable Being introduced in a purely conventional way, whom man cannot perceive or know[8], and whose place for all practical purposes is taken by His Word. Every manifestation of the divine Spirit, every act of divine power must be ascribed

[1] *Apol.* i. 33 and 36. [2] *Apol.* ii. 8 and 10.
[3] *Apol.* i. 46. [4] *Apol.* i. 5 and ii. 8. [5] *Dial.* 75.
[6] *Apol.* ii. 10. This, as Otto *ad loc.* notes, is exactly what Apollinarius taught.
[7] *Apol.* i. 10; *Dial.* 108.
[8] Cf. *Apol.* i. 13, 61; ii. 6; *Dial.* 4, 127, etc.

unhesitatingly to the Logos and to the Logos alone[1].

In spite of the simplicity of its methods and the comparative crudeness of its results, the Logos-theology in the hands of the Apologists of the second century provided Christians with a philosophy of the universe at once impressive in breadth of outlook and adapted to the needs of the time. It had the immediate virtue of making the most of the common ground, of disguising somewhat of the novelty of Christianity, and of presenting Christ not as the destroyer but as the consummation of the aspirations of mankind. If God is the Father of all and the source of every good gift, such an attitude towards the saints and sages of the past is more appropriate than the self-satisfied narrowness, bitter invectives and revolutionary clamour of Tertullian and the Latins. If Christ is Son of Man, the analogy between the Logos in Him and the seeds of Logos in us enables us to do more justice to His manhood than the frank dualism of the Gnostics. If He is Lord and Saviour and His religion the religion of Incarnation, His value is better preserved by emphasising the belief that He is the image of God and we made in that image, than by explaining the analogy in terms of inspiration and Christ as the greatest of the prophets. Moreover, in the hands of later and less superficial thinkers this Christian philosophy was capable of a sublimity, a comprehensiveness and a sanity which make it peculiarly attractive to the modern world. And in this nobler form it soon found expression.

[1] *Apol.* i. 33. The "Prophetic Spirit" is indeed mentioned as an angel or power in *Dial.* 116, and as "in the third rank after the Logos" in *Apol.* i. 13, but is little more than a name and has no distinct significance or function.

Clement of Alexandria, though less lucid than Justin in his exposition of the doctrine, is vastly his superior in breadth of learning and imaginative insight. Unlike his predecessors, he is concerned not with *argumenta ad homines* but solely with the search for and statement of truth. His theme of the gradual training of mankind by a loving Father[1] in the principles of the true Reason involves a majestic treatment of the evolution of religious knowledge and is illustrated by a wealth of allegory and lore widely gathered in the fields of philosophy, poetry, mythology and history. The story of humanity is to Clement the revelation of one steady and ever-unfolding purpose: its motive is the love of God to men; its goal the love of men to God. Wherever men have learnt to live nobly, wherever glimmerings of light have fallen on their darkness, there we may recognise the loving work of God and of His Logos, labouring together in perfect harmony of will to prepare men for the full manifestation of the divine splendour which is goodness and truth and beauty, for the full illumination of divine love. Wherever there are sin and degradation there we must feel that man's outlook is distorted by ignorance, that he has not learnt to know the true Reason which all men recognising will follow. Perfect enlightenment and knowledge of God are the object of this educative process, and in its course various methods have been employed. The chief of these are the gifts to the Greeks of philosophy and to the Jews of the Mosaic Law, both of which, if inter-

[1] Though he lays great stress on the love of God for mankind (cf. *Paed.* i. 3, 8, etc.), Clement "starts from the current philosophical conception of God as the highest abstraction and simplicity" (Gwatkin, *Knowledge of God*, II. 96). Cf. *Strom.* ii. 16.

preted by one who can read the spiritual meaning often concealed but always present in them, contain a clear revelation of the Logos and point the way to still fuller knowledge of Him. They predict His coming and enable men to prepare for it. Their sequel and completion are, of course, the appearance of the Instructor Himself in the flesh, that men might not only learn from hearsay what are the qualities of the perfect life, but might see such a life actually lived on earth and seeing might model their own conduct upon it. So the Logos became incarnate, "assuming the rôle (*προσωπεῖον*) of man and fashioning Himself in flesh[1]"; "manifestly becoming flesh and revealing that the same virtue is at once practical and speculative[2]"; "assuming flesh which is by nature passible, He trained it to the habit of impassibility" and "assuming flesh capable of being perceived (*αἰσθητὴν σάρκα*) He came to show men what could be done by obedience to His commands[3]." And even as incarnate the Logos is wholly unlike humanity, omniscient and impassible: "He ate not for the sake of His body, which was sustained by a holy energy, but that the false idea might not arise in the minds of His companions that He had been manifested only in semblance. He was altogether incapable of suffering: there entered into Him from without no emotion whether of pleasure or of pain[4]." And the result of it all, if a man will but take advantage

[1] *Proptrept.* x. fin.

[2] *Paed.* i. 3.

[3] *Strom.* vii. 2. These passages are characteristic, and prove that Clement believed, like Justin, that the nature of Christ consisted of Logos and animate flesh—Logos, *ψυχή* and *σάρξ*.

[4] *Strom.* vii. 3. Cf. the passages collected and translated by Tollinton, *Clement of Alexandria*, II. 290–2, especially *Paed.* i. 12.

of his heavenly schooling, will be the true Gnostic, Clement's version of the "Sapiens" of the Stoic, whom he describes in glowing words: "a portrait godly, close-conformed to God, is the soul of the righteous, wherein through the practice of obedience to His commands is enshrined and enthroned the Guide of all things mortal and immortal, the King and Sire of the beautiful, who is Law personified, and Covenant, and Word eternal, who is alone Saviour for each and for all[1]."

Clement's great trilogy is the work rather of a religious dramatist than of a strict theologian, tracing in its three stages the rise and growth and perfection of Greek Christianity. It is a biographical sketch of the conversion, probation and triumph of an ideal man, an early *Pilgrim's Progress* reflecting even more strongly than Bunyan's the characteristics of its author's nationality and outlook. Even from this standpoint it is bewilderingly unsystematic. Clement never bridles his fancy, never neglects an allusion, never hesitates to digress. His love of allegory leads him into labyrinths of symbolism in which he often seems himself to lose his way and where a modern reader becomes hopelessly perplexed. His wide knowledge of the classics makes portions of his work more like a thesaurus or anthology than a guide to the Christian life. His taste for popular sermonising leads him constantly to break off his theme in order to deliver vigorous and searching attacks upon the follies and vices of his countrymen. And the effect of it all is to destroy the unity and order of his scheme. Even so, much that is strictly irrelevant is of absorbing interest. The very qualities that mar his work as a

[1] *Strom.* vi. 9.

theologian give its details an unique value. As a guide to those regions of speculation in which human ingenuity can only grope its way by the aid of symbol and allegory, Clement stands alone. As a pioneer in the attempt to find in the gospel a principle which shall give harmony, proportion and meaning to the whole sphere of human knowledge, his effort deserves our gratitude and his success our admiration. As a representative of the abiding features of Christian Hellenism alike in its faults and in its virtues, his work is typical of the Greek church at its best. Nevertheless, as a contributor to scientific theology Clement could never have attained widespread influence. And it was left for the methodical labours of Origen to crown his purpose by constructing the first exposition of Christianity as a systematic theory of the universe. To Clement we owe an invaluable collection of material available for the solution of doctrinal problems; like David he made abundant preparation for the building of the Temple: to complete the actual structure was a task given not to him but to his successor. It is to Origen, not to Clement or the Apologists, that Christianity owes its first *Summa Theologiae*.

Indeed, in the sphere of Christology there was as yet hardly a problem. Man possessed in common with the animals a body and an animating soul, endowed with instincts and sense-perceptions: he differed from them in having also the divine faculty of reason (τὸ λογικόν) which gave him knowledge of reality and of God. That was common ground to the Christian philosopher and his opponents. So long as Christ was regarded as the Logos, it was obvious that His Incarnation could consist only of the assumption of flesh and animating soul;

for He was Himself the true Reason, the fulness of that which men possessed in part, the original or archetype of which they were imperfect copies. In this sense He was perfect man, though no Greek could or ever did say, until the end of the fourth century, that He had assumed a perfect man, or would have hesitated for a moment to endorse the Apollinarian doctrine that the Logos took in Him the place of the rational soul in us. Origen, as we shall see, tried by the use of his theory of pre-existence to give a larger content to Christ's humanity, and specifically repudiated the doctrine of archetypal relationship[1]. But his attempt was not really successful, and when his successors rejected his teaching of pre-existence, they fell back upon a Christology identical with that of Clement. It is this traditional belief which made Monophysitism so natural to the Greek churches, and entitles Apollinarius to be regarded as an authentic representative of the theology of Hellenic Christendom.

Origen possessed all Clement's industry and many-sided knowledge, but combined with it a power of concentration and a clearness of insight which enabled him to survey, parcel out and set in order the whole field of theology, and to lay firm foundations on which all ages might build. His work on the textual criticism and exegesis of Scripture gave the first impulse to Christian study of these subjects. His literary activity supplied the Church with a series of books which not only recorded the progress already made, but defined

[1] He mentions it as held by Heracleon, the Valentinian Gnostic, in an extreme form, but dismisses his argument summarily as neither supported by obvious proof nor by general probability (*In Johan.* ii. 21 (15), ed. Brooke, I. 85). In Heracleon the theory was heavily coloured by his dualism.

the lines on which future enquiry must proceed. His massive learning enabled him to attempt a synthesis of the whole content of contemporary knowledge. His genius for metaphysical speculation emboldened him to pursue the quest of truth with a freedom and zest undaunted and unrivalled. His skill in argument and his familiarity with other systems of thought afforded him the means of answering the ablest objections of educated paganism. His mastery of every department of learning qualified him to construct a course of study in which theology took its proper place as the queen of sciences. His fame as a teacher and his gift for infecting his pupils with the love of learning gave his school an immense influence upon the thought of the time and stimulated an interest in Christianity throughout the Greek-speaking world. Rarely has one man living the life of a scholar effected so much. With him the old epoch of unbridled individual interpretation, of chaotic and unclassified beliefs, closes, and the definite and progressive study of religious problems begins. Few will deny that the change from a multitude of private opinions to a single authoritative creed was essential to the life and organic growth of the Church. And if we allow that the change was beneficial, we must recognise our chief benefactor in Origen. To no one since New Testament times does constructive theology owe more[1]. A meaner generation for political motives laid undue stress on those aspects of his speculations which were rejected by subsequent Catholicism, and ventured on an act of parricide to his memory. But there can be

[1] "Even Jerome, before personal feelings had warped his judgment, styled him one 'confessed by all competent to judge to be the Master of the Churches after the Apostles'" (Westcott, *Religious Thought in the West*, p. 220).

few sincere students of the early Church and of the character and work of its champions who would not sooner be damned with Origen than canonised with Cyril of Alexandria[1].

It is impossible within our limits to treat his work in detail: nor is it necessary to do so. For the very quality that raises his writings and especially the *Contra Celsum* so vastly above the level of his contemporaries, their startling modernity of outlook and method[2], is naturally that which has left least traces upon his successors. He was too great for his age: and it is scarcely surprising that his noblest conceptions were either neglected or caricatured, and that when his honour had been desecrated by the attacks of a Jerome and the defence of a Rufinus the Church which owed more to him than to any other of her children should have condemned him to the flames whose eternal existence his larger charity had denied.

His system as a whole, save for the points like the eternity of the universe, or the pre-existence and transmigration of souls, or the ultimate salvation of all rational beings, points which he reaches on general grounds, puts forward with all modesty and regards merely as matters of private speculation, is not only orthodox but the very foundation of later orthodoxy. It is so many-sided, and his writings are so voluminous that if certain passages by themselves suggest error others can readily be found to counterbalance and explain them. Thus in

[1] Cf. Vincent of Lerins (*Commonit.* 44) who, paraphrasing a famous saying of Cicero's, asks "who would not rather be wrong with Origen than right with anyone else?"

[2] Compare, *e.g.*, the brilliant account of the Struggle for Existence in his handling of the problem of Evil in *C. Cels.* iv. 76; or contrast his answer to the question "Why did not the Christ come sooner?" in *C. Cels.* iv. 7 and 8, with that of Athanasius in *De Incarn.*

some places he uses language which clearly conveys the impression that God is the Absolute and the Son His subordinate and cosmic representative: in others he emphasises their equality and essential unity so strongly as to satisfy the most rigid Nicene: and we can only conclude that if his definitions are occasionally misleading, his belief in Subordinationism is not more than is warranted by the fact that the Son, not the Father, is believed to have become incarnate, or than is implied in the clause "the Father is born of none." And if we make allowance for the conditions under which many of his books were composed, for the translators who have preserved several of the most important and for the loss of very much of his work, we shall feel that few scholars are more liable to be misrepresented by excerpts and casual quotations. Even in the relatively small number of his books that have survived there is scarcely a point raised by later theologians on which he has not said something. His immense range of learning and intimate acquaintance through educational work not only with various shades of opinion but with actual human lives enable him to bring very varied resources to bear upon the harder problems and prevent his ideas from ever becoming stereotyped or mechanical. The intense devotion to study which makes his life an ideal for scholars of all time, the readiness to recognise truth in all its forms which led him to compromise his reputation by attending the lectures of Ammonius Saccas, the distrust of catchwords which will never let him rest content with a convenient paradox, and the fearless insight which never shrank from enquiry into the mysteries of God and yet was never ashamed to confess that it had failed fully to understand them, are all characteristics which make him unique among the theologians of his own or perhaps of any age, and by this very uniqueness weaken his influence and invite misunderstanding.

If the work of Origen be contrasted with that of Clement or any other patristic thinker, the most striking differences are seen to be all due to the same cause. Put briefly he is never content with history. His theme is always the eternal relationship of God to man. He is concerned not so much with the series of facts by which God has revealed Himself as with the interpretation of those facts in terms of eternity. He turns, indeed, from the Stoic to the Platonic view of the universe, and treats theology not primarily as a drama in progressive acts, but as a presentment of the changeless truth of which all temporal and spatial happenings are but a shadow and a symbol[1]. Like Plato he seeks for the underlying unity in the apparent diversity, believing that it is the presence of this unity alone which gives existence and meaning to phenomena, and confident that in and through the phenomenal is revealed to the seeing eye a knowledge of the real. The application of this desire to view everything *sub specie aeternitatis* led him in two particular instances to discoveries of remarkable importance. Believing that divine action can never be determined by arbitrary and temporal considerations but must always represent the essential attributes of the divine nature, he interpreted the generation of the Son, not, like all his predecessors[2], as a definite act in

[1] Cf. the comparison between Origen and Augustine in this respect, as drawn by Westcott, *l.c.* pp. 247–9.

[2] They borrowed the Stoic distinction between the Unspoken and the Spoken Word (Λόγος ἐνδιάθετος and προφορικός) to describe it. The Logos always existed potentially in God—else were God ἄλογος!—but for creation He is issued forth or uttered, and thus given distinct and personal existence.

pre-mundane history closely connected with the task of creation, but as a perpetually existing relationship without beginning or end, a necessary condition of the life of God. Thus he was the first to clear the way for belief in a consubstantial Trinity by answering in anticipation the Arian objection that fatherhood implies priority. Similarly, with regard to the Incarnation he was not satisfied to consider it as a sudden and isolated episode in the history of God's dealings with men. The life of Jesus Christ upon earth cannot be a mere consequence of the Fall, a special and drastic remedy for human sin: it must be the symbol of an eternal inclination of God towards His creatures, the expression of an all-embracing redemptive instinct in the inmost heart of Deity. Origen thus takes his place as a combatant in the great controversy of which traces can be found in the records of the next century, and which rent asunder the later Scholastics into Thomists and Scotists. And the attempt to follow in his steps is probably responsible for the popular charges against Apollinarius of teaching that Christ's body was from heaven and consubstantial with the Godhead.

For the rest, apart from this insistence on the static and eternal, his world-scheme, the evolution and training to perfection of free souls, is not very different from that of Clement. He lays more stress upon the individual than upon the race, since human life is to him only one stage on a journey which began in the dim past and will continue through many future epochs. But the general conception of the Logos as the truth and life of all things individually and collectively, of sin as a misuse of the freedom of choice due to ignorance of this Logos, and of the method of salvation as consisting in obedience to given precepts and imitation of a given model, is the same in them both. Indeed, it is in these respects that Origen shows himself a disciple of the Logos-theology and an authentic Hellene, although in them he makes the doctrine even more attractive than it was before. For in addition to the Stoic and Jewish strains employed from the beginning, he brings in a third, the Platonic theory of ideas. To Plato a sphere of abstract concepts, the archetypes of things seen, is interposed between the plurality of phenomena and the unity of the supreme good: and Origen transfers this belief in a "universe of actualities and intelligibles[1]" to the Logos who thus becomes at once the ground and reality of all the objects of sense and the link whereby they are brought into connection with the Father. The Logos is the image of God and men are images of the image[2]: the Logos is the archetypal reason, truth and righteousness[3] personified, and the prototype of those qualities in men[4]. All rational beings participate in possession of the Logos, and since they are free agents this participation is determined by and proportionate to their love for Him[5].

This conception of the Logos, though applied in the first instance to His relationship with the universe, is carried over into Christology and employed with equal skill. In this field indeed Origen's direct influence upon his successors is disappointingly small; for his views on it were bound up with his belief in the pre-existence of souls and on that account regarded from the first with suspicion. Nevertheless, his doctrine of the Incarnation

[1] The κόσμος νοητός of the Platonists.
[2] *In Johan.* ii. 2.
[3] *Con. Celsum*, iii. 41.
[4] *In Johan.* vi. 6 (3).
[5] *De Princ.* ii. 6. 3.

is very noteworthy because in it all the chief tendencies of later thought are anticipated. In the chapter of the *De Principiis*[1] in which he treats the subject many of the phrases and ideas employed casually by him are the catchwords in the later controversies. Thus, although he describes Christ as possessed of a perfect and self-determinating human soul, he insists that this soul is so inseparably united with His deity as to become one spirit. We may say "either that the soul with the flesh assumed by it exists in its fulness in the Son of God, or that it receives the Son of God in His fulness." "The words of Scripture 'The twain shall be one flesh' are more true of the Incarnate than of any other: for the union of the Word of God with the human soul is more truly one flesh than that of man and wife[2]." The two natures, each remaining true to itself, are so united that the Godhead is not degraded by any unworthy change and the manhood is no illusion or phantasm. In consequence of this union we can apply the epithets proper to each nature to the other and say that it is the Son of God who died and the Son of Man who will return in glory with the holy angels. The whole is aptly illustrated by the famous simile of the lump of iron in a furnace which while remaining iron takes all the properties of brightness and heat that belong to fire and itself may be said to become fire[3]. The mode of this perfect union in the Incarnate is apparently explained in two ways;

[1] *De Princ.* ii. 6. The passages quoted are in §§ 3–6. The psychology of Origen and the meaning of "soul" in his work are discussed below, pp. 196–8.

[2] Compare with this the use made of the same text by Theodore and the Nestorians.

[3] Used also in a passage of great importance by Apollinarius. See below, p. 209.

and it is interesting, and significant of Origen's greatness, that these two are exactly those which later became characteristic of the two great schools of thought. It is argued, firstly, that there is nothing unnatural in the belief that a rational soul can be wholly received into oneness with the true Reason which is at once the ground and the archetype of its existence. Their fundamental kinship explains their final union. Secondly, a fuller explanation can be found in the proposition that this particular soul was not assumed arbitrarily but because of its love of righteousness. The perpetual practice of virtue removed all possibility of alteration and produced a fixed habit of sinlessness. What began as an act of its will became through long usage a property of its nature. The soul is at once perfectly human because possessed of the fundamental human quality of free choice, and at the same time utterly unable to sin because completely at one with the divine.

These two theories of the mode of union are characteristic respectively of the two greatest schools of Greek philosophy and of their counterparts in Christian theology. The former, which is the more in harmony with the bulk of Origen's thought, is Platonism pure and simple: the second adopts, perhaps unconsciously but with close similarity, the method and standpoint of Aristotle: the difference between them is exactly that which in the fifth century separated the theology of Alexandria from that of Antioch. It is plain that the former, if pressed, would lead to a belief in the merging of the human soul whose essential quality is its possession of Logos in its divine original: the Logos would take the place of the highest human element, as He does in the thought of Justin and of Clement, being, indeed, the perfect prototype or idea of which all human souls are reflections. Similarly, the second is in reality not far from Ebionism: for the first impulse towards Incarnation starts from the free choice by the human soul of union with the Logos and this union only becomes complete progressively[1]. Origen himself, to some extent, avoided these consequences by placing the whole matter far back at the beginning of time, and representing the union as indissoluble long before the historic birth of Jesus. But even so the difficulties remain, and when the theory of pre-existence was abandoned[2] they became at once obvious and were made the subject of the Christological controversies. These two contrasted points of view thus found combined in Origen are not again brought together until a compromise was reached in the verdict of Chalcedon.

One point remains to be considered. Origen, by placing the completed union of the human and divine at a point before history, might avoid pressing to their logical conclusion the theories by which he explained it. But as a student of the whole body of Scripture he still had to face the difficulty which no other supporter of the Logos-doctrine had ventured to approach, that the Gospels assign to the child Jesus a period of infancy and growth, and that the existence of such a period appeared inconsistent with belief in His changelessness and therefore to Greek minds with His divinity. How

[1] Cf. Dorner, *Doctrine of the Person of Christ* (Eng. trans.), I. ii. 143.

[2] This and the rest of Origen's less orthodox speculations seem to have been tacitly dropped by the majority of his followers. Methodius, whose work is still little known, while a Platonist and in many respects very close to Origen, was apparently the first to make a definite attack upon them.

could the Logos, the Word and Wisdom and Power of God, have ever been a speechless, ignorant, helpless babe? How could He have grown in wisdom and stature and in favour with God and men? The Apologists are content to note the contrast between His divine power and His human weakness with a reverent refusal to enquire: and the passage in which Origen comments on the famous verse of St Luke[1] with one similar reference to the subject[2] is the first attempt of the theologians to deal with the problem. In both of them he employs the familiar text in the Epistle to the Philippians[3] which has furnished the accepted method of explanation ever since. The Son of God is able to be filled with wisdom because He had first emptied Himself by a deliberate decision of His own will. He assumed the form of a servant of which infancy and growth, like suffering and death, are an integral and necessary condition. Yet this temporary condescension does not invalidate the fulness of His revelation: for (so Origen declares) the powers thus surrendered He speedily recovered when once He began His life on earth. Even during the brief interval there is no absence and no real limitation of His Godhead: for in one striking passage the Son is represented as saying dramatically to Himself, "Now I am ignorant of speech, for I am too young." Indeed, throughout his treatment of the subject, the noticeable fact about Origen's theory of kenosis, as compared with those propounded later, is that the self-limitation is not a permanent condition of the incarnate life, equivalent to the whole circum-

[1] *Hom. in Luc.* xix. [2] *Hom. in Jerem.* i. 7 and 8.

[3] *Phil.* ii. 7. The original meaning does not concern us. ἐκένωσεν, whatever its significance to St Paul, was interpreted in its theological sense by the Fathers.

stances of earthly existence, but a single act completed before that life begins and equivalent to the descent from the glory of the Father, an act so transient in its effects as to last only until the end of His adolescence, and even during that time self-conscious, theatrical and unreal. The theory is in fact introduced solely for the exegesis of a few texts which, if taken at their face-value, would give a very different meaning to the Incarnation from that which Origen and Greek Christians generally attached to it. Their whole interpretation of Christ was dramatic: He came as a spectacle for men to behold, an example to copy, a teacher to obey. And in so far as stress is laid on this side of His mission, the significance of His humanity falls into the background. The evidences of that humanity, invaluable as they are to the sinful and the despairing, to those whose discipleship is of the heart rather than of the intellect, must be explained away lest the presence of His human limitations cast a slur upon the infallibility of His divine authority. And in that fact is contained the whole burden of the history, the whole secret of the failure of the Greeks. The two great defects inherent in Hellenism come out unconcealed when we pass from Origen to his successors.

He had taken the Logos-theology as the ground-plan of his structure, but his mighty intellect had seen much of its inevitable weakness and corrected many of its shortcomings, by introducing features from other schools of design and devising refinements and improvements of his own. He had in fact modified the original scheme so extensively, and so cleverly produced an appearance of symmetry and completeness, as almost to conceal its underlying imperfections. His followers who by their numbers and influence established for the first time a norm of doctrinal orthodoxy in the Greek churches, were less catholic in their tastes, less broad-minded in their outlook. While remaining pathetically loyal to the memory of their teacher and sincerely convinced that they were following in his steps, they were blind alike to the deep principles and to the fine touches which made his work so majestic and harmonious, and exhibited as his something which is in reality almost a caricature upon his predecessors. His many-sidedness secures the shelter of his name for any perversion however distorted: Origenism, which is at first the catholicism of the East, sinks rapidly into disrepute: and within two generations the stoutest champion of the school is the muddle-headed Eusebius of Caesarea whose theology is stigmatised by Dorner as "a chameleon-hued thing, a mirror of the unsolved problems of the Church of that age[1]."

There is little enough evidence of the views of his immediate successors. Few of them were eminent as theologians, and even among those who have left works behind them—Pierius, Gregory Thaumaturgus, Theognostus, and Dionysius the Great—there is not much that is notable save their inferiority to their teacher. Yet in spite of this lack of distinction the school acquired a predominant influence, and in the generation after Origen's death in 253 A.D. all the principal bishoprics in the Eastern Church were in the hands of his pupils. Dionysius of Alexandria and Firmilian of Neo-Caesarea were the leaders: but Hymenaeus of Jerusalem, Theotecnus of Caesarea, Helenus of Tarsus, Nicomas of Iconium, Athenodorus of Pontus the brother of Gregory,

[1] Dorner, *Person of Christ*, I. ii. 218.

and Maximus of Bostra, besides many others whose names have been preserved, were among its members. In consequence this debased Origenism became the normal orthodoxy of the Greek Christians, being actually introduced into the creeds of many Eastern churches[1], and so controlled a body of united support and was used as a standard and test of belief. To this uniformity, coinciding as it did with an increase in the power of the episcopate, is largely due the rapid development of the practice of synodal action against errors of doctrine or breaches of discipline[2]. Origen in his lifetime had been asked to act as champion of the Church against at least one prominent heterodoxy, that of Beryllus of Bostra[3]; and after his death it was natural that the fellowship of his pupils should assume the same prerogative. A series of small disputes on such various topics as the treatment of the lapsed, the re-baptism of heretics, the date of the Paschal festival, and the canonicity of the Apocalypse, gave the school an opportunity of showing its influence, and made it probable that its tenets would gradually be imposed upon the whole East. In regard to Christology this would have meant the unchallenged supremacy of the Logos-theology, a result likely enough and perhaps then satisfactory if all the Church had been Greek.

In order to understand the reaction which led to the famous controversy between the Origenists and Paul of

[1] Cf. the letter of six bishops against Paul of Samosata, the creed of Gregory Thaumaturgus (probably genuine) and the letter of Alexander of Alexandria against Arius; also Harnack, *H.D.* III. 113–7.

[2] Tertullian, *De Jejun.* 13, first mentions *concilia* as held *per Graecias*, but as held for devotional purposes and fellowship. Firmilian, *ap.* Cyprian, *Ep.* 75, assigns them disciplinary functions.

[3] Cf. Eusebius, *H.E.* vi. 33.

Samosata and so prepared the way for the struggles of the next century, it is necessary to summarise those defects in the Hellenic interpretation of Christianity which have already become apparent from our survey of its development.

Its initial error is undoubtedly the preference for metaphysics rather than for ethics. The sense of sin, of personal responsibility and the need for salvation, which is so fundamental to the highest Jewish thought whether of Jeremiah or of St Paul, is entirely strange to the Greeks. Sin is for them at worst only an unfortunate accident of bodily existence, a leaden weight encrusted upon the soul but alien to it: remove it and the soul will rise of itself[1]. Clement had written that sin was ignorance[2]; and his belief that it could be conquered by education in the principles of right reason would have been accepted by every Platonist. A true philosophy, a correct solution of the questions which the childlike curiosity of the race was always ready to ask, and their childlike confidence in man as the measure of all things always ready to answer, was therefore the one needful means of salvation. That being provided and sin being duly recognised, all would be well. Hence the facts of the Gospels are only of importance as the starting-point of Christian metaphysics. The historic Jesus is entirely superseded by the eternal Logos. The crucifixion and resurrection which are the hope and boast of St Paul are unnecessary and even embarrassing to the Greeks. The ideas of a fall and a restoration, of penitence and redemption and atonement, are almost repugnant. Christianity is not a new life or even a new

[1] So Plato, e.g. *Rep*. vii. 4.
[2] *Paed*. i. 13; *Strom*. ii. 15; cf. also *Strom*. vii. 16.

religion: it is simply a new theory of the universe. It is as such that it recommends itself to people who always delighted in nothing else but to hear or to tell some new thing.

The predominant intellectualism, while in a few rare cases a fine and spiritual thing, becomes for most a shallow and self-satisfied delight in the subtleties of dialectic, and involves a concentration upon the mental at the expense of the emotional and practical sides of human nature: it thus contracts and distorts the ethical and psychological basis of Christ's appeal. He had chosen Peter, the hard-handed rough-tongued fisherman, above the rest, not because he possessed a highly trained mind, but for his capacity for passion, that dangerous but splendid gift of which the Church has so often been afraid and ashamed. "Simon, lovest thou me?" is the condition and justification of the command "Feed my sheep." The Greeks in substituting cleverness for love, enlightenment for the glowing enthusiasm and loyalty of the Apostle, were led not only into a perverted presentation of the Christian life, but into grave doctrinal errors. For their God is not the God of religion, but rather the Father of lights in whom is no variableness neither shadow of turning—which is, with all due deference to St James, a very different conception. Human logic by itself will always tend so to conceive of Him: for if He be infinite, as must surely be assumed, all attributes are limitations and inconsistent with His nature. This dilemma besets Greek thought and drives it to two conclusions: first, if God the Father be thus infinite, He cannot Himself enter into any connection with the finite except in some unexplained way through a mediator or cosmic representative who is therefore inevitably regarded as different from and inferior to the Father; and second, although this representative is inferior, yet since He alone is knowable He becomes for the practical purpose of religion by far the more important. The Subordinationism of the former conclusion must, and for the less religious inevitably did, lead to Arianism and the denial of the Son's divinity. The second arising from the need of some God more amenable to worship than the Absolute checked this tendency, and the consequence was ditheism, God and His Logos being regarded as essentially distinct and yet alike divine. Dionysius of Alexandria, explain it as he would, could hardly escape this conclusion[1]: Eusebius of Caesarea frankly accepts it, and regularly styles the Son "a Second God[2]." No doubt some such method of solving the problem of Absolute and Relative, Transcendent and Immanent, by rigidly dividing the two spheres and assigning one to the Father and the other to His Logos, is an inevitable consequence of any physical concept of the Godhead. Little else could be done so long as Uncaused Being, "which is and was and is to come," was treated as the fundamental quality of the divine. But both in itself and in its results, when judged either by the test of Scripture or of experience, it is seen to be plainly unchristian. Its pagan affinities stand revealed if we compare it with the belief of any educated heathen of the time. The emperor Constantine, for example, both before and after his conversion has exactly the same concept of God and of religion. He was from the first a monotheist, in the sense that he recognised as the

[1] Cf. Athanasius, *De Sent. Dion.* 12–25; Basil, *Ep.* 9.
[2] Cf. *H.E.* i. 2, etc.

first cause and underlying principle of things one almighty but unknowable being. The multitude of gods he accepted as representatives of the various aspects of this one true God, as channels through which worship might be paid to Him, as means whereby He might and did reveal Himself to men. The variety of cults had in his view simply been devised in order to meet varying needs and lead various minds to the service of the one Supreme. No man could be expected to pay equal honour to all the members of a much overcrowded pantheon: each was free to select for himself the particular godling best suited to his own character and station in life. The principle is the same as that which led to the worship and choice of patron saints in mediaeval times. Constantine the soldier naturally chose the soldier's favourite god, the Unconquered, the Sun, Apollo, Mithras, as his special protector and object of devotion. All that happened when he became converted was that he shifted his allegiance from one representative of the Supreme to another. Christ superseded Mithras as his patron saint: he remained an eclectic monotheist not a Christian. Under the circumstances it is appropriate that when at last he received baptism it should have been at the hands of the arch-Arian Eusebius of Nicomedea.

The comparison with paganism yields results less striking than a comparison with Scripture. Life, Light, Love, the great Johannine Trinity, represent an entirely different conception of God, a conception which alone enables men to pray "Our Father" and alone gives an adequate explanation of the motive of Incarnation. And if the Greeks' theory of the divine essence is false, so is their theory of the mode under which that essence exists. Ditheism is opposed alike to the First Commandment and to the Baptismal Formula: it dissolves the Unity without realising the Trinity. By its emphasis upon the Logos it virtually deposes God the Father: it also appropriates to the Second Person the work and attributes of the Third. It is the Logos not the Spirit who is the Lord and Giver of life, who spake of old through the prophets, who moves now in the hearts of men. How complete and how persistent was this appropriation is strikingly proved by the Epiclesis or Prayer of Invocation in the Prayer-book of Serapion, bishop of Thmuis, the friend of Athanasius. All the other known liturgies are either later in date or come from sources outside the influence of the Logos-theology, and in them the Epiclesis is invariably addressed to the Holy Spirit: in Serapion's the Logos is invoked. Indeed, there is really no room for any appreciation of the Spirit in Greek theology. Like the Christians whom St Paul found at Ephesus, the Apologists and Origenists seem scarcely to know if there be a Holy Ghost. Whenever they are driven to explain His mention in the New Testament, they can only surmise that He is the chief of the hierarchy of heaven, the first of angels, the captain of the seven spirits of God. Even Origen's own account is unsatisfactory and confused, and no real element of his system. To this neglect are due not only the rise and popularity of the Macedonian heresy in the later days of Arianism, but to some extent the lack of clear ideas on the matter which is so obvious a shortcoming of present-day Christianity.

If the Greeks' doctrine of God is thus open to strong criticism, similar objections may be raised to their doctrine of Christ. In early days when the case was based upon a belief in the incarnation in Christ of that Logos which was incarnate to some degree in all men, this analogy not only admirably served the interests of contemporary apologetic, but was a reasonable corollary to acceptance of the divinity of Jesus, and a satisfactory starting-point from which to study the revelation of God and man given by Him[1]. For we must needs begin with what we ourselves know and share, interpreting His nature in the light, the very insufficient light, of our own experience. An Incarnation implies that those who accept it can found their theology upon the admitted oneness of God and man in Jesus, and can learn the nature and relationships of each as they are seen in Him. But if once God and man are regarded as by postulate irreconcilable, if we admit the validity of the sceptical attitude which defined deity in negative terms as the very antithesis and opposite of humanity (and the Greeks speedily found themselves doing this), the analogy from which they started and with it ultimately all belief in an Incarnation break down. Regarding God as unknowable, impassible, super-essential, a dilemma confronted them: either the Logos like ourselves is passible, in which case *ex hypothesi* He cannot be divine—which is Arianism; or He is impassible and therefore not man at all—which, disguise it as you will, is Gnosticism: in either case there is no Incarnation. The history of the Christology of the fourth century, of Athanasius and Apollinarius and Cyril, is the record of the struggle to avoid being impaled upon one horn or the other. The typical Greeks, ingenious as are their

[1] This analogy is plainly maintained by Clement and by Origen. To Clement, "the difference between human and divine is one of measure and degree, but not of kind" (Tollinton, *Clement of Alex.* II. 30): to Origen, Christ, like ourselves, possesses full human nature and the Logos, in His case alone perfectly united.

efforts to escape, reject the manhood and lapse into Docetism. In the end the Church accepted a middle course which is in reality no solution at all. Surrendering the analogy between the Logos and the seeds of Logos, and separating divine and human into mutually exclusive compartments, Churchmen thought to unite the two by setting them side by side in Jesus, linking them by sophistries like the doctrine of *Communicatio Idiomatum*, and frankly distributing between them the whole series of His earthly actions. Starting from their postulates no other result was possible. Their postulates were unchristian.

The original analogy was first definitely abandoned when Paul of Samosata asserted that the indwelling of the Logos in Jesus was rather that of a quality than of a person. But even when this had been condemned, so long as the ideas centring in the title Logos survived, the significance of the change was hardly recognised. Only during the Trinitarian controversy when much more definite notions of the Son's personality were formulated and pushed to the verge of tritheism, was the separation between Christ and ourselves generally accepted.

And the portrait of Christ enforced upon them by their wrong idea of God is again both pagan and unscriptural. The deepest Christian experience is one of salvation, of a real atonement, a vital union with God, a new birth, a life out of death. That is the gospel of St Paul and of St Paul's Master. Here in Christ is God reconciling the world to Himself. But if God is remote and penitence a matter of intellectual training, then perhaps a demigod after the Arian pattern or an actor thinly disguised in the make-up of humanity will serve.

An example is what is required; and such a being is at least worthy of our imitation even if, being other than ourselves, He cannot evoke our love. In consequence, the reality of His manhood does not matter: is indeed something of a stumbling-block. His body, however real its stuff, is only a cloak assumed that the Logos may render Himself visible and play His part on the world's stage. The Incarnation is only a theophany. And such a belief, if it does outrage to the Christian conscience, is also irreconcilable with the narratives of the Gospels. Not only to St Mark but to St John and St Paul it is the man Christ Jesus who has wrought salvation. The picture given by those who knew Him after the flesh is of a true man: there is nothing of unreality or self-consciousness about His emotions and His needs. Greek exegesis might be forced by doctrinal presuppositions to read into the Gospels what is virtually imposture and fraud: the actual story gives no basis for such a charge: spontaneity and a total absence of affectation shine out from the Jesus of history. Nor among the many substitutes which limited understanding, conventional piety, temperament or prejudice has preferred to Him, is there any, save perhaps that of the Latin church, less like the original than is this etherialised philosopher whose childhood and growth, hunger and thirst, sufferings and death, are but the local colour of his part, whose lightest utterance is a fantastic allegory, who comes to appeal rather to the wise than to the simple and with the moralisings of a pedant, not the challenge of the Cross.

It is ironical that the Hellenic Christianity which could produce in the hands of Origen a theology of such learning, breadth and insight, could be so easily debased by his successors. But, in fact, it is the very qualities which are his peculiar glory that when imitated by shallower and less devout minds become the causes of their failure. The learning which he had used to adorn and enforce the practice of righteousness tempted them to turn religion into a system of philosophy and to develop a coldly ascetic habit travestying Origen's sympathy and enthusiasm, and wholly alien from the full vitality of Apostolic times. The breadth which made him try to harmonise all things as one great sacrament of divine love degenerated into an easy optimism blind to the fact of evil or to the reality and true conduct of the moral struggle. The insight which could see behind the events of history the revelation of eternal truth lapsed into a trick of allegorising which, professing to explain, effectually explained away. The latter half of the third century is admitted even by the prejudiced historian to have been a time of grievous corruption and decay[1]. The scarcity and quality of its literary remains bear out his warning. It is not surprising that the diffused and popularised Origenism should be deeply involved in the general deterioration and should have been impotent to check it. Nor is it surprising that the mass of Christians who after all were not Origenists should have made their protest and initiated a reaction in theology from abstract speculation to the practical study of human need, from the allegories of Christian Gnosticism to the plain words of Scripture, from the Logos incarnate to Jesus the Son of Man.

[1] Eusebius, *H.E.* viii. 1.

CHAPTER II

THE FIRST CONTROVERSY

In surveying the literature of the first three centuries we are apt to think that the line of apologists and philosophers from Aristides to Dionysius represents a *consensus fidelium* on theological subjects. The few, who on this supposition disagreed with them, can be labelled as either Ebionite or Gnostic and classified in a pedigree which implies that the members of each family are closely related. Thus the mysterious Ebion, the eponymous hero and mythical ancestor of one race of heretic, is the spiritual grandfather of Theodotus of Byzantium called "the Tanner," who is in turn the sire of Asclepiades or Asclepiodotus, Apollonides, Hermophilus, and another Theodotus "the Banker," from whom descends Artemon or Artemas the direct progenitor of Paul of Samosata. It is a convenient scheme and looks well in coloured chalks upon a blackboard: but, as we have seen, it is based upon and fosters a false estimate of the facts. So far as catholicity goes, it is certain that the followers of the Logos-doctrine do not (at least until the period of evil peace after Origen's death and probably till the end of the century) represent more than a small proportion of the Christians of the East. Outside the ranks of "nimble-witted Grecians" such a refinement of the simple gospel met with little approval. The vast majority, especially in Syria, Palestine and the farther East, while accepting Jesus as the Christ and entering fully into the way of life revealed in Him, did not feel the need of strict metaphysical definitions and, if they did, approached the question from a very different angle. Instead of stárting with His divinity and setting Him up at once as a second God alongside the Father, they began like the Apostles from the First Commandment and, while admitting that Jesus stood in a unique relationship to God and had the value of God for mankind, insisted that any theory of His person and nature must be made compatible with belief in the divine monarchy[1]. That this theology was universal in the Church until the close of the second century, as the followers of Artemon boasted[2], is no doubt an exaggeration. But that it is not a total falsehood is plain enough from the attitude of the Roman popes Zephyrinus and Callistus towards Noetus the Monarchian whom they heard with sympathy and towards Hippolytus, a strong supporter of the Logos-theology, whom they censured as a ditheist[3] and who has in consequence covered their memory with invectives. Certainly the prevalence of such an attitude among the average Christians of the time is abundantly proved by a study of its popular literature. Many books are confessedly heretical propaganda and rather Gnostic than Ebionite: but the most important, the *Shepherd of Hermas*, which so narrowly escaped being included in the canon, the

[1] Thus, *e.g.*, even in Ignatius we have the famous definition in *Ephes.* vii. 2: "There is one physician fleshly and spiritual, begotten and unbegotten, God becoming in flesh, true life in death, of Mary and of God, first passible and then impassible"—which is technically both Apollinarian and Adoptianist.

[2] *Little Labyrinth, ap.* Eusebius, *H.E.* v. 28. His claim is supported by the attitude of Tertullian (*Adv. Prax.* i. 3) towards the pope.

[3] *Refutatio*, ix. 6. Origen, *In Johan.* ii. 3, states that "the mass of those reckoned believers" rejected the whole Logos-theology.

Clementine Homilies and Recognitions, and several of the apocryphal Acts, reflect a vague Monarchianism which often comes near pure Ebionism. To catalogue all these varying shades of thought, to classify them under the appropriate name, and to represent them as definite schools of heresy is a general and diverting procedure borrowed from the unhistorical method of authors like Epiphanius who read back their own time into the past and regarded the faith as from the first a complete and static *regula fidei*. The truth seems to be that the multitude of believers then as now was not vitally interested in theology, was content to take the fact of Christ without minute explanation, and deeply distrusted movements like Montanism or the Logos-doctrine which from their tritheistic and ditheistic tendencies seemed to be steps towards polytheism and away from the Gospels[1]. Accepting the authority of the Old Testament with its emphasis upon the one true God and its warnings by example and precept against infringement of the divine monarchy, they felt that insistence upon the fulness of Christ's inspiration and the uniqueness of His person, however emphatic, must stop short of establishing a belief in a plurality of deities. The attempts of Marcion and the Gnostics, with their irritating claim to superior illumination, to decry the God of Israel would only strengthen this resolve.

In the West this attitude is traceable in the Adoptianist tendencies which Loofs[2] rightly notes in the tra-

[1] Cf. Tertullian, *Adv. Prax.* 3.

[2] *Nestorius*, pp. 110–2. His suggestion that these tendencies were due to Irenaeus who brought them from the East (*l.c.* pp. 123–5) is plausible: but probably they were general if not universal in early times among "simple" believers.

ditional Christology from Tertullian and Novatian to Augustine and Leo; and is typified by the so-called Modalistic Monarchianism which dominated Roman Christianity under four popes and harmonised the revelation in Christ with the oneness of God by treating His deity as an expansion of or effluence from that of the Father. Among the Syrian churches a different method prevailed. Dwelling in the atmosphere of the New Testament among scenes and people which would constantly remind them of the life portrayed in the Gospels, they had little temptation to regard Christ as a metaphysical abstraction. If a visit to the Holy Land can even now powerfully stimulate our appreciation for the details of our Lord's life on earth and bring His manhood vividly before us, we can realise how strong an effect constant association with the actual conditions under which He lived would exert. Jesus as He was in the days when He went in and out among us was the picture on which the Christianity of the East fastened. Conceptions of Him as the World-force and life-giving Reason, or as the Second Person of the divine Trinity, might come as a doctrinal afterthought. To the unsophisticated He was first and foremost the Son of Man, the prophet of Nazareth, the teacher and the friend; and at the same time one who in virtue of His character and history and of their experience of the reality of His resurrection was acclaimed with conviction but without precise definition Saviour and Son of God. Geographical affinity was further supported by two more concrete influences. The quarrel with Gnosticism in which the Easterns were so long engaged was especially keen in the Syrian churches. For not only were many of the chief Gnostics of Syrian birth, but the tendency to esoteric religions was strong. Those who escaped it naturally viewed with distrust all attempts to spiritualise the gospel or to make Christianity a field for speculation; and as Gnosticism declined they felt that their prejudices had been justified by results and were ready to direct them anew against the Christian Gnosticism of Alexandria. Equally important as making for an Ebionite Christology was the presence of large and friendly Jewish colonies. Whereas in Alexandria the Jews lived in a regular ghetto and were the constant foes of the Christians, in Antioch and the Syrian towns[1] quite a different relation between the two existed. Even as late as the fourth century there was the closest friendliness between the Church and the Synagogue. Chrysostom[2] is never weary of rebuking his flock for their visits to Jewish places of worship, observance of Jewish feasts and swearing of Jewish oaths. The brotherly love between the two communities was positively embarrassing; and was no doubt influential in formulating that type of Christian theology which its critics repeatedly call "the new Judaism[3]."

If the environment of Syria thus favoured the maintenance of a type of thought very different from that of the Greek cities, Paul of Samosata was admirably fitted to act as its champion and to develop out of the general Syrian attitude a new school of scientific theology. Of his education and early career, and indeed of his life in general, we know little; and that little is contained in the Synodal Letter of the bishops who con-

[1] *E.g.* in Edessa; cf. *Doctrine of Addai*, p. 32, and Burkitt, *Early Eastern Christianity*, pp. 16 and 34.

[2] Cf. *Adv. Judaeos*(especially Or. ii.) and *Comm. in Ep. ad Galat.* ii.

[3] Epiphanius, *Haer.* lxv. *passim*; Chrysostom, *De verb. apost.*, etc.

demned him and in references by Athanasius, Epiphanius, Theodoret and a few others to whom his name was an abomination. Eusebius, in whose *Church History* is preserved all that remains of the letter, has omitted the doctrinal sections, which would have been of the greatest interest, and only gives us a long indictment of Paul's morals. The charges of bribery, immorality, blasphemous pride and inordinate luxury may have truth in them: Paul was a courtier and the Prince Bishop had not yet become a familiar figure. But it is significant that his accusers admit that they have no first-hand evidence, and that Church Councils usually supported their verdict on their victim's theology by aspersions upon his character[1]. Athanasius and Eustathius, both canonised saints, were accused in exactly the same way by the councils which condemned them. It is to the facts of his life rather than to the letter that we must turn if we would discover what manner of man was this first Antiochene theologian.

Paul's birthplace is an unimportant outpost on the Euphrates whose situation is described by Strabo and whose fame rests upon its two great sons, Lucian the satirist and Paul the heresiarch. The story of Christianity and indeed of secular events in this region of the farther East is extremely obscure. Only the church and school of Edessa are at all well known, and there is nothing to connect Paul with the Edessenes. Indeed, but for one circumstance he would probably have remained an unknown member of an unknown church, and have died without notoriety or influence. But just at this time a career was opened out for him by the

[1] Cf. the ironical comment of Socrates, *H.E.* i. 24: "It is a matter of common occurrence for bishops to load with abusive epithets and pronounce immoral those whom they depose—and to give no grounds for so doing."

sudden rise to power of the astonishing kingdom of Palmyra. When Sapor, king of Persia, had defeated and captured Valerian, overrun Asia, sacked Antioch and Tarsus and threatened the whole stability of Roman dominion in the East, Odenathus and after him his wife Zenobia alone succeeded in resisting the invaders. They built up with amazing rapidity a powerful state out of the No-man's-land between the rival empires, pushing back the Great King to the walls of Ctesiphon and extending their sway until Antioch itself fell into their hands. Under their rule the type of Christianity, to which, as we have seen, the Syrian church was naturally inclined, seems to have received considerable stimulus, and Paul, who was a prominent member of their household, probably developed there his peculiar position. It is not unlikely that Zenobia was herself a Jewess either by birth or by religion: for this is definitely asserted by Athanasius[1] and by Theodoret[2], whose accounts are obviously independent, and is only opposed by the evidence of Trebellius Pollio in the *Historia Augusta*[3], who says that she boasted of being "of the race of the Ptolemies and Cleopatras"—a boast plainly part and parcel of her fondness for taking Cleopatra as her model[4] and as proof of descent from the Lagidae wholly worthless[5]. At any rate it is recorded in the Talmud[6] that she showed marked favour to the Rabbis and with them encouraged no doubt an Ebionite

[1] *Hist. Arian.* 71.

[2] *Haer. Fab.* ii. 8, where Paul's lapse into Artemon's error is ascribed to his desire to present Christianity to Zenobia in a form as like Judaism as possible. So Neale, *Patriarchate of Antioch*, 47.

[3] *Tyran. Trig.* 30. 2.

[4] Cf. Trebellius, *l.c.* 30. 19; Vopiscus, *Aurel.* 27. 3.

[5] Syriac, not Greek or Coptic, was her native tongue: cf. Vopiscus, *l.c.* 27. 6 and 30. 3.

[6] *Talm. Jer.*; Ter. viii. 46.

or Judaising Christianity. Political reasons at this time would certainly encourage her to do so: for Manes the Persian was now making his first attempts to combine the revived Zoroastrianism with Christianity and so reawakened Gnostic tendencies; and Manes, like Marcion, entirely repudiated Judaism, apparently employing a similar series of antitheses from the Old and New Testaments to support his dualism[1].

These influences combined to bring the theology of the Syrian church into close affinity with what had been characteristic of the Nazarenes or Church of the Synagogue. The Ebionite attitude, which had hitherto been rather an undefined tendency than a formulated body of opinion, at this time received precise expression, and although in Paul it took its most scientific form his case was no isolated exception: he was one of a school. In the East this school manifested itself in various directions. It produced and popularised the *Acts of Archelaus and Manes*, a book whose language is strikingly close to that of Paul, Jesus being described as a man, virgin-born indeed, but not endowed with divine power until His baptism, when by the descent of the Spirit He became the Christ, and as attaining this Godhead by moral progress not by nature[2]. It trained Aphraates the

[1] Epiphanius, *Haer.* lxvi. 70–5; cf. Legge, *Forerunners and Rivals of Christianity*, II. 278.

[2] The date, authorship and original language are very obscure. It is extensively quoted by Cyril of Jerusalem, *Catech.* vi., and Epiphanius, *Haer.* lxvi., and mentioned by Jerome, *De Vir. Illustr.* 72, as having been translated from Syriac into Greek, and being very popular in the East. The critical problems concerning its origin and value, on which many scholars from Beausobre to Kessler, Nöldeke, Rahlfs and Bardenhewer have written, do not concern us. For our purpose, whatever its importance to students of Manichaeism, it is clear evidence of the widespread influence of this type of Christology in the late third or early fourth century.

Persian sage, whose whole cast of thought is biblical and ethical rather than speculative and metaphysical, and who defends the application to Christ of the title Son of God on the ground that Israel was in the past called by God His son, and that Moses and other righteous men have been already named gods[1]. It may probably have had a representative in the learned Beryllus of Bostra whose teaching was refuted by Origen in 244, and who was certainly a Monarchian and in all likelihood, as Harnack has shown, an Adoptianist[2]. It became so powerful as to survive the scandal of Paul's condemnation and to establish on the very scene of his fall a traditional theology which made Antioch the worthy rival of Alexandria. It made the Far East Nestorian more than a century before Nestorius.

From a position of influence in the cultured circle which Zenobia and Longinus had formed at the court of Palmyra Paul was transferred to the see of Antioch some time between 260 and 264 A.D.[3] Once established there he found speedy opportunity to display his views: for he was now confronted not with the simple theosophy of Bardaisan or the speculations of Christianised Zoroastrians, but with the Christian Gnosticism of Alexandria. Against this in its popular form, with its double danger of representing Christ as a second God and as the Logos veiled in flesh, all his instincts rose in revolt. He saw that there was need to assert in his new bishopric

[1] *Dem.* xvii. 3, 4, 8 and 11: cf. Burkitt, *Early Eastern Christianity*, 91–5.

[2] Cf. Harnack, *H.D.* III. 36–7. Our sole knowledge of Beryll's doctrine comes from a sentence in Eusebius, *H.E.* vi. 33, and Origen, *In Ep. ad Tit.* Socrates, *H.E.* iii. 7, is unreliable.

[3] Demetrian the bishop probably did not survive the sack of Antioch shortly after Valerian's fall in 260, and Paul must have been enthroned when order was re-established there.

the truths of the unity of God and the real manhood of Jesus which had been familiar to him in his birthplace, and he displayed skill and learning in the method of his assertion[1].

The sources for our knowledge of Paul's system are not numerous[2]. The Synodal Letter is, as we have stated, useless in this respect. Although most of the fourth century writers mention him either as connected with Artemon or with Marcellus and Photinus, Epiphanius[3] is the only one to give an account of his views and even this is of the most general kind. Theodoret[4] is absurdly brief, and we find little fresh before Leontius[5], who in his writings against the Nestorians has quoted some valuable extracts from the lost portion of the Synodal Letter to prove the resemblance between Paul and Theodore of Mopsuestia, and also from the record of the debate at the Council between Paul and Malchion. The most important source, however, is five fragments reputed to be from a treatise of Paul to Sabinus, quoted in an anonymous work which is traditionally ascribed to Anastasius the Presbyter and certainly not written earlier than 650 A.D. This book is generally called the *Doctrina de Verbi Incarnatione*[6] and consists of extracts from the Fathers followed by a few

[1] A. Réville, "Christologie de Paul de Sam." (in *Bibl. de l'École des Hautes Études*, VII. 189–208), takes Christology as Paul's starting-point and regards his Monarchian doctrine of the Logos as an afterthought. This seems to me in all respects less probable than the interpretation which makes his Monarchianism primary.

[2] The most recent collection of them is by Lawlor, *Jour. of Theol. Studies*, XIX. 20–45, 115–20.

[3] *Haer.* lxv.

[4] *Haer. Fab.* ii. 8.

[5] *Adv. Nest. et Eutych.* iii. (Migne, *P.G.* LXXXVI, I. 1392, 1393.)

[6] First published in a translation by Canisius, *Thes.* II. 255–6, and in Greek by Mai, *Script. Vet. Nov. Coll.* VII. 1–73.

from the chief heretics. Among these are some very valuable fragments of Apollinarius, of Eudoxius and Lucius the Arians, of Ebion, Paul, Nestorius and Theodore. The quotations from the four last-named are suspiciously alike, and the presence of Ebion gives one pause: but Harnack[1] allows the genuineness of those from Paul despite their bad company, and so many parallels between the language of Paul and the Nestorians are preserved by Leontius that, save for Ebion, hesitation on the score of resemblance may be dispelled.

The Christology of Paul, although the most interesting part of his work, is only a consequence of his insistence on Monarchianism. He starts from the First Commandment[2], from the conviction that belief in a pre-existent personal Logos is polytheism, and that the Logos and the Spirit, although eternally present in the one God, are no more distinct Persons on that account than are the Logos and Spirit in a man. As a consequence of this denial it follows that the Logos cannot be the centre of personality in Christ, but only an impersonal force, inspiration or energy, issuing from the Godhead and acting upon the human Jesus from without. In this respect he is sharply opposed to Noetus who taught that it was the personal Godhead of the Father that became incarnate. Paul, claiming that inspiration was in fact incarnation, insisted that the Logos had become incarnate: but insisted also that this indwelling was not personal or essential, but only as a quality, being effected in a fashion similar to but more complete than that in which He dwells in the prophets.

[1] He conjectures that the Ebion fragments also belong to Paul, *H.D.* III. 44. They add nothing to our knowledge.

[2] Epiphanius, *Haer.* lxv. 2.

Jesus, although born of a virgin, is a man like other men. In God's foreknowledge and by the constant exercise of virtue He received a special gift of divine power either at conception or at baptism, and was given the title Christ and by adoption the position of Son of God. Thus, as Réville[1] admirably puts it, Paul "enforces the contrast between a Christ descended from on high and displaying before the eyes of men a perfection inherent in the divine nature, and a Christ sprung from beneath, sharing our humanity, raising it by His moral activity to indissoluble communion with God, and deified through the perfection which He has acquired at the expense of struggle and suffering."

His account of the cause and mode of this deification is the most remarkable portion of his theory. The fragments in which they are explained present so striking a contrast to the theology which we traditionally associate with the third century and so important a contribution to Christology as to deserve full reproduction. Paul bases his position upon the character of Jesus "who was born holy and righteous, who by conflict and toil overcame our inherited sin, and by so doing made His own position steadfast, who was conjoined by His virtue to God and gained by His progressive performance of good deeds a unity and identity of will and energy with God. This unity He preserved inseparably, and so receives as the reward of affection bestowed on Him the name which is above every name." "Do not be surprised," he continues, "that the Saviour possessed unity of will with God. For as Nature reveals that in diversity there is an underlying unity and identity of essence, so the fixed habit of love

[1] *L.c.* p. 199.

effects in diversity a unity and identity of will, revealed by a unity and identity in objects of desire." "After being anointed by the Holy Spirit He received the title Christ: He suffered according to nature; He wrought miracles according to grace. By the changelessness of His disposition He was made like to God and continuing pure from sin was united to Him and was inspired to receive the power to work miracles. Thereby being proved to possess one and the same energy of will with God, He was named Redeemer of the race and Saviour." The two remaining fragments contain a very cogent vindication of his theory. He claims, firstly, that no other mode of union is possible; for "different natures and different persons have only one means of union, namely concurrence of will from which springs a oneness of activity between those who are thus brought into contact": and, secondly, that no other mode is meritorious; for "what are controlled by the condition of their nature have in them nothing praiseworthy: what are controlled by the fixed habit of affection are highly to be praised; for they are controlled by a unity and identity of purpose confirmed through unity and identity of activity, and their impulse towards further increase never ceases: in this way is the Saviour conjoined to God and never again undergoes separation from Him for ever, but possesses unity and identity of will and activity with Him, ever impelled onwards by the revelation of the good."

Such, if we may trust the authenticity of the fragments, is Paul's most complete statement of his belief. Parallels to it might be found in a few isolated sayings of Origen: but otherwise nothing else at all like it has been preserved from this period, nothing which shows so clear a grasp of the vital importance of conduct, so strong an insistence that goodness not reason is godlike, so earnest an attempt to understand the human realities and to interpret them in the light of psychology and commonsense.

The two elements which after him became characteristic of Antiochene theology, literal exegesis of Scripture, and Aristotelianism, appear very clearly in these fragments. His method in using the Bible is indeed less plain from them than it is from the accounts of critics like Athanasius[1] or Vincent of Lerins[2]: but his theory certainly does justice to passages in the New Testament which are hard to reconcile with more orthodox opinion. For example, the belief that before the opening of the public ministry there was a period of growth and progress spiritual as well as bodily is the only fair deduction from the reference to these years in St Luke[3], a reference which the Alexandrians either evaded or explained away. Similarly, the stress laid on the anointing with the Holy Spirit and on the development of power and of gifts, though this is not so explicitly connected with the baptism by Paul as it is by the later Antiochenes, is thoroughly in accordance with the importance attached to the opening of the ministry in the New Testament, with the absence of narratives of miracles wrought previously to it (a point which separates the canonical from the apocryphal Gospels), and with the words "This day have I begotten Thee[4]"

[1] *Con. Arian.* iv. 30.
[2] *Commonit.* 35.
[3] ii. 52.
[4] Inserted in Luke iii. 22 in cod. D, and read by Justin, *Dial.* 88 and 103, Clement Alex. *Paed.* i. 6, and Methodius, *Conviv. Virg.* viii. 9.

which had been introduced at a very early date into St Luke's account and were the reading of Paul's contemporaries.

As to his Aristotelianism the fragments supply indubitable evidence. The whole standpoint from which they approach the problem is in sharp contrast with the idealistic and imaginative philosophy of the Platonic and Pythagorean schools. Paul, unlike the Alexandrians, finds his chief interest in the concrete and particular not in the abstract and general, in the scientific analysis of human nature rather than in the metaphysical principles of which it is or may be the embodiment, in the study of the facts of history and experience more than of the eternal relationships by which those facts are to be interpreted. His resemblance to Aristotle is one of outlook and goes far deeper than similarity of phraseology. Nevertheless, a few quotations will prove it more vividly than any description. "It is by practising goodness," says Aristotle, "that we become good[1]." "Habits of mind arise from the exercise of the corresponding activities[2]." "Activities exercised on any particular object develop the character correspondingly: for example, athletes achieve success in this way. Every sane person knows that habits of mind are formed by exercising activity in any direction[3]." And again, on another point raised by Paul, "Equality and similarity, especially similarity in respect to virtue, are the ground of affection[4]." "Perfect affection is the affection of good men who are alike in regard to virtue: their affection endures so long as they are good and their virtue is constant[5]." Finally, Paul's argument that Christ's

[1] *Eth. Nic.* ii. 1. 4. [2] ii. 1. 7. [3] iii. 5. 11, 12.
[4] viii. 8. 5. [5] viii. 4.

goodness is only praiseworthy if dependent on His freedom of will, may be paralleled by such sayings as "Voluntary actions excite either praise or blame; involuntary only pardon or perhaps pity[1]." "The involuntary is what is done under constraint, and constraint arises from a source external to ourselves, a source of such a quality that its victim contributes nothing to the result[2]"—which is exactly Paul's objection to the belief that Christ is necessarily and by nature incapable of sin.

It is certainly this use of the ethical teaching of Aristotle that distinguishes Paul's theology from the unscientific Ebionism of the *Acta Archelai* or the blurred rhetoric of Aphraates. Its employment is a discovery of the first importance; and the question naturally arises, whence did he derive it? One is tempted at first sight to suppose that the Aristotelianism of the early Church may have been obtained from the same source as that of the mediaeval, and that the rabbinical schools had already learnt to value the philosopher whose works they introduced into England in the fourteenth century. If so, we might find a single origin for Paul's beliefs and for his methods; and should feel that the title "the New Judaism" was doubly earned. But there is little if any evidence for connecting the Rabbis of that time with Aristotle: and if there were we must not press too far the evidence for Jewish influence upon Paul; for even his foes admit that he did not enjoin observance of the Mosaic Law or of circumcision, and all Ebionism was traditionally regarded as of Jewish origin. We are, therefore, left to enquire whether, as many have suggested, he borrowed it from the schools of Artemon

[1] *Eth. Nic.* iii. 1. 1. [2] iii. 3.

or Theodotus with whom his opponents ironically invite him to enter into communion and all writers against heresy insist that he was in some way connected.

Both on general grounds and from the lack of all proof of contact[1] it seems vastly unlikely that the powerful and self-reliant patriarch of Antioch should have borrowed his ideas from unimportant and already condemned heretics, much less have attempted to revive their heresy. Students of doctrine, then as now, have been too eager to assume that similarity of opinion necessarily involves conscious relationship, and in doing so have greatly underestimated the frequency of parallel development and the influence of widely diffused ideas. Nevertheless it is certainly striking to find so curious a resemblance between the methods ascribed to the Theodotians and those of Paul. A contemporary writing, called the *Little Labyrinth* and quoted by Eusebius and Theodoret, gives an interesting and suggestive account of them. Although claiming that belief in Christ as "mere man" was primitive, their movement seems in no way connected with the Church of the Synagogue. Rather are they scholars and scientists, reflecting a type of humanistic culture and critical ability very different from that of the Alexandrian Platonists. The *Little Labyrinth* comments sarcastically on their fondness for the construction of syllogisms, on their "earthy" studies in Euclid, their admiration for Aristotle and Theophrastus, and their reverence for Galen. Their attitude

[1] The Theodotians had attempted to found a church at Rome in Victor's time (*Little Labyrinth*): Artemon was also influential only in Rome, apparently living there from the papacy of Zephyrinus until after Paul's condemnation. Paul had never had any possibility of contact with Rome; for all his working life was spent outside the Empire.

towards Scripture also rouses the unknown author to satire: "They claim that they are rectifying it," he exclaims, "and yet they cannot even agree with one another. Either they disbelieve that the Scriptures were uttered by the Holy Spirit, or they reckon themselves wiser than He!" For their critical attitude they are classified by Epiphanius[1] as an offshoot of the sect of the Alogi, the obscure party or person that first ventured to contrast the Synoptists with the Fourth Gospel to the latter's disadvantage[2]. Although we have no reason to suppose that Paul adopted what we should now call the "higher criticism," his affinities in this respect are with the critics rather than the allegorisers: and these two characteristics of the Theodotians survived his condemnation and became the distinctive features of the Antiochene theologians, Eustathius, Diodore, Theodore, Nestorius and Theodoret.

If Paul derived his views neither from Jews nor Theodotians, we must conclude that the ideas which we find shared by so many Syrian and Byzantine Christians represent a type of culture, the extent and influence of which have been underestimated by most students of Church history. It is generally assumed both by them and by classical scholars that the Peripatetics produced little effect upon thought in the Graeco-Roman world as compared with the Stoics on

[1] *Haer.* liv.

[2] The identification of the Alogi with Gaius, the opponent of Montanism (Eusebius, *H.E.* vi. 20) and apparently of Hippolytus, by Gwinn (*Hermathena*, VI. 397 *seq.*) is plausible but not certain. Whether the Alogi attacked the Johannine writings through dislike of the Logos-theology, as their name and Epiphanius' account suggest, or of Montanism and the chiliastic ideas of the Apocalypse, as Gaius seems to have done, is unknown: possibly both are true.

one side and the Neo-Platonists and Neo-Pythagoreans on the other[1]. The affinities and rivalries of the two latter with Christianity are so notorious that they have completely overshadowed the significance of the Christian Aristotelians, and created an impression that the scientific method and pursuits of the school had wholly failed to attract popular attention. Yet there are numerous indications both from contemporary sources and from the evidence of later events that in the first five centuries of the Christian era the influence of the Peripatetics both in philosophy and in critical studies was constant and, especially in the farther East, widely diffused. Scanty as is our knowledge of Mesopotamia and of the extent to which Greek education still lingered in the countries conquered by Alexander, it is significant that the schools which the Mohammedans found and developed at Baghdad and elsewhere under the Caliphate should have been permeated by the very authorities whom the Theodotians are accused of admiring[2]. Aristotle and Theophrastus, Euclid and Galen came to Europe from her Moslem invaders: in the seventh and eighth centuries these names had been the glory of Eastern learning[3]. May we not suppose that what they found was not simply the creation of those exiled philosophers who had been driven from the Empire by the bigotry of Christians[4], but a traditional culture

[1] Cf. *e.g.* Gomperz, *Greek Thinkers*, IV. 506.

[2] Cf. Margoliouth, *Early Development of Mohammedanism*, pp. 205–8.

[3] Cf. Bury's account of the influence of Baghdad upon the revival of learning at Constantinople in the ninth century (*Eastern Roman Empire*, pp. 436–9).

[4] Justinian closed the schools in Athens and expelled the philosophers in 529 A.D. Damascius, their head, with six associates emigrated to Persia, but speedily returned.

which had survived on the confines of Persia from a much earlier period?

Paul's attack upon the Origenists was speedily recognised by them, and before he had been long at Antioch they took measures against him. The records of their procedure are obscure, and the number and results of the Councils actually held cannot be determined with accuracy. Theodoret[1] describes a first meeting to which Dionysius of Alexandria, being too old to attend, sent a letter: Paul denied the charges against him and gave his assent to apostolic doctrine. Afterwards, when fresh rumours of his errors were circulated, a letter was addressed to him and another gathering took place: here again Paul escaped condemnation, perhaps owing his acquittal to the influence of the great Firmilian[2]. Finally, a third Council was convened, and Paul was examined in detail by Malchion who had been a sophist and was evidently skilful in debate: as a result of his replies he was convicted of heresy and his name was struck off the list of bishops. The victim, strong in the support of Zenobia, refused to recognise the sentence or to surrender his position; and it was only after her defeat by Aurelian that an appeal to the emperor secured his expulsion from his church nominally on the ground that one who resisted the vote of his fellow-believers should be cut off from their company, but actually, no doubt, from political motives.

Of the documents purporting to descend from this controversy the letter of Dionysius[3] is almost certainly spurious: but that of the six bishops[4], Hymenaeus,

[1] *Haer. Fab.* ii. 8.

[2] So Réville, *l.c.* Firmilian died before the final Council.

[3] In Mansi, *Conc.* I. 1031.

[4] In Routh, *Rell. Sacr.* III. 289.

Theophilus, Theotecnus, Maximus, Proclus and Bolanus, is much more likely to be genuine both by reason of its characteristic theology and from the resemblances to it in the strange series of anathemas appended to the first creed of Sirmium against Photinus[1]. The full report of the argument between Paul and Malchion[2] survived at least until the time of Justinian and is quoted by him and by Leontius, and these fragments have lately been collected and arranged by Lawlor[2], and give a clue as to the ground of his condemnation.

The letter is an interesting statement of the Origenists' position and displays all the peculiarities of the Logos-theology in its crudest form. The six bishops start by granting that God is one and insisting that He is unoriginate, unseen, unchanging, incomprehensible to man save in such imperfect notions as are obtainable from the revelation in His Son. The Son who thus discloses to us the Absolute is defined as "Wisdom and Word and Power of God, pre-existent not in the divine foreknowledge only but in essence and hypostasis, God and Son of God"; and whoever denies this or says that it is ditheism is excommunicate from all the catholic churches. In proof of the doctrine of personal pre-existence which they evidently regard as the chief seat of Paul's heresy, they adduce a long series of quotations from the Old Testament, many of them those first employed by Justin against Trypho and showing that the Son was the agent of God in creation, in revelation to the patriarchs and in the giving of the Law. They

[1] Quoted by Athanasius, *De Synodis*, 27: especially noticeable are the references to Abraham's visitors, to Jacob's wrestling and to the text: "The Lord rained down fire from the Lord" (for the use of which against Photinus cf. Epiphanius, *Haer*. lxxi. 2).

[2] *Journal of Theological Studies*, xix. pp. 20–45, 115–20.

conclude with a brief and elementary statement of Christology to the effect that this same Son sent by His Father came down and assumed flesh from a virgin, flesh which has thus been changelessly united to the Godhead and deified, whence also Christ is proclaimed as God and man. So far as this goes it agrees with the views of the later Logos-theology, of Athanasius and of Apollinarius: but it is not sufficiently definite to prove that they realised the central difficulty and consciously anticipated future attempts to meet it.

It was indeed natural that the bishops should lay more stress upon the personal pre-existence of the Son than upon the nature of Christ. For since Origen had substituted the word Son for Logos in speaking of the Godhead, Greek thought had begun to question the possibility of conceiving of the Second Person of the Trinity as a faculty or attribute: and when Paul revived this they were ready to confute him. But in Christology they had no such clear case. For Paul's doctrine (strange as the statement may appear) was too similar to their own to be easily crushed. Both sides were at present agreed in maintaining the analogy between Christ and ourselves. They might accuse Paul of representing Him as a prophet excelling other prophets only in the degree of His inspiration. But Paul could fairly retort that they did likewise by their theory that the Logos which dwelt fully in Him dwelt also potentially or in germ in all other men. And they were not yet in a position to deny it. Different as were their respective premisses, they did in fact accept the same conclusion, the similarity between Christ and mankind, Paul maintaining that Jesus was God inasmuch as all men and He with them were inspired of God, and his opponents that the Logos was man inasmuch as all men were but images of the Logos. It was in consequence of this difficulty that the Council, recognising the inadequacy for themselves of a doctrine which interpreted the Incarnation in a sense inconsistent with their conception of deity, sanctioned an innovation which was of the gravest import for the whole future of Christianity.

The fragmentary condition of the report of the argument, and Eusebius' folly in omitting the important part of the Synodal Letter, make it impossible to give a full account of this momentous decision. But enough remains to prove the general course of the procedure. Both questions, the personal pre-existence of the Son and the distinction between Christ and mankind, were raised, and it seems clear that in each case the solution was obtained by means of a single term and its cognates, *οὐσία, ὁμοούσιος, οὐσιώμενος*, and *οὐσιώδης*. The precise significance of these words to the Council has long been a matter of debate among scholars[1], largely owing to the development in their use after the outbreak of the Arian controversy, and to the consequent uncertainty as to Paul's meaning displayed by Athanasius and Basil. As generally understood in Greek thought from Aristotle until at least the middle of the fourth century, *οὐσία* has two distinct meanings: it stands either for a particular entity, for what the creed calls a person, or for the common element shared by a class of particulars, in theological language a substance. By Athanasius and the orthodox Nicenes it was probably

[1] It is briefly discussed by Bethune-Baker, *Texts and Studies*, VII. 1. pp. 74 *seq.*, and more fully by Robertson, *Athanasius*, pp. xxx–xxxiii; cf. Zahn, *Marcell. von Ancyra*, pp. 11–32.

used in Trinitarian doctrine only in the latter meaning[1], although even by them the former is not infrequent when they are speaking of the Incarnation[2]. But in Paul's time it seems to have been regularly, if not universally[3], applied to that underlying and individual reality which constitutes the ego in any subject, and to which personality is the closest modern equivalent[4]: and in this sense it was employed by both parties to the dispute. Bearing this in mind, the Council's action becomes plain. Paul in his doctrine of the Godhead had used the term ὁμοούσιος to mean not that the three Persons were consubstantial but that God was unipersonal[5], the Logos being only an impersonal attribute

[1] How far ὁμοούσιος changed its meaning during the controversy is of course keenly debated. Marcellus, who regarded the Logos as an impersonal ἐνέργεια, championed the ὁμοούσιον at Nicea and must have understood it to mean unipersonal.

[2] Cf. below, pp. 221–4, for its use in Apollinarius.

[3] In Clement, *Strom.* iv. 13, and Origen, *In Ep. ad Hebr.* Fr. 3, ὁμοούσιος seems to bear the meaning "homogeneous": and οὐσία no doubt was never wholly restricted to the sense of person, although in Greek theology from 250–325 A.D. this was its technical significance.

[4] For this use in Origen's time, cf. *De Orat.* 15, "The Son is different in οὐσία from the Father," and Bigg, *Christian Platonists*, p. 179. Of Paul's contemporaries Dionysius of Alexandria, when he called the Son ξένος κατ' οὐσίαν from the Father, meant "different in person"; cf. Athanasius, *De Sent. Dion.* 12, and Bethune-Baker, *Introd. to Christ. Doct.* p. 116: Pierius of Alexandria is said by Photius, *Biblioth.* cod. 119, to have spoken of Father and Son as two οὐσίαι and two natures, and Photius adds that "it is clear from the context of the passage that he used it instead of hypostasis or person and not like the Arians": the letter of the six bishops against Paul speaks of Christ as "one and the same in οὐσία although interpreted under many categories," and here too οὐσία must mean person. The objection of the conservatives, that is, of the majority of Greeks, to the ὁμοούσιον at Nicea was due to their conviction that it meant unipersonal and was Sabellian.

[5] Hilary, *De Synod.* 81, explains Paul as meaning *negata personarum proprietate*: Athanasius, *De Synod.* 45, and Basil, *Ep.* 52, though less definite are not irreconcilable with this explanation: cf. Tixeront, *Hist. des Dogmes*, I. 432, and Lawlor, *l.c.* pp. 30–4.

attached to the one *οὐσία*, God. The Council, accepting the word in this sense, definitely forbade its use. Similarly, in dealing with Christology Malchion forced Paul to admit that the Logos dwelt in Christ "not personally (*οὐσιωδῶς*) but as a quality"; and the Council established against him a definition maintaining that the Godhead incarnate was "a personality personally existent in the body[1]." In doing so they represented the manhood of Christ as incomplete: they destroyed, except for any who might care to admit that the Logos and a perfect human personality are identical (an admission which under the influence of Hellenic deism no Christian of that age would make), the reality of the Incarnation: they sacrificed the analogy between Logos and seeds of Logos, Christ and the saints, which had been so successfully employed in Christian apologetics and had become so familiar that it appears, although its use is no longer logically legitimate, in the *De Incarnatione* of Athanasius. The conclusion that Christ differs from man not in measure and fulness but in kind, a conclusion which, conceal the fact as we will, removes Him from our species and reduces His Incarnation to a Gnostic theophany, was, no doubt, to the Council primarily an expedient adopted in controversy. Perhaps they hardly recognised the significance of their innovation. For Hellenic Christianity had been gradually moving towards such a result, and the circumstances of the conflict with Paul simply occasioned what was inherently inevitable. Nevertheless, their verdict is one of the landmarks in the history of doctrine. It may have

[1] *οὐσία οὐσιωμένη ἐν σώματι* preserved in Leontius, *Adv. Nest. et Eutych.* iii. (Migne, *P.G.* LXXXVI. i. 1393): cf. Routh, *Rel. Sacr.* III. 312.

been inevitable so long as the nature of God was interpreted in terms of pagan philosophy: that it was disastrous was barely discovered as the result of nearly two centuries of struggle, and is by no means yet generally recognised.

In the long run it was disastrous: under the circumstances it was inevitable. Paul and his followers, necessary as was their emphasis upon the manhood of Jesus, seemed to the Origenists to be treating Him as a mere prophet; and Apollinarius' dictum, "a Prophet cannot be the Saviour of the world[1]," is a fair summary of a conviction fundamental to Christendom. The Apostles would have had no reason to break with their fellow-countrymen had they found in their Master one who differed in degree, and in degree only, from themselves. That was not their experience of Him. At His Ascension, if not before, they had learnt that He was in the full sense one with God: at Pentecost they had entered upon a new life of fellowship with Him and with one another, a new life in Him. He had done something unique in history: by His own unbroken union with God, His sinlessness as we call it, He had proved Himself different if not in nature at least in moral quality from mankind: and it was in virtue of this difference that He initiated a new relationship between humanity and its Father. At its deepest and truest the experience of Christ and of love and life and light in Him has always forced those who share it to proclaim Him divine. To the sinful and despairing, to those whose failure drives them to cry that in them dwells no good thing, it is not as a prophet but as a Saviour that Christ appeals. If He is simply a pattern

[1] Cf. *Anacephalaeosis*, 1, *ap*. Lietzmann, *Apollinarius*, p. 242.

of glorified humanity, of humanity as it ought to be but save in Him is not, then He is to the sinner something near a mockery. The instinct which insists that He is Very God is wholly sound; Very God is the only title which does justice to His value and to our experience of Him. For the Origenists to condemn Paul was to vindicate the uniqueness and the saving power of the Master: it was the testimony of Christians to the reality of their way of life. But so long as they conceived of God in physical rather than in moral terms and tried to interpret the Incarnation not under the categories of personality but under chemical metaphors as a mingling of gold and silver or wine and water, they were compelled to face the issue "either God or man" and to reject either history or experience: for if they said "man" they betrayed their conviction of His efficacy; if "God," they were false to the records of His life which could not by any ingenuity be reconciled with their concept of the divine. The next century disclosed a number of ingenious attempts to escape this dilemma, attempts in which Apollinarius is the pioneer, attempts which are still too widely accepted. What was wanted was a frank recognition that their preconceptions were wrong, a recognition that Very God and Very Man are neither contradictory nor separable, that man is only perfect if perfectly united with God, that Very God for us men at least (and with this alone we are concerned) is necessarily Very Man. That is perhaps a legitimate explanation of the adverbs of the Creed of Chalcedon. It is a result unattainable by the great Greeks, by Athanasius and Apollinarius, Cyril and Dioscurus.

All the circumstances of the case combined to make the condemnation of Paul the most notorious event of the time for the Christian world. In later years the spectacle of heresy in high places became so common as scarcely to attract special interest: but as yet there was no precedent for the fall of a patriarch. The length of the struggle, the difficulty of reaching a verdict, the inability to enforce it, and the political significance of the controversy, helped to impress the memory of the unhappy event upon men's minds, and the attitude, no less than the references, of subsequent Churchmen shows how deep the impression was. If Paul had been the saintliest of men and his ruin had possessed the glamour of a martyrdom, we should hardly expect that his opinions would have survived save perhaps in a small circle of admiring disciples. Being what he was, a man whose conduct both at the Council and in its sequel bears out the charges of his enemies, and whose character no one of his followers attempts to defend, a worldling lax and vainglorious in success, subtle and evasive in controversy, obstinate and undignified in defeat, the immediate reappearance and permanent influence of his beliefs are a striking satire upon the futility of a policy of repression. Still more amazing is it to find that the very city which had witnessed the scandal of his bishopric and the greater scandal of his excommunication should have dared to revive and perpetuate during two centuries of conflict the characteristic features of his theology. Here is clear proof that the Origenists, although their personal eminence and the fame of their teacher had raised them to the chief sees of the East so successfully that a Council of bishops was little more than a reunion of old schoolfellows, were still a clique whose doctrine had as yet little support from the mass of believers. Greek theology in the third century was the possession of a small group of intellectuals: the *communis sensus fidelium* was not ready to endorse it for at least another generation.

We have already suggested that a theology of a distinctly Nestorian type was traditional in the Syrian churches, and that the geographical and ethnic affinities of the city where the disciples were first called Christians should have made Antioch a centre of belief in the humanity of Jesus. The influences which create and sustain a particular form of popular doctrine are never easy to gauge exactly. Cultus and the emphasis given in public worship to special aspects of religion are vastly more important than the work of scholars and thinkers, as is plainly shown in the Christianity of our own time. Ceremonial and hymns and festivals make an impact upon the uneducated which will survive long after the beliefs inculcated by them have ceased to be taught or even accepted. In particular the associations and memories engendered by a great feast-day are far more permanent than the opinions of a multitude of theologians: even the creed of preacher and teacher cannot but be coloured by the occasions of his discourses and the valuation of those occasions in the minds of his hearers. It is not a subject on which it is safe to dogmatise: but we suggest that along these lines may be found a strong reason for the vitality of the Antiochene Christology.

Nothing is more characteristic of this position than the importance which it attaches to the baptism of Jesus as the time at which He received the chrism and the sealing of His divine Sonship. It is, indeed, the strength of their doctrine that it enables them to do justice to an event which was obviously regarded by the Evangelists as of supreme importance in the life of the Master. At no city in the ancient world were the Christian festivals celebrated with such enthusiasm as in Antioch. The temperament of its population, lighthearted, emotional and easily excited, led them to mark the great days of the Church's calendar with an unusual display of religious ardour. Chrysostom's sermons to the Antiochenes contain a number of complaints that the people only come to church readily on feast-days and will only receive the sacrament at the Epiphany and in Lent[1]; and Julian the emperor, who knew them by bitter experience, acted strategically when he tried to win them back to paganism by multiplying its pageantries. By far the most important of the festivals at this time and place, a festival outstripping even Easter itself in its dignity, was the Epiphany. A vigil service lasting all night preceded it[2], after which crowds of the less regular church-goers flocked to the Eucharist and to hear the popular preacher of the day. And at Antioch the Epiphany was primarily if not solely a commemoration of the Baptism of Christ, "the day on which He was manifested to the people[3]," "the day on which the gates of heaven were unbarred[4]." If any other times of "manifestation" were included, they were kept entirely subordinate[5]; for it is with the Baptism[6] that all the

[1] Cf. *De Baptismo* and *In Ep. ad Eph.* ch. I. iii.

[2] Severianus of Gabala (Migne, *P.G.* LXV. 15).

[3] Chrysostom, *De Bapt.* 2.

[4] Chrysostom, *In S. Lucian. Mart.* i.

[5] The Nativity was probably included: for Ephraim's hymns point to the existence of a Birth-festival and Chrysostom (*In Diem Nat.*), preaching in 386 A.D., tells us that the 25th December was first kept as Christmas in Antioch ten years previously. Epiphanius, not an Antiochene, connects Epiphany with Birth (*Exp. Fid.* 22).

[6] Both Chrysostom, *De Bapt.* 2, and Jerome, *Comm. in Ezech.* i. 1. 3 say that it commemorates not the Birth ("for then He was

Eastern homilies then preached connect it, affording in this respect a strong contrast to the sermons of the West[1]. Furthermore, there was an additional reason which should impress this date indelibly on the public imagination. For the ceremony of baptising new converts, which in the West[2] has always been associated with Eastertide, was in the East regularly performed not at Easter but at the Epiphany. So unique a celebration must have fostered an Adoptianist tendency in popular theology, and have constrained the leaders of Church life to lay emphasis upon the significance and doctrinal meaning of the event thus celebrated. When once such ideas had become associated with the festival, they would become part of the whole religious atmosphere, and display a vitality independent of individual teachers and impervious to external attack. The growth of Mariolatry and the history of the Iconoclastic Controversy prove that argument is almost futile when opposed to popular sentiment and established practice. Paul's theology was, we believe, in the main an expression of existing tendencies. At any rate it found in Antioch a soil eminently congenial to its development. Henceforward Christological history resolves itself into a series of struggles between Antiochenes and Alexandrians—Diodore, Apollinarius and Theodore; Nestorius

obscure"), but the Baptism. Cf. Chrysostom, *De Beat. Philog.*; *Apost. Constitutions*, v. 12 and viii. 33; Gregory Thaum. (?), *Hom.* iv.

[1] *E.g.* Augustine, in all six sermons *In Epiph. Dom.* (*Serm.* 199–204), refers solely to the Magi and never to the Baptism: whereas Chrysostom, who frequently mentions the Magi, never connects them with the Epiphany.

[2] Siricius ordered Easter and Pentecost to be kept as days of general baptism: Leo expressly forbids baptism at the Epiphany "the commemoration of the visit of the Magi" (Dion. Exig. *Coll. Decr.* in Migne, *P.L.* LXVII. 232, 281).

and Cyril; Flavian, Eutyches, Dioscurus and Theodoret —until after many failures Antioch was victorious and drove from the Church the characteristic Christian philosophy of the Greeks.

The task of founding the Antiochene School was undertaken not by Paul but by one of the most interesting and perplexing personages in early Church history, Lucian of Antioch, who died a confessor to the faith in the persecution of Maximin Daza, apparently in 309 A.D. The evidence on which our knowledge of Lucian's history and opinions is based is not only scanty but very conflicting: indeed, the only point on which all are agreed is that he was a man of great sanctity, eminence and influence: in every other respect the accounts of his contemporaries, of later writers and of modern historians are notoriously contradictory, ascribing to him a variety of theories not only inconsistent but mutually destructive. Thus Alexander, the bishop of Alexandria who quarrelled with Arius, in the letter to Alexander of Byzantium[1], states as an accepted fact that Lucian followed in the footsteps of Ebion, Artemas and Paul of Samosata, and remained outside the orthodox communion during the episcopates of Paul's successors. On the other hand, Eusebius[2] is warm in his praise, and the Confession of Faith preserved as Lucian's by Rufinus[3] and almost universally accepted as genuine, clearly shows that its author rejected Paul's Christology and maintained the belief that the Logos assumed flesh but did not possess a human soul—a point which Epiphanius[4] expressly declares that he taught. The evi-

[1] In Theodoret, *H.E.* i. 3.
[2] *H.E.* ix. 6.
[3] In his translation of Eusebius on *H.E.* ix. 6.
[4] *Ancoratus*, 33.

dence of later generations is not less contradictory. Chrysostom[1] describes him as a sainted martyr; Epiphanius[2] as the fountain-head of the abominations of Arius and as only called a martyr by Arians. The Council of the Dedication in 341 A.D. produced as Lucian's a creed which, although the Nicenes could not accept it owing to the absence of the actual word ὁμοούσιος, is yet thoroughly orthodox in its definition of the Son; Philostorgius, the Arian historian, who is naturally eager to claim the great teacher as the founder of his own party, gives an imposing list of the Arian leaders who had been Lucian's pupils[3] and evades the unpleasant evidence of the creed by the incredible suggestion that Asterius, whom Athanasius[4] had quoted as an arch-heretic, had interpolated into it the orthodox phrases[5]. Nor are modern scholars more in agreement. Dr Harnack, who labels him "the Arius before Arius," and is followed by most English scholars, says that he combined the two irreconcilables by teaching that Christ was at once the Logos clothed in flesh and also capable of moral progress and deification—a blend of two heresies which led inevitably to the belief that the Logos was imperfect, changeable and totally distinct from the essence of the Father. Harnack's main argument for this is the evidence of Philostorgius, a bad

[1] *Hom. in S. Lucianum Mart.*

[2] *Haer.* xliii. 1.

[3] Antonius of Tarsus and Leontius of Antioch, "who preserved their faith unshaken at Nicea," Eusebius of Nicomedea, Maris of Chalcedon, Theognis of Nicea, who forsook it for a time but soon returned, Menophantus, Eumenius, Eudoxius, and Asterius the Cappadocian, the black sheep of the flock.

[4] *De Syn.* 18.

[5] Philostorgius may have been misled by Asterius' use of ἀπαράλλακτον εἰκόνα (the phrase in Lucian's creed) in his book against Marcellus (Epiphanius, *Haer.* lxxii. 6).

witness unless strongly supported: but it is a convenient theory if we are to reconcile the contradictions in the statements that have come down to us. At the same time its plausibility must not be allowed to conceal its weakness. For it does violence to the two facts about Lucian which no one disputes, that he was a scholar and a man of profound intellect, and that he was a martyr and a man of devoted piety[1]. It seems frankly incredible that such a man should have professed and taught publicly for many years opinions at once notoriously illogical and incapable of satisfying the needs of a religious life. To suppose that he was an Arian, and muddle-headed Arian at that, is to rob him of his claim either to sainthood or to intelligence. Nor is it necessary to make Lucian responsible for the development of Arianism when the whole circumstances of the time, secular and ecclesiastical, led inevitably to it: Origen's case ought to warn us against inferring the master's teaching from the views of his disciples. On the other hand, Gwatkin seems to go too far in the opposite direction when he writes that "there is really nothing against him except the leaning of his disciples to Arianism," and that Alexander's statement may be set aside on account of its "reckless tone[2]." To throw over the contemporary evidence in this way seems arbitrary. The Confession of Faith, to which Gwatkin does not allude, may possibly be spurious: but no strong argument has yet been brought against it, and the fact that we owe its preservation to Rufinus is not enough in itself to destroy the possibility of genuineness, even if its doc-

[1] Eusebius, *H.E.* viii. 13. "One who proclaimed Christ's Kingdom first by word in its defence and then by action."

[2] *Studies of Arianism*, p. 17, note.

trine were not supported by Epiphanius. Alexander's letter has even greater claims to respect: for the bishop, after writing a sound and accurate account of the teaching of Arius, would not be likely to spoil his case on such an important issue by an unguarded and slanderous attack upon one so revered as Lucian. His statement seems to ring true; and indeed when the facts must have been familiar to all, deliberate falsehood seems as impossible as reckless ignorance.

When there is such a difference of opinion among the greatest authorities it seems presumptuous to suggest that it is possible to appreciate the position of Lucian without either casting a slur upon his memory or throwing over the contemporary evidence. For a careful consideration of that evidence supplies a clue to the real facts. Alexander's letter, which seems of first-rate importance, simply states that Lucian was for the earlier part of his active career outside the orthodox communion, and that during this period he taught the doctrine of Paul, implying that he then maintained the distinction between Father and Son as between unbegotten and begotten and the human progress and adoption of Jesus. This form of Paul's theology, modified as it is by the recognition of the pre-existent personality of the Logos, is exactly what his Arian pupils afterwards agreed to maintain, and in that time of uncertainty it would not seem far removed except in Christology from orthodox opinion. It is, however, clearly inconsistent with the views which he held later on in life after his admission to communion and at the time of his martyrdom, when the Confession of Faith was delivered[1]. For in the Confession (and we believe

[1] So Rufinus, *l.c.*

it to be genuine) there is not a word about distinction of essence in the Trinity or moral progress in Jesus. It is a simple expression of the principles of the Logos-doctrine: Christ the divine Word and Wisdom has become incarnate by assuming flesh, and has thus given to mankind the perfect example of perseverance in virtue. Such a statement might in fact be used as a recantation of Paul's views; for its wording is in complete agreement with the letter of the six bishops. That Lucian did actually change his early teaching in the direction of the dominant Logos-theology is implied, indeed demanded, by the fact of his reconciliation with the Church: and such a change is what would naturally occur when once his studies and devotion had discovered the inadequacy of Paul's position. No doubt his conversion was a gradual process of which the reconciliation was only the completion. Starting from the Ebionite view of Jesus as man it may have been the work of years to arrive at the conviction that this did not adequately explain the experience of Him as Son of God and Saviour. But such a change follows the natural lines of development for religious temperaments. Had he lived a century later he might have seen that the two aspects, human and divine, were not irreconcilable, and might have helped to formulate the doctrine of their union. As it was he could only see that his new vision was inconsistent with his old, and be driven sooner or later to pass from the one extreme to the other. The stages of his passage may well have been as follows: first the acceptance of the texts of the Old Testament which almost all Christians at that time regarded as proofs of the personal pre-existence of the Son, and consequently the rejection of Paul's belief that the

Logos was a mere faculty of God: then the application of analogous arguments to the incarnate Logos, and the conviction that in Christ also the Logos must be personal: finally, the conclusion that belief in an indwelling divine personality was inconsistent with belief in the possession of a human soul, and the denial of those attributes of change and progress which, suitable enough for an inspired man, were unworthy of the Logos made flesh. That some change of this kind did in fact take place seems not only consistent with the evidence, but the only method of explaining it. It accounts for the ascription to him of opinions mutually incompatible: it accounts for his change of attitude towards orthodoxy: it accounts for the Arian tendencies of his pupils: it accounts for the reverence paid to him by the Church as scholar and as saint.

The only point in this reconstruction of Lucian's beliefs that needs further explanation, if we are to understand the work of Apollinarius, is that raised by Epiphanius' statement that Lucian and all the Lucianists denied that the Son of God assumed a human soul: "I suppose they do so," adds that uncharitable controversialist, "in order that they may assign to the divine Logos human suffering and all that He underwent during His sojourn in the body[1]"—an insinuation simply due to the subsequent course of history, and an ascription to Lucian of motives which undoubtedly influenced Eunomius and the Anomoeans, but which were neither present in Lucian's mind nor recognised as a necessary consequence of the denial until after his time. Never-

[1] *Ancoratus*, 33. Gwatkin, *Studies of Arianism*, p. 17, n., rightly remarks that the accusation "is no clear case for a charge of heresy in Lucian's time."

theless, that Lucian, who died an orthodox supporter of the Logos-theology, should be said to have taught this belief may seem strange to those who refuse to recognise that such Apollinarianism was the accepted and universal doctrine of the typically Greek Churchmen of the time. Lucian in denying to Christ a human soul was only doing what all the Origenists, when once they abandoned their master's theory of the pre-existence of souls, found themselves obliged to do, and what Justin and Clement had already done. He was merely accepting an integral part of their theology[1].

The truth of the statement that this was the traditional opinion of Greek catholicism, as well as the causes which made it more inevitable at this time than previously, may be studied very clearly in the only Christological work of this period, the *De Incarnatione* of Athanasius, a book in which the Logos-theology and denial of a human soul to Christ are put forward frankly as the Catholic Faith. In Athanasius at least no unworthy desire to degrade Christ can be assumed from such a belief; and where the protagonist of orthodoxy agrees with him it is not fair to sneer at Lucian.

In view of the comparatively recent studies of Hoss[2] and Stülcken[3] on the Christology of Athanasius, studies naturally based upon his one uncontroversial dogmatic treatise and incidentally somewhat over-emphasising

[1] The words of the creed quoted by Alexander of Alexandria to his namesake of Byzantium (in Theodoret, *H.E.* i. 3) are proof enough: "Our Lord Jesus Christ who wore a body in truth not in semblance from Mary Mother of God and sojourned among the race of men." Cf. also the fragments of the *De Divin.* of Peter of Alexandria, martyred 311, quoted at the Council of Ephesus 431, Act. I.

[2] *Schriftum und die Theologie des Athanasius.*

[3] *Athanasiana* (Texte und Unters. N.F. IV. 4).

the importance of its evidence, it may seem unnecessary to do more than comment upon their conclusions. But the *De Incarnatione* is so interesting in itself and so significant of the position adopted by Greek thinkers of this age, that in order to trace the course of doctrinal history we cannot pass it over. It is, in fact, the last of the great series of Apologies, and to a large extent its scope and arguments are dictated by its purpose. Like the works of Justin it falls into two sections, one addressed to Jews and consisting almost entirely of quotations from and explanations of the Old Testament, and the other addressed to philosophic pagans. This latter follows earlier precedents in basing its argument on the two ideas which such readers would admit, that there is perceptible in the universe a rational purpose or Logos manifesting itself through the laws of nature, controlling the order of events and making for unity and harmony, and that there is an analogy between the universe and the individual, so that if it is allowed that the former contains evidence of an immanent principle of reason a similar conclusion must be accepted with regard to the latter. This portion therefore developed into an exposition of the Logos-theology, and although lacking in originality and not strictly in harmony with much of its author's thought, is yet one of the most systematic, lucid and concise statements of the doctrine. The characteristic belief, traceable through all the Greek Apologists right back to the Apostolic age, a belief in the Logos as Himself the image of God and as the source of that image in men, as the creator and sustainer of the world, as the giver of life and reason, as the revealer of God through nature, through the Law and prophets, and, finally, through His own Incarnation, is pressed home upon unbelievers. The resemblance to the Alexandrian School is in general very striking: but it is a resemblance of expression rather than of thought; the language is the language of the Apologists, but the ideas are the ideas of St Paul.

That is, here as elsewhere, the great feature of Athanasius' work. All his power, all the splendid contribution which he made to Christianity, spring from this fundamental fact that he alone, at a time when men were tempted to substitute a monistic philosophy for the gospel, when Platonism was dominant and much of the value and uniqueness of Christ neglected, felt keenly the sense of sin and failure and the need for redemption and atonement. This changed attitude towards sin naturally affects even the arguments that he borrows from his predecessors. Their doctrine contemplates religion as an ever-developing process of evolution, a steady education of God's divine children by their Father, in which although perfection has not yet been attained the end is sure and will come when once man's ignorance has been enlightened. Athanasius is the first of his countrymen to abandon this cheerful faith. To him the world is rather the scene of an eternal struggle. Men are not ignorant so much as wilfully and perversely rebellious. The first man chose evil rather than good, death rather than life, and his descendants have inherited his preference. No mere imitation of a good example will suffice to raise the fallen: for humanity not only will not but cannot rise of itself. A death unto sin and a new birth unto righteousness, a complete break with the old, a fresh start upon the new, can alone achieve improvement. Mankind, originally created in the image or according to the Logos of God, has in

Adam defiled the image, rejected the Logos. Christ comes to recreate and restore. Whereas the Origenists borrowed from Plato his vision of the ascent of man from the phenomenal to the real, Athanasius borrows his antitheses of becoming and being, semblance and actuality, and applies them to the condition of man who without Christ is the prey of sin and death, a phantom devoid of all true existence, who can only obtain through Christ the special gift of grace which bestows righteousness and immortality. To the Alexandrians it is the birthright of every man to be in the image of God, the heir of an eternal heritage: to Athanasius, as to Apollinarius after him, that birthright once given has now been lost and lost irrevocably unless He who first made the covenant be pleased in His mercy to renew it.

This fundamental quality of his thought had naturally a large effect upon his Christology. To the typical Greek it did not vitally matter whether Christ were Son of God or Son of Man: in either case what was wanted was a perfect pattern for men to copy. Holding their views about the divinity of the human race as a whole, they did in fact find no difficulty in confessing the special divinity of the archetype of man. But the indifference of the conservative majority to the issue raised by Arius is proof enough that they did not feel the constraining force of the claim for co-essential Godhead. To Athanasius the matter was different: to him to interpret Christ as in any sense an inspired man, whether as possessing a full share of the Logos which His brethren had in part, or as maintaining continually the allegiance to goodness which they continually repudiated, was to misunderstand the true scope of Christ's work. That work was twofold: "He reversed the death sentence by the offering up of His body, while He corrected error by His teaching, thus by His power setting upright the whole state of man[1]": the second function which had alone been fully recognised by his predecessors might be fulfilled by purely human means; the former which is to Athanasius indispensable could only be achieved by God Himself. No substitute, no inferior deity, is sufficient. The sin-tainted could only secure the sure hope of salvation if the giver of the promise be very God of very God. That is why Athanasius was ready to face exile and the fear of death in defence of a word, and why the deity of Christ mattered so much more to him than to the others.

And yet in stating his belief he met with a great difficulty. The argument against pagan philosophy proceeded from its admission of a general indwelling of Logos in the universe and in the individual to the assertion of a particular indwelling of special fulness in one individual, Christ. It was a chain of reasoning hallowed by long usage, and Athanasius sets it out forcibly and with plausibility. But at the same time its cogency can only be maintained if the mode of indwelling in Christ and in other men be similar. At Antioch Malchion's distinction between the Logos as an essence and the Logos as a quality had really destroyed the validity of the analogy. To Athanasius also, although he uses the argument, it would have been fatal to allow for a moment that the mode was similar: for it must then follow that Christ differs only in the quantity of His inspiration from us and is not God but God-inspired man. If the Logos dwells in Him as in us, then He is a prophet after all, and the Samosatene

[1] *De Inc.* x. 1.

was right. Such a consequence must be avoided at all costs. Athanasius must vitiate his logic if he would escape heresy. He did so by accepting the traditional Gnosticism of Alexandria, by making the Godhead the centre of Christ's personality and by denying tacitly but indubitably His possession of a human soul. There was no other means of escape open to him. The Christology of the treatise is forced upon him by sheer necessity.

The chief passage in which it is expressed is worth quoting in full in order to compare its language with that of Apollinarius. "When the theologians speak of Christ as eating and drinking and being born, remember that it is only the body as body that is born and nurtured with appropriate food, but that He who is present in the body is God the Logos. By the works that He wrought in the body He revealed Himself to be not man but God the Logos. This language is applicable to Him since the body which eats and is born and suffers was the body not of any other but of the Lord, and because when He became man it was but fitting to speak about Him as though about a man[1], that it may be proved that He has a body in reality not in semblance[2]." This is the most definite statement of the subject: but there are a great number of other phrases in which the manhood of Christ is described, and in every one of them it is called only His body, His shrine, His instrument[3], and never regarded as complete or

[1] Robertson, *Athanasius*, p. 46, wrongly translates "to be predicated of Him as man," a rendering incompatible with the order of the Greek which plainly implies that He only appeared to be, and was not, man.

[2] *De Inc.* xviii. 1, 2.

[3] Cf. *De Inc.* viii. 2, 3; ix. 1, 2; x. 4; xiv. 8; xx. 2; xlii. 6, 7.

personal. This body it is which is offered to death to fulfil the debt and redeem mankind. "The Logos," he says, in another striking sentence, "could not die; for He is immortal, the Son of the Father. So He took to Himself a body able to die, in order that this becoming partner with the almighty Logos might be paid to death as an adequate ransom for all men, and at the same time might remain incorruptible owing to the indwelling Logos[1]": and the same thought is continually repeated. Clearly the conception of a perfect manhood and a human soul was not needed so long as the idea of Godhead expressed by the term Logos prevailed. It would further seem to lead to Samosatene heresy. So Athanasius at this time in his life definitely rejected it, and, as we shall show, persisted in so doing at least until his last years.

Yet, although in his case there was a peculiar motive for the rejection, he was only following the universal habit of his time. The whole trend of theology made it impossible for the Hellenic churches to attach any meaning to the formula of Two Natures. Probably it is strictly fair to say that no orthodox Greek Christian since the close of the first century, unless Origen be included among the orthodox, would have felt any hesitation in denying that Christ had a human soul as distinct from the Logos. "Veiled in flesh the Godhead see. Hail the incarnate Deity" had no savour of heresy to them. The human nature of our Lord was interpreted in the sense that Christ was perfect man because the Logos was the archetype of humanity, rather than that He satisfied our need for God most fully because He possessed and had experienced all the weakness, all the

[1] *De Inc.* ix. 1.

temptations of a man amongst men. Until Paul's condemnation the denial had been rather implied than expressed, though Clement stated it plainly enough: but the definite confession that in Christ the Logos was an οὐσία οὐσιωμένη made such a denial an explicit tenet of formal orthodoxy, and by the readiness with which it was accepted proves that it was not regarded as anything of an innovation. Our study of the attitude of Arius and his opponents will amply confirm what we have already seen in the cases of Lucian and Athanasius.

CHAPTER III

THE ARIANS AND THEIR OPPONENTS

It has generally been the custom among students to regard the great controversy with Arianism as concerned solely until its latest phase with the doctrine of the Godhead: it is classified as Trinitarian, not Christological: and the significance of the Arian attitude towards the Person of Christ has been entirely neglected. Hence in great part has arisen the mistaken notion that there was almost no formulated thought on the nature of the Incarnate until Apollinarius, a notion which has led to the belief that he invented not only the particular heresy ascribed to him but all that chaos of ideas which we see described in such a treatise as Athanasius' *Ad Epictetum*. To suppose that Christology started with Apollinarius is unjust to him: even the error for which he was condemned was, as we have seen, common property at least a century before his death: and, attractive as it is to certain minds to make a notorious heresiarch a scapegoat upon whom can be safely laid all the sins of the orthodox, it is in this case a proceeding historically unjustifiable.

As a matter of fact, Christology was an important element of the earliest Arianism as is made plain by the first documents of the controversy. The letter written by Alexander of Alexandria to his namesake of Byzantium[1] to explain the grounds of his quarrel with his presbyter, and already quoted for its evidence upon

[1] In Theodoret, *H.E.* i. 3.

Lucian, is quite definite. Arius, according to it, had been teaching that Christ was not co-eternal with God but had been created out of nothing: that is what Alexander condemns. But having stated this, the letter goes on to lay bare the considerations which had led Arius to this error, and accuses him of saying that the Saviour was not by nature Son of God, but that "although capable of change He yet by habitual diligence and practice never did incline towards evil and so was adopted Son of God." Alexander adduces many texts to counteract this by proving that Christ's Sonship was due "not to this diligent practice of moral progress but to peculiarity of nature," and that He was therefore incapable of the possibility of falling; and adds that other proofs are unnecessary since his learned readers will recognise that this is the old heresy of Ebion and Artemas, Paul and Lucian. If this letter stood alone we might suppose that Alexander was attempting the familiar trick of fastening upon his victim the charge of teaching errors that had been already condemned. But although practically all the early writings of the Arians have perished, there remains in the fragments of their leader's poem, the *Thalia*, a statement which bears out Alexander's accusation. Arius himself had written[1] "the Logos is capable of change, but of His own free-will continues good so long as He wishes. He is capable of change even as we are. God foreknowing that He would remain good, gave Him in anticipation the glory which as man and in consequence of His virtue He afterwards possessed. God from foreknowledge of His works made Him become already what He after-

[1] Quoted by Athanasius, *Or. c. Arian.* i. 5.

wards was." This extract proves that Arius accepted an estimate of Christ's ethical development identical with that of Paul, disagreeing with him only in assigning this development not to the inspired man Jesus but to the incarnate Logos. Arius in fact combined the two theories which, according to our reading, Lucian held at different times, the Adoptianism of the School of Antioch and the Logos-theology with its denial of a human soul to Christ, and so was inevitably led to ascribe all the attributes of the manhood to the Godhead and to deduce His inferiority to and estrangement from the changeless Father. The Arian argument at the opening of the controversy is a simple syllogism; Christ is the Logos incarnate: Christ is capable of change and suffering: therefore the Logos is capable of change and not equal with God.

Such an argument was exceedingly difficult for the orthodox to answer, since it could only be met by them in one of two ways. The major premiss might be denied, and a doctrine of the perfect manhood as distinct from the Godhead be boldly developed, Christ being represented as possessed of two natures, two spheres of personality, so that His sufferings and death might be ascribed only to His humanity. Or the minor premiss might be attacked if it was asserted that the human growth and emotions, ignorance and hunger and pain, of Christ were unreal, and the mass of texts which emphasised His manhood was explained away. So long as both sides agreed that changelessness and impassibility were the essential qualities of deity, there was no other possible reply to Arius: and of these two neither was very satisfactory. To the Greeks who could never avoid the habit of treating will and nature materially as if these terms referred to physical entities, the former answer seemed to assign to Christ an unthinkable dualism: the coexistence in one person of two natures mutually exclusive and antagonistic was inconceivable: in the last resort they might be forced to accept it; but they resisted the conclusion as long as possible and the Monophysites went into schism rather than agree to it. The second answer, as Alexander's letter indicates, appeared the easier: rather sacrifice the plain evidence of Scripture, and vindicate the impassibility and Godhead of the Incarnate by ingenuities of exegesis, or as was attempted later by a theory of self-emptying: this might be Gnosticism, but at least it safeguarded the philosophic concept of God and the reality of the divinity of His Son. So far as Athanasius touches Christology during the first half of the controversy he shows himself wholly in favour of this second method of interpreting Christ.

Fortunately for the orthodox, the subject was practically dropped and the dispute was soon confined to the strictly Trinitarian issue. For the Arians were not in a position to press their syllogism. Although it was at once the starting-point and the mainstay of their position, all reference to it seems to have disappeared from their propaganda until the second generation of heretics, Eudoxius, Lucius and Eunomius, arose and revived it. If Athanasius and the Nicenes were unable to meet the argument, Arius and his early associates were equally unable to force them to do so; and the reason for their inability is plain. At Nicea and indeed throughout the first phase of the struggle the Arians were fighting not primarily for Arianism but for their own right to be considered orthodox: they wanted recognition of their opinions as consistent with the Catholic Faith. So when once Alexander had demonstrated that the minor premiss of their syllogism was borrowed from the heresy of the notorious Paul of Samosata, further insistence upon it would have been suicidal, and would merely have scandalised those moderates like Eusebius of Caesarea whose support they strained every effort to secure. Only when in Eunomius' time the desire to conciliate the conservatives had passed away, and Arianism made its bid for supremacy, was their best argument brought out from the armoury to which it had been relegated and employed in the conflict.

For some thirty years Christology disappears from the writings of the chief combatants; and it is only from scattered allusions that we can trace the content of thought on the subject. Athanasius' position which is important both from his representative character and from his relation to Apollinarius, can, however, be stated with considerable clearness. The *De Incarnatione*, surely the most amazing piece of theology ever produced by a boy still in his teens[1], shows us his views before the controversy opened: but throughout his earlier writings against the Arians we find the same ideas expressed with one significant change of terminology. The only allusion to the doctrine of the Incarnation in the Creed of Nicea is contained in the insertion of the words "and was made man" to explain "incarnate." This at first sight seems to overthrow our contention that Greek thought was essentially Apollinarian. As a matter of fact the addition was due solely to a quibble

[1] Athanasius was born probably in 298: the *De Inc.* was certainly written before 319.

of which Athanasius explains the character[1], and which illustrates the change referred to in his statement of his doctrine. The Arians, denying the human soul of Christ, refused to describe Him except as the Logos incarnate or made flesh, σαρκωθείς; "made man" they could not accept. The orthodox who agreed substantially with them in their denial nevertheless admitted that the Logos and His body together constituted and could be properly called "man," and introduced the word into the Creed in this sense. Thereafter Athanasius himself regularly gives the title to what he had in his earliest work always called "the body": "man" and "manhood," when applied to Christ in his anti-Arian writings, mean "the Son of God incarnate," "the Logos veiled in flesh." Thus in the *Expositio Fidei*, which if genuine[2]

[1] Cf. *Or. c. Arian.* iii. 30, 31. Flesh is used in Scripture, e.g. *Joel* ii. 28, to represent man: but Christ is not a man. St Paul, *Col.* ii. 9, is quoted by Athanasius to vindicate the Nicene definition and he explains it as meaning "Being God He had His own body and using it as His instrument He became man." Hence the Logos incarnate can be said to have been "made man" and be called man because He was "in the body."

[2] The *Expos. Fid.* is very similar to the *Sermo Major de Fide* (Migne, *P.G.* XXVI. 1261 ff.), which is quoted by Theodoret and Gelasius as Athanasian. The *Sermo Major* consists of an epitome of the arguments of the *De Inc.*, many sentences being verbally identical, expanded into an attack upon Arianism on lines exactly similar to those of the *Expos*. Thus *Sermo Major*, 5 and 6, reproduce *De Inc.* ix; *S.* 7 *De Inc.* xvii. 1; *S.* 8 *De Inc.* xxvi. 6; *S.* 9 *De Inc.* xxxi. 4; *S.* 10 *De Inc.* xliii. 7, etc. *Sermo* 22 contains the same explanation of *Jeremiah* xxxi. 22, and of its versions in LXX and Aquila as *Expos.* 3; and the curious phrase ὁ κατὰ τὸν σωτῆρα νοούμενος ἄνθρωπος (*Sermo* 18) is paralleled in *Expos.* 3. At the same time the *Sermo* in many respects resembles the *Orations against the Arians*, *e.g.* the explanation of *Luke* ii. 52 in *Sermo* 18 and *Or. c. Ar.* iii. 51 ff. The Christology of the *Sermo* is thoroughly Athanasian, differing only from the *De Inc.* in its use of ἀναλαμβάνειν and φορεῖν ἄνθρωπον instead of λαμβάνειν σῶμα: in the *Sermo* ἄνθρωπος and σῶμα are both used of Christ's man-

must be very early[1], he speaks of the Son as having assumed "our man" from Mary and twice calls the humanity of Christ "the man of the Lord[2]," though he is equally ready to call it "the body of the Lord" and obviously uses the terms interchangeably. That the alteration is one of words and not of thought is made abundantly clear by a number of passages in the *Orations against the Arians*, which reflect his teaching at the period when his opponents were beginning to return to their arguments from Christology. Thus he writes that "the Son did not become different when He assumed flesh, but remaining the same was veiled by it[3], putting on a body which came into existence and was made[4]." In all this section of the book he is occupied with texts quoted by the Arians to prove that Christ was a creature, and in every case he argues that the words refer not to the uncreated Logos but to the "flesh" or "body" or "manhood." "It is not in regard to the essence of the Logos, but only in so far as His manhood is concerned, that He was made. How could the bodily aspect of the Logos be indicated except by the words 'He made

hood, but their meaning is exactly the same. It seems plain that both *Expos.* and *Sermo* are genuine and represent Athanasius' Christology during the early years of his episcopate.

[1] Robertson, *Athanasius*, p. 83, suggests 328 A.D., and that it was issued as a statement of belief on accession to his bishopric.

[2] κυριακὸς ἄνθρωπος, a curious phrase quoted by Rufinus (*De Adult. Libr. Orig.*) and Theodoret (*Dial.* iii. ed. Schulze, IV. 240) as Athanasian, but occurring elsewhere in his works only in the *Sermo Major de Fide*, in the exposition of Psalm xl (xli), and in the spurious Fourth Dialogue on the Trinity. In the *De Inc.* xxxi. 4 κυριακὸν σῶμα occurs in exactly the same sense as in the *Sermo Major*, where κυριακὸν σῶμα and κυριακὸς ἄνθρωπος are used interchangeably, as σῶμα and ἄνθρωπος are in the *Expos.*

[3] Thus he twice speaks of the body as a garment, ἱμάτιον, in *Or.* i. 47 and ἐσθής in *Or.* ii. 8.

[4] *Or.* ii. 8.

it[1]'?" The most illuminating passage is that in which the crucial text in St Luke is discussed, and there Athanasius asks "Is Jesus Christ a man like all the rest of mankind, or God wearing flesh?" and answers "if He is in truth an ordinary man like the rest of men then let it be granted that as a man He makes progress: this, however, is the doctrine of the Samosatene which in actual practice you accept, though nominally and for fear of public opinion you repudiate it. If He is God wearing flesh which is the explicit meaning of 'the Word became flesh,' what kind of progress could He have who was eternally equal with God?...The progress belongs to the body[2]." Here, indeed, Athanasius shows his own mind. The fear of Paul's heresy, the dread of any suggestion of humanity lest it should impair the Godhead of Christ, constrains him to explain away the Scripture and assert in plain words that the manhood of the Master is confined to the assumption of a human body, that in Jesus there is no room for a human soul. Just as in the passage quoted His growth is explained away, so His want and weakness and ignorance are all interpreted simply as necessary conditions of the part which He has to play while incarnate, as concessions to the understanding of His followers and as tests of their faith: they are a pretence and nothing more[3]. "He showed that His body was passible by permitting it to weep and hunger[4]." Apollinarius himself could scarcely

[1] *Or.* ii. 12: numerous similar passages are to be found: cf. *Or.* iii. 31, 32, 38, 39, etc.

[2] *Or.* iii. 51, 52.

[3] Cf. *Or.* iii. 37 (ignorance); 40 (weakness); 56 (fear); and *Ad Serap.* ii. 9.

[4] *Or.* iii. 55. Newman's notes on these *Orations* prove that Catholic doctrine has far outstripped Athanasius in artificiality and docetism.

have been more definite; and Athanasius at this time of his life at least must have endorsed all his friend's teaching on the subject[1]. That is one of the certainties of history; and even the Catholic scholars who have the strongest motive for reconciling his doctrine with that of Chalcedon, have lately given up the attempt to defend the views of his earlier years[2].

The prevailing uncertainty and lack of definite Christological teaching during the first phase of Arianism were due partly to the motives that we have been describing, and partly also to the absorbing character of the Trinitarian dispute. If in one sense the doctrine of the Trinity is only a consequence of the claim that God and man have come together in the person of Jesus Christ, it was none the less natural that when once the controversy had begun no progress should be attempted in the explanation of this union until it had been settled what was meant by God. Arius and his followers devoted themselves to the task of overthrowing the verdict of Nicea and of winning over the conservatives or moderates who had formed the majority of the Council. With this end they searched the Scriptures for proofs of the unity of God, and compelled their opponents to turn from philosophy and dogmatics to exegesis and an endless discussion of epithets. Meanwhile, with the leaders of thought fully occupied, the way was opened

[1] Cf. Dr Rashdall, "Plain Words to Bishop Gore" (*Modern Churchman*, XII. 6–28), a brief but convincing exposition of the Apollinarianism of Athanasius. The evidence to any honest student of the *Orations* is overwhelming. Almost every section could be quoted.

[2] Tixeront, whose book is able and honest save for its omissions, dismisses the Christology of all his writings prior to 362 in a footnote and without discussion (*H.D.* II. 116). Cf. Ottley, *Doct. of the Inc.* II. 33.

for a revival of all kinds of wild speculation. The stability of the faith which had been temporarily secured by Origen's efforts had been shaken: the graves of dead heresies were opened and their inmates came forth. Marcellus, who regarded personal existence as a limitation imposed upon the Logos by His circumscription within the bounds of flesh, and Photinus, his little-known follower, who brought this theory into conformity with Paul's by saying that the flesh, not the union of flesh and Logos, was the seat of personality, and that this being originally human was adopted as His own by the impersonal Logos, added to the confusion. That Marcellus was never condemned by Athanasius although several criticisms of his work were made by more orthodox writers than Eusebius of Caesarea, shows how great was the general uncertainty. Indeed, language like that of Athanasius, describing Christ as Godhead veiled in flesh, language which being used by Arians and Nicenes alike must have seemed to the ordinary Christian indisputably orthodox, encouraged the reappearance of the barest docetism. So long as there was a danger of Samosatene heresy in any ascription to Christ of a complete humanity, and of Arianism if the attributes of man were attached directly to His Godhead, men would naturally ask in perplexity whether He could be called human at all. Was not even the possession of a human body a proof of the inferiority of His divinity? Would it not be safer to merge this meaningless and embarrassing manhood entirely in the deity and return to the belief of the old-fashioned Gnostics that Christ was simply and wholly a divine being who had indeed been made visible to human eyes and had in appearance undergone the ordinary conditions of human life, but who had never been in any sense a man among men? Some such refuge as this was very widely accepted and various long-buried heresies were revived. The old beliefs that the body of Christ was "heavenly" in substance, that He brought it with Him when He became incarnate, and that in His birth He took nothing from His mother, were again given expression; and a mass of other crudely docetic teaching was proclaimed and became widespread.

Very clear proof of this tendency to repudiate the reality even of the human flesh of Christ is to be found in the great treatise on the faith composed by Hilary of Poitiers during his exile in Asia Minor between 356 and 359. The Christology of the *De Trinitate* is admitted to be indisputably docetic, though attempts have been freely made to conceal the extent of its errors, and orthodox interpolations contradicting his plain meaning have appeared in many places in some of the manuscripts. Hilary is concerned with the problem of the ignorance and weaknesses of our Lord, and like Athanasius sets himself to explain them away. In doing so he is more radical than the great Alexandrian. Christ said that He did not know the hour of the Second Coming: such a denial is "due to the economy of His hidden wisdom[1]," and is "a divine plan of silence[2]." "He says that He does not know in order that others may not know; that the Father alone knows, to show that He also knows[3]." And in this sense the apostles understood Him; for they asked the same question later, and then He did not plead ignorance. So of His human needs, "He ate and drank as a concession not to His own necessities but to

[1] *De Trin.* ix. 71. [2] *L.c.* ix. 75. [3] *L.c.* ix. 71.

our habits[1]." And of His fear, "He cannot fear death whose purpose is only to die for a moment[2]." But it is in his explanation of our Lord's suffering that Hilary comes nearest to Gnosticism; for he then gives an account of the quality of Christ's person. He admits, indeed, the reality of the human birth: but, like Aeschylus[3], declares that the mother contributes nothing to it except the nurture of the germ, nothing more than the soil does to the seed. Thus "His body did not owe its origin to her[4]": "He is the origin of His own body[5]": "Since He is 'the bread which comes down from heaven,' His body cannot be supposed to have sprung from a human conception, because it is proved to be from heaven[5]." Certain heretics declare that "since the body and soul of Adam both sinned, the Lord must have taken from the Virgin the body and soul of Adam, and therefore that she did not conceive the whole man from the Holy Ghost[6]": to which Hilary replies, "If it is from God alone that the Virgin received the flesh that she conceived, it is far more certain that from God alone came the soul of that body[7]." In consequence, such a body could feel no pain: "That flesh is from heaven; that humanity is from God. He had a body to suffer and He

[1] *L.c.* x. 24. [2] *L.c.* x. 12.

[3] *Eumenides*, 627–43. Cf. *De Trin.* x. 15–16. Plutarch, *De Stoic. Repugn.* 41, quotes Chrysippus as holding this view, and in *Sympos.* iii. Q. iv. 3, mentions it himself. Aristotle knew better: cf. *De Gener. Anim.*

[4] *L.c.* x. 16. [5] *L.c.* x. 18.

[6] *L.c.* x. 20. This is absurdly explained both in a footnote and in the introduction to the volume of the Nicene and Post-Nicene Fathers (*Hilary*, pp. 186–7 and lxx–lxxi) as an argument refuting Apollinarianism. Hilary's whole point is, of course, that neither body nor soul is really human.

[7] *L.c.* x. 22.

suffered: but He had not a nature capable of feeling pain[1]."

It is unnecessary for us to discuss whether this represented the fulness of Hilary's thought on the subject, or the extent to which his other writings modify it. It is at least clear proof that in arguing with the Arians of the East he lapsed into crudely Valentinian ideas and thereby testifies that the orthodox had no more appreciation than their opponents of the reality of Christ's manhood. At least as early as 351 when the conservative First Council of Sirmium anathematised those who interpreted the text "The Word became flesh" as implying that He was transformed into flesh or had been changed by assuming it, and those who declared His Godhead to be passible[2], Christology had been brought back into the controversy. Hilary shows with what uncertainty it was handled.

This reappearance within the Church of errors long ago condemned and apparently driven from it is very characteristic of the middle years of Arianism, and has been strangely misunderstood by students of Church history. And their misunderstanding has led them to ascribe all this variegated docetism to Apollinarius. It is too often forgotten that the Marcionite churches were still strong in many quarters and particularly so in Syria[3], that there were Valentinians active in Egypt[4], and that the Manichees were serious rivals to the Chris-

[1] *L.c.* x. 23. For a still clearer statement cf. *Tr. in Psalm.* cxli. 4.

[2] Creed in Athanasius, *De Synod.* 27; Hahn, *Bibl. der Symbole*, pp. 197–8.

[3] Cf. Theodoret, *Ep.* 113.

[4] Epiphanius, *Haer.* xxxi. 7. In *Haer.* lxxvii. 15 Epiphanius admits that the crude errors which he wrongly ascribed to Apollinarius were derived "from men estranged from the Church and akin to Valentinus, Marcion and Manes."

tians. Furthermore, as we have seen, Paul of Samosata had a living representative in Photinus; Athanasius had in his early years been a forerunner of Apollinarius; Eunomius had revived Arius' insistence upon the absence of a human soul in Christ; and the school of Antioch was combatting him by teaching which anticipated Nestorianism. All the evidence goes to show that there was an atmosphere of uncontrolled speculation abroad in matters of Christology, and that even the fathers of the Church were bewildered, not knowing how to locate the error or when located how to correct it. In consequence, when once Apollinarius was condemned and the orthodox recognised him as a heresiarch, all the floating misbeliefs with which they were familiar were recklessly ascribed either to him or at least to his influence—Polemon and Timothy of Berytus, two disciples who exaggerated his teaching, lending some slight colour to the charge[1]. Basil no doubt furnishes the explanation when he states that Apollinarius is a voluminous writer and that prominent ecclesiastics have no time for modern theology[2]. Authorities like Ambrose[3] and Gregory Nazianzen, who could not avoid

[1] They maintained that the flesh was "from Mary" and therefore ἡμῖν ὁμοούσιον, *i.e.* neither pre-existent nor of the substance of the Logos—thus repudiating the docetism of the time: but unlike the other Apollinarians and the heresiarch they held that its complete union with the Godhead rendered it ὁμοούσιον θεοτῆτι: cf. Timothy, *Ad Homonium*, *ap.* Leontius, *Fraud.* p. 138. The few extracts from Apollinarius which, if they stood alone, might support this view are discussed later.

[2] *Ep.* 244.

[3] The influence of Ambrose, *De Incarn. Dom. Sacr.*, also called in early times the *C. Apollinaristas*, in promoting belief that the *Ad Epict.* was an attack on Apollinarius, has been very great. Its §§ 49–51 are little more than a translation of the *Ad Epict.* but contain one reference to a saying presumably Apollinarian in origin. Hence sprang the conviction that Athanasius' letter was itself

the responsibility of pronouncing an opinion upon the new heresy, knew much about the current Gnosticism and if they had not read Apollinarius, as Ambrose, despite one supposed quotation, had not[1], found it easier to attack what they knew than to discover his opinions—especially as for the Easterns these were remarkably like their own. Athanasius and Basil long before Apollinarius was even suspected of heterodoxy had written against various forms of docetic speculation[2]. Their successors after his condemnation, following the lead of Epiphanius and Ambrose, assumed that these works were directed against him, and that therefore he must somehow have taught the errors attacked in them; and in this assumption seized upon any phrases of his which could support it. So it came about that wherever any Christological aberration appeared there it was assumed that the wily heresiarch or his disciples must have been at work: in Corinth, in Cyprus, in Palestine, in Egypt, in Asia Minor, Apollinarianism is as ubiquitous as it is protean[3]. The bishop of Laodicea must surely, according to these critics, have combined in himself the nebulosity of Eusebius of Caesarea, the meddlesomeness of Lucifer of Calaris and the duplicity

directed against the heresiarch. The fact that Ambrose is writing against the Arians and makes in this book no mention by name of Apollinarius proves at least that the various Christological errors which he attacked were not connected by him with Apollinarius.

[1] Cf. § 50. "I have read in a certain writer's books that in Christ the instrument and He by whom it is moved are of one nature." One fragment from Apollinarius, *Ad Heracl.* Lietzmann, Fr. 117, is the only parallel to this, and may have been sent to Ambrose. His treatise and other references to Apollinarius, *Eps.* 46 and 48, and *Enarr. in Psalm.* xxxix. 26, prove that he had read nothing else.

[2] For Basil cf. *Eps.* 261, 262 and below, pp. 254–6.

[3] And yet Sozomen, *H.E.* vi. 27, declares that the country affected by Apollinarianism was from Cilicia to Phoenicia.

of Cyril of Alexandria. The theologian beside whom Athanasius was reckoned a mere babe[1] is supposed to have employed all the catchwords of the crudest Gnosticism. The greatest thinker of his time is credited with opinions which even third-rate divines like Ambrose and Chrysostom knew to be untenable and which Epiphanius, most uncharitable of doctors, though he cannot resist the temptation to parade and criticise them in his chapter on the Dimoeritae[2], declares that he never held. And yet when we study his own works and character we discover not only that he is transparently sincere and singularly clear and consistent, but that he repeatedly anathematises and ridicules the errors which he is accused of having initiated[3]. After all, as Gregory of Nazianzus aptly reminds us[4], Christology began with Christ not with Apollinarius; and though to ascribe all the speculations of the time, especially those easiest to criticise, to the one heretic was no doubt a temptation to the harassed leaders of the Church, it was just neither to him nor to his predecessors.

[1] Philostorgius *ap*. Suidas, *Lex*. i. 115.

[2] *Haer*. lxxvii. Epiphanius had read the *Ad Epict*. and come across a variety of Christological errors, loosely connected in certain cases with Apollinarius. He investigated Vitalis' doctrine at Antioch and found that it had no relation to the *Ad Epict*. He admits that the cruder errors come rather from Valentinus, Marcion and Manes: but none the less criticises them in the same section as that of Vitalis, thus leaving his readers under the impression that Apollinarius is responsible.

[3] Cf. in Lietzmann, *l.c.* Frs. 112, 159, 162, 164. Apollinarius expressly anathematises such ideas in his letter to Jovian, l, p. 253, and to Terentius, l, Fr. 163, and his Synodal Tome, l, p. 263. Even more striking is the fact that Theodoret in his Dialogue quotes a large number of passages from Apollinarius to prove that he condemned the notions that the body of the Logos was "heavenly" and that the Logos was changed into flesh.

[4] *Ep*. 102.

And yet this habit of assigning all the loose Christology of the fourth century to his influence has been imitated and emphasised by almost every historian of recent times. Catholic students, who bring to their work the conviction that from the first there has existed a rigid and consistent tradition in matters of doctrine, naturally refuse to admit that in Christology there was as yet no definite *regula fidei*: the prevalence of manifold misbelief must be due not to the perplexity of Churchmen, but to the guile of an arch-heretic. For them, as for Basil, Apollinarius "may be expected to say anything[1]." Or if, like Voisin, they know that he was honest and frank of speech, then "pseudo-disciples" can be made responsible. But that less prejudiced historians should accept so false an estimate of the man and his times is hard to explain, unless it be that only lately the true fragments of Apollinarius' writings have been collected, and that the convention of past ages dies hard. Probably the chief cause of the misunderstanding has arisen from the influence of mistaken views of Athanasius. Until recently it was generally assumed that the two books against Apollinarius were genuine[2], and that, therefore, the great Alexandrian was aware of his former friend's lapse. Admitting this, it became natural to see in the *Tome to the Antiochenes* a censure of Apollinarius; and if the *Tome*, then surely also the *Ad Epictetum* which was so freely quoted against him in patristic times. Hence colour was given to the idea that he was in some way responsible for the mixed assortment of heterodoxies found at Corinth, and the phantasies of every contemporary Gnostic were labelled as Apollinarian in origin. It is one of the ironies of history

[1] *Ep.* 263.

[2] For these, see below, pp. 242–53.

that the most lucid and unambiguous of all Greek theologians, one so consistent that even his enemies, to whom we owe the collection of fragments from his works and who would have strained every nerve to convict him of crude heresy, could hardly ever detect a doubtful phrase, should have been made the parent of so diverse a brood of speculations. It is worth while before considering his work in detail to expose the mistake which has done him such unmerited dishonour.

As we have said, it is the letter of Athanasius to Epictetus of Corinth which has chiefly occasioned the false estimate of Apollinarianism. This was regarded in antiquity as the standard work on Christology, and is quoted as such by Cyril of Alexandria[1] and by Epiphanius[2], and used by Ambrose[3], Valentinus the Apollinarian[4], and the authors of the two books against Apollinarius and of the letter to Caesarius[5]. Only Epiphanius[6], among those who were in a position to know the truth, connects it in any way with Apollinarius, and he demonstrates plainly that the errors in it were never taught by him. Nevertheless, the majority of recent scholars[7] see in it evidence of the activity of the bishop of Laodicea and make his disciples responsible for

[1] *Ep.* 40, to John of Antioch: cf. also *Ep.* 45.

[2] *Haer.* lxxvii.

[3] *De Incarn.*: cf. above, p. 99, note.

[4] *Capita Apologiae*, 9.

[5] Ascribed to Chrysostom.

[6] The fact that Epiphanius mentions the letter after referring to the Council of Alexandria in 362 has been used as an argument for its date (*e.g.* by Dräseke, *l.c.* pp. 28, 29). Epiphanius is simply quoting the evidence of official action against errors which he connects with Apollinarius—quite unjustifiably. Obviously, therefore, a conciliar verdict precedes a private letter.

[7] Dorner, *Person of Christ*, whose treatment of the Christological confusion in the middle of the fourth century is very able and accurate, ridicules the idea: cf. *l.c.* I. ii. p. 524.

Epictetus' troubles. In order to do so, they date the letter as late as possible, most of them following Montfaucon and putting it in 371. We believe that both the supposed allusions to Apollinarianism and the late date are wholly mistaken, that Athanasius had no idea of connecting his friend with the crude opinions which he attacks, that Apollinarius was in no way the cause of their existence, and that his own beliefs did not incur a breath of suspicion until at least 374.

In the first place it must be noted that by common agreement the *Ad Epictetum* is one of a group of three letters[1] written at the same time, the two others being that to Adelphius, an Egyptian bishop, and that to Maximus, who is probably the Cynic philosopher connected with Gregory of Nazianzus. The three letters all deal with similar Christological errors, the Adoptianism of Paul of Samosata and the Antiochenes on the one hand, and on the other various docetic errors which Athanasius points out to be akin to those of Valentinus, Marcion and Manes[2]. Much the fullest account of them, based upon memoranda[3] supplied by the Bishop of Corinth, is contained in the *Ad Epictetum*, a formal and official utterance. But the two others unquestionably refer to the same topics in less detail. The *Ad Adelphium* is the only one to associate these errors with any particular source; and it assigns them explicitly to the Arians, who "seeing themselves universally proscribed, prove themselves 'inventors of evil.'" In view of what has been said there is no reason to doubt the truth of this assertion; and if so we may refer the dis-

[1] *Eps.* 59, 60, 61.

[2] *Ad Adelph.* 2.

[3] It is not clear whether these were heretical pamphlets (as *e.g.* Tixeront, *Hist. des Dogmes*, II. 109, supposes), or reports compiled by Epictetus. The Greek makes the latter much more likely.

turbances at Corinth and the efforts of Maximus, a zealous opponent of Arianism, to the same source. This alone shows that Apollinarius was in no way involved. And his innocence is further demonstrated by the fact that the *Ad Epictetum*, the longest and most important of them, was sent to him for his approval and comments. We possess among his remains fragments of the letter to Serapion of Thmuis[1], the trusted supporter of Athanasius during his later exiles, in which the Bishop of Laodicea acknowledges the receipt of "the master's letter to Corinth," expresses warm commendation of its contents, and especially condemns "the utter madness" of those who say that the flesh of Christ was consubstantial with His Godhead—the very belief which, according to some of his critics, he was actively propagating. The tone of the fragments is one of friendly deference, but Apollinarius writes with a clear sense of the value of his opinion and an entire absence of anything which could suggest that he knew himself to be implicated in the errors under criticism[2]. He is the expert to whom a draft has been submitted. The contents of the *Ad Epictetum* make any connection of it with Apollinarianism inconceivable; for it deals with seven phases of docetic error, every one of which is explicitly and repeatedly condemned in the extant writings of Apollinarius.

We have suggested that this group of letters has only been placed late in the life of Athanasius from a notion that they referred to the bishop of Laodicea. There is,

[1] In Leontius, *Adv. Fraud.* pp. 129 and 138 (Lietzmann, Frs. 159–161).

[2] Voisin, *L'Apollinarisme*, pp. 64–6, suggests that Athanasius sent the letter to him to test his orthodoxy—a theory wholly at variance with the style of his reply.

in fact, only one indication of the time of their composition in the three, the allusion at the beginning of the *Ad Epictetum* to "the assembling of diverse synods in Gaul and Spain and great Rome, which unanimously anathematised those who were still secretly supporting Arius, Auxentius of Milan, Ursacius, Valens, and Gaius of Pannonia, and wrote everywhere that no synod should be quoted in the orthodox Church save that which was held at Nicea." The identification of these synods is a notable problem, and some of the efforts of those who place the letters in 371 are curious in the extreme. Lietzmann[1], for instance, invents a special meeting of Nicenes, held where or under what circumstances he does not know, with a series of anathemas against Apollinarius and a protocol signed by Epictetus. Others see in it a reference to the synods at Rome, in Gaul and Italy, mentioned in the first sentence of the *Ad Afros*[2], and held during the pontificate of Damasus, that is, after 366; or more specifically to the synod at Rome when Auxentius was condemned in 369–70[3]. Others, again, identify it with the synods held in so many places during the reign of Julian[4], when the return of the exiles gave opportunity to other bishops, as it did to

[1] *Apollinaris*, p. 11.

[2] The identification of these and the dating of the *Ad Afros* are obscure. Gaius is not mentioned in it.

[3] So Voisin, *l.c.* p. 62, note, and Catholic historians generally. Apollinarius' letter to Serapion makes this vastly unlikely, since Athanasius was restored in 366 and did not then use Serapion as his agent. There is no evidence that Serapion was alive, though he may have survived till 368.

[4] So Robertson, *Athanasius*, p. 566, of the synods in Spain and Gaul mentioned in Athanasius, *Ad Rufin.* (*Ep.* 55) which are no doubt the same as those in *Ad Epict*. The date of *Ad Rufin.* is uncertain, but it alludes to Athanasius' synod of 362 and was probably written soon after it.

Athanasius, to convene meetings freely. The fact is that the meetings in Gaul, Spain and Rome cannot be certainly fixed, and may have taken place almost at any time; for while the East was suffering severely the West was relatively unpersecuted except when terrorised for a moment in 357 just before the Arian triumph at Sirmium. We know of synods held in Gaul to protest against the Blasphemy[1] and at Paris to ratify the Nicene faith and excommunicate the Arians of the West[2]. The principal point to notice about the description in the *Ad Epictetum* is its almost exact resemblance to the account of the Council of Ariminum given in Athanasius' *De Synodis*[3], where he tells us that these same four and two other secret Arians were condemned, that it was declared that no attempt must be made to revise the Nicene Creed, and that a letter was sent to Constantius to this effect. The parallelism is indisputable, and convincing. It must be to this phase of the Arian controversy that the *Ad Epictetum* refers, and the synods must be those held so frequently at this time or in the next year. 360 or 361 will be the date for the group of letters[4].

[1] Phoebadius took the lead: cf. his *C. Arian.* and Gwatkin, *Studies of Arianism*, p. 163.

[2] Hilary, *Frag.* 11, gives their letter to the East. De Broglie, *L'Église et l'Empire Rom.* IV. 93, dates this in 361. It may well have been earlier.

[3] §§ 9–11.

[4] The synod in Gaul will be one of those mentioned: Athanasius, *Hist. Arian.* 45, implies that Hosius of Cordova made a public recantation of his lapse, and tradition strongly supports the belief that he died in Spain: a council there in 358 is at least possible. Liberius restored from exile in 359 was not at Ariminum and may well have mooted or even held a synod to reassert his adherence to Nicea. After their disappointment at the results reached at Ariminum and Seleucia, and Constantius' withdrawal to the East, the Westerns were roused to activity and a multitude of meetings took place.

A further proof of this is provided by the total absence in all three of any allusion to Athanasius' own very important council at Alexandria in 362[1]. As we shall see, this meeting was definitely concerned with Christology and in the Synodal Letter, the famous *Tomus ad Antiochenos*, clauses defining the nature of the Incarnate were expressly included. It is unthinkable that the great bishop should quote councils in the West which had no direct connection with Christology if his own synod, the first at which the question was debated, had already been held. Especially is this impossible in the case of the *Ad Adelphium*; for this same Adelphius[2] was present in 362 and in writing to him Athanasius must certainly have reminded him of the very relevant decisions then taken. The *Tome* was one of its author's most significant writings, and its Christological clauses were actually used at Rome as a test of orthodoxy when the case of Vitalis the Apollinarian was discussed there in 375[3]. To place the three letters after 362 seems frankly impossible: only a misconception of the situation and of Apollinarius' connection with it has made it seem desirable.

The three letters deal, as we have said, with similar topics. The Arians in the last phases of their theology had reverted to the interest in Christology, and showed a tendency to deny the reality of the body of Christ: Athanasius describes them as "neither acknowledging Him as God, nor believing that He has become man[4]." Their great opponent attacks this Gnostic error in all three letters, insisting upon the reality of the flesh

[1] Such as occurs, *e.g.*, in the *Ad Rufin.*

[2] Adelphius of Onuphis is among the signatories (*Tom. ad Antioch.* 10).

[3] Cf. below, p. 141.

[4] *Ad Adelph.* 1.

assumed by the Lord, but in such a way as to prove that he is still thoroughly Apollinarian in his own outlook[1]. It is unnecessary to survey the two shorter letters, since their contents are amplified and extended in the *Ad Epictetum*.

Epictetus had discovered wide variety of opinion among his quick-witted but superficial flock, and reported his difficulties to Athanasius with a request for advice. The great bishop in his reply cites from the memoranda supplied to him a number of these, and they are an interesting comment upon the Christological position at the time and upon the need for clearer study. Most of the quotations refer to various forms of docetism; that the body of the Logos was of the essence of the Godhead; that this essence was transmuted into flesh and bones and hair; that this body was in no sense human; that therefore the Godhead was the seat of suffering; that the body was not from Mary; that if it was from Mary there would be not a Trinity but a Tetrad; and that it had existed eternally in the God-

[1] He uses the words *γέγονεν ἄνθρωπος* and *ἐνανθρώπησις* occasionally as does the Nicene Creed: but it is *σωματικῶς ἄνθρωπος* (*Ad Max.* 3): and far more often the manhood of Christ is *σάρξ* or *σῶμα* or even *ναός* (*Ad Adelph.* 8). Thoroughly Apollinarian is his treatment of the charge of worshipping a Tetrad (*Ad Epict.* 8–9): "How can they think that the body ransomed and quickened by the Logos made an addition in Godhead to the Logos who quickened it? Rather was there a great addition to the human body by the partnership and union of the Logos with it. From being mortal it became immortal: being 'psychic' (*ψυχικόν*) it became spiritual." It is true that Athanasius is arguing against docetism: but there is not a word to indicate that he believes in the perfect humanity, and human soul of Christ. Indeed, where he argues that our salvation affects our whole manhood, soul and body, though he says that the Saviour became man, yet "salvation came by the Logos, for the body of the Lord was human and real" (*Ad Epict.* 7).

head, since it consists of the essence of the Logos[1]: these are the same errors as those attacked by Basil[2], and were known to most of his contemporaries. In addition, there are a few quotations of an Ebionitic character, that the Christ who suffered was not the Son of God but a holy man on whom the Logos descended as upon a prophet, and that these two, the man and the Logos, are quite separate. All these beliefs were collected from the orthodox members of an ordinary and unimportant see; and it is not surprising that Athanasius began to feel the need for closer thought than he had yet given to the subject or that he sent his letter to the recognised expert, his friend of Laodicea.

Certainly in his later years he followed the movement of the time in its return to the study of the Incarnation. When he returned from exile the whole issue was raised at the Council of Alexandria in 362 A.D., at which Apollinarius was unable to be present but was represented by certain monks who are honourably mentioned in the Conciliar Letter. Few questions have been more variously explained than the causes which led the Council, whose main purpose was Trinitarian, to a consideration of Christology, or the particular system contemplated by its verdict. Dräseke[3], Harnack[4], Loofs[5], Kattenbusch[6] and Gwatkin[7] suppose that Apollinarian-

[1] Every one of these seven propositions can be found condemned and ridiculed in the fragments of Apollinarius. Compare with the first, Lietzmann, Frs. 112, 153, 162, 164; with the second, Frs. 117, 121, 122, 128, 163; with the third, Frs. 149, etc.; with the fourth, Frs. 107, etc.; with the fifth, Frs. 116, 125, 160; with the sixth, K. M. II. 31; with the seventh, Lietzmann, Fr. 42, *Ad Jov.* 1. And yet critics still imagine that the *Ad Epict.* attacks Apollinarianism!

[2] Cf. below, pp. 254–6.

[3] *Apollinarios*, p. 28.

[4] *H.D.* IV. 157.

[5] *Leitfaden*, p. 161.

[6] *Apostol. Symbol.* I. 281.

[7] *Studies of Arianism*, p. 210: he reckons Arianism as equally under consideration.

ism[1] was under discussion: Robertson[2] and Stülcken[3] that it was some form of Arianism: Dorner[4] that it was the Ebionism of Antioch: while Voisin[5], whose study of Apollinarianism is always imaginative, reconstructs a lively picture of a dispute between Apollinarius and the Antiochenes, and his account is followed by Tixeront[6] who allows, however, that Apollinarius himself was in no way suspect. The tone of the Council's decision seems purely general, much more so than would have been the case if any of these many suppositions were correct. The phrasing of the Conciliar Letter, the *Tomus ad Antiochenos*, is, as Gwatkin notices[7], certainly not technical enough to exclude Apollinarius; and we have no reason to suppose that he was as yet suspected of error, indeed quite the contrary: for in his second letter to Basil[8] he refers to this Council with warm sympathy and uses its decision to support his own belief. If Arianism had been directly responsible for the raising of the question, much more drastic language would have been employed; and the Council had been summoned not to devise attacks upon the heretics or even to discuss them, but to promote mutual understanding among the orthodox. Again, though there is a definite clause excluding Paul's error, Ebionism, at least in its simpler forms, seems inadequate as an

[1] The mention of Apollinarius' representatives may probably indicate that Athanasius, having consulted him about the *Ad Epict.*, desired his support and advice.

[2] *Athanasius*, p. 481.

[3] *Athanasiana*, p. 61.

[4] *Person of Christ*, I, ii. 526–7.

[5] *L'Apollinarisme*, pp. 41–8.

[6] *Hist. des Dogmes*, II. 103, 108–9.

[7] *Studies of Arianism*, p. 210.

[8] Printed in Basil's works as *Ep.* 364. He accepted the Christological views of the *Tome* equally emphatically, though giving them his own interpretation.

inspiration for so wide a debate. Probably the motive was at first in no sense particular, but arose from Athanasius' knowledge through Epictetus' memorandum of the prevailing confusion. In addition, the Council was largely concerned with the affairs of the church of Antioch, and must have been aware, probably from the evidence of the monks sent to represent Apollinarius, that, as we shall shortly show, the Antiochene School was specially interested in Christology, and have feared their tendency to follow Paul. The Council's report reads like a gentle warning to them that though the Alexandrians are prepared to resist all docetic interpretations of Christ's humanity, they cannot countenance any such duality as might seem to be deducible from the teaching of Eustathius and Diodore; and a suggestion that a position midway between the rival errors may be found by adopting some such definition as the Council submits and that this if accepted would supply a peaceful solution of possible difficulties[1]. The terms in which Paulinus, the head of the Eustathian party, signed this statement[2] support this view of the Council's policy.

The Conciliar Letter thus drafted shows the final stage in Athanasius' Christology[3]. Whereas he had after Nicea modified the expression of his views in the *De Incarnatione* so far as to call Christ's body His manhood,

[1] This is substantially the view advocated by Stülcken, *Athanasiana*, p. 100.

[2] *Tom. ad Ant.* 11.

[3] It will be proved later that the two books *De Incarnatione et contra Apoll.*, ascribed to Athanasius, cannot be genuine. Here we may note that their acceptance has seriously hindered a right understanding both of Athanasius' Christology and of Apollinarianism, and is largely responsible for the notion that the *Ad Epict.* and the *Tom. ad Antioch.* refer to Apollinarius.

he now extends this modification still further. Shrinking from the docetism which was encouraged by a belief in Godhead veiled in flesh, and realising the importance of Christ's death and the impossibility of attaching death to the Logos, he now allowed that the Incarnate did not take a mere body deprived of soul and senses and intelligence, but united to Himself all the attributes proper to one who being Son of God became also Son of Man. At the same time, though allowing thus much humanity, he expressly condemns the belief that the Logos descended upon a perfect man. His object is twofold, to maintain the unity of the agent and to provide a double sphere for His activity; and this is explained by the series of clauses in which he goes through the chief events of the Gospels, distributing them appropriately between the Godhead and the manhood: the Christ who enquired for Lazarus and who raised him up was not two but one; He asked in His human capacity, He restored to life in His divine[1]. This seems at first sight a striking approach to the standards of a later orthodoxy: in reality it is a change of phrase rather than of belief[2]. In his youth Athanasius had treated Christ's body as the centre of His human attributes, the source of His human actions. Now he has realised that a body alone cannot constitute such a centre, and has accordingly modified the terms of his definition, so

[1] The case of Lazarus had been discussed by Athanasius in *Or. c. Arian.* iii. 37, 40, 41: some phrases are like those of the *Tome*, but the reality of the human ignorance is strongly disputed, and there is no suggestion of full manhood in Christ.

[2] That Athanasius' theology altered during his life's struggle is not improbable: certainly he modified his definitions. Failure to recognise any change in him is the chief weakness of Bethune-Baker's admirable thesis *The Meaning of* Ὁμοούσιος (*Texts and Studies*, VII. 1).

as to include explicitly what he had before understood and implied, namely something human in Christ sufficiently vital to be the seat of those experiences which could neither be assigned to the Godhead nor explained away. But there is no thought of a real humanity: Christ is still the Logos, not a man, nor even in any true sense man: the veil has been made a little thicker, that is all. Athanasius is still an Apollinarian at heart. Apollinarius, whose representatives at the Council must have been consulted as to the phrasing, could accept as his own opinion this whole section of the *Tome*; and, in fact, does so in his letter to the bishops exiled in 374 from Egypt to Diocaesarea[1], in which the crucial passage is cited in full with definite approval, though its clauses are explained and the exact significance in which they are taken is stated. His chief follower, Vitalis, who expressly anathematises those who do not accept its chief phrase, does the like[2]. That the thought not only of Athanasius but of the great school of theology to which he belonged was far too close to the heresiarch to be able to criticise him effectively we shall discover when we consider the anti-Apollinarian writings of the Gregories.

This revival of interest in Christology, if it owed much to the desire to clear up the existing confusion, owed still more to the work of the later Arians. When the few Eastern supporters of the Nicene Creed had been suppressed and the imperial support secured, it was safe for Arianism to leave conciliation and proof-texts and to develop a theology of its own. The man who

[1] In Leontius, *Adv. Fraud.* 146 (Lietzmann, *l.c.* p. 255).

[2] In his confession of faith, quoted by Cyril Alex., *De recta fide ad reg.* 10 (Lietzmann, *l.c.* p. 273).

undertook this task was Eunomius, the most capable, honest and outspoken member of the party, one of the few Arians who was neither a time-server nor, despite his attacks on the Nicenes, a wanton blasphemer. His skill in detecting and penetrating the weak places in his opponents' position is sufficiently proved by the length of the volumes which the most illustrious contemporary theologians composed against him. It is not easy to estimate his work at first hand; for his books have been destroyed and we can only judge them from the polemics that they provoked. But what can be gathered in this way supports belief in his insight and ability. He saw the impossibility of the attempt to maintain a metaphysical concept of God as the Uncaused Cause, the super-essential Absolute, and to combine this with acceptance of a consubstantial Trinity of Persons in the Godhead, and assailed it with vigour and shrewdness. So, too, in Christology he carried the war into the enemy's camp and boldly confronted Basil with the dilemma that either the Logos incarnate must be identical with the pre-existent Logos, or there must be two Christs, the pre-existent Logos and whatever was assumed by Him at His Incarnation, declaring further that if the latter alternative is accepted then ultimately salvation is the work of this manhood since it alone is the seat of the suffering and death by which we were redeemed[1]. His own views on the subject are nowhere more clearly stated than by his follower, Lucius the Anomoean, who became bishop of Alexandria in 374 A.D. and whose Christology is preserved in the *Doctrina*[2].

[1] Eunomius' argument is to be found in Gregory Nyssen., *C. Eunom.* v. and vi. (Migne, *P.G.* XLV. pp. 705 *seq.*).

[2] *Doc. de Inc.* 9.

"John," writes Lucius, "proclaims the truth 'the Word became flesh,' meaning that He was compacted with flesh but not with soul as these hucksters of the faith declare. He was united with the body and became one with it. How can Christ be anything but one person, one nature compacted as we know that soul and body are compacted to form man? If He possessed a soul, the impulses of God and of the soul would be conflicting; for each of them is self-impelled and led to display different forms of activity." The last sentence is a very cogent criticism, one that we shall find urged strongly by Apollinarius. The main contention of the Eunomians is summarised in the "Blasphemy" of Sirmium, "Christ assumed flesh or a body that is a man[1]"; and in the creed of Eudoxius, one of the least reputable of the party, but perhaps politically its most influential leader, who declares his belief in the Son of God "incarnate but not made man: for He did not assume a human soul: instead of a soul there was God in the flesh: the whole when combined was one nature[2]."

These arguments, which are in reality just those which Arius had originally propounded and withdrawn, although for the student of Apollinarianism they are of the highest interest both in their resemblance to and their difference from that heresy, did not at the time receive much separate consideration from the Nicenes. They were too obviously inspired by desire to degrade the Godhead of the Son to distract orthodox attention from the central objective, the establishment of His consubstantial deity. The Greek Fathers were content to leave Christology until it could be interpreted and if

[1] Hahn, *Biblioth. der Symbol.*

[2] *Doc. de Inc.* 9.

need be reconstructed on that basis[1]. Nor could they make it a satisfactory battlefield; for they were much too like their opponents in their general view of what actually constituted the Lord's manhood and in their desire for real unity of person to attack them with security. Both then and thereafter the Alexandrians refused to accept the most satisfactory means of escape and assert a doctrine of two natures. And if they had been alone, it is likely that on this issue the Arians would never have been met. But throughout the controversy there was a school, small in numbers and at first almost without influence, that chose this better way. While Athanasius and his fellows attacked only the minor premiss of the Arian syllogism that Christ was capable of change, the School of Antioch remained faithful to the Syrian tradition and attacked the major premiss that Christ was the Logos. The teaching of Eustathius and Diodore, the only Antiochenes of this period of whose writings we know anything, is preserved in fragments, but enough survives to prove that they were worthy predecessors of Theodore, Nestorius and Theodoret. Their strenuous assertions that Christ possessed a complete human soul may have been partly responsible for the modification of Athanasius' views in the Conciliar Letter of 362. Consideration of them has been reserved until now, partly because they are by far the most courageous and lucid exponents of Christology during the Arian controversy, and partly because they

[1] Cf. the very characteristic attitude of Cyril of Jerusalem in *Catech.* xii and xiii, where he uses *ἀνθρωπότης* and *ἐνανθρωπήσας* frequently, but without definite indication that Christ did more than assume flesh *ὁμοιοπρόσωπον* and *ὁμοιοπαθές* with ours: cf. xii. 13, 14, 26. His doctrine is less elaborate, but similar to Athanasius'.

supply the natural starting-point for the study of Apollinarius, their great opponent.

Eustathius, who may justly be reckoned the immediate founder of the typical Antiochene theology, is a man of whom we know very little in spite of his obvious importance. Holding at Nicea a position of special prominence[1], he made himself obnoxious not only to the Arians as a zealous opponent of their doctrines, but also in all probability to the moderate or conservative majority through his disapproval of the principles of Origenism. So when the Arian reaction began, he was the first of the Nicenes to be driven into exile, immorality and perhaps Sabellianism being the alleged cause of his condemnation. He was sent to Trajanopolis and seems to have spent the rest of a long life there, apparently surviving until after or only just before the orthodox confession of Meletius in 361 A.D.[2], and possibly till 370[3]. Although he died in Thrace, "he was entombed," says Chrysostom, who speaks of him as a martyr in will if not in fact, "in the hearts of the people of Antioch." Certainly he exercised great influence upon the Nicene party in the city which, during his absence, was led by the priest Paulinus and was still called by his name. Unfortunately, all his writings on Christology have perished, though many fragments of a book *On the Soul*, of a sermon on Proverbs viii. 22,

[1] "Primus in Nicaeno concilio," says Facundus: but his exact status there is obscure.

[2] So Chrysostom, *In S. Eust.* 2, whose evidence is strong but not precise, and Theodoret, *H.E.* iii. 4, who says he died before Meletius' election. Gwatkin, *Stud. of Arian.* p. 78, note, surveys evidence and dates his death 356–360. Cavallera, *Le Schisme d'Antioche* (Paris, 1905), pp. 65, 66, criticises Gwatkin and tries, not very successfully, to prove that he died before 337.

[3] So Socrates, *H.E.* iv. 14, 15, and Sozomen, *H.E.* vi. 13.

and two sentences from a commentary on the Psalms are preserved in the *Dialogue* of Theodoret[1], and a series of brief quotations from a large work against the Arians is contained in Facundus' *Defence of the Three Chapters*[2]. These prove that he attacked the Arian denial of a human soul to Christ and propounded against it a modification of Paul's views which seems to have been even more outspoken than that of his successors. "Why," he writes, "are the Arians so anxious to assert that Christ assumed only a soulless body? It is because, if once they can win acceptance for this, they can go on to ascribe passibility to His divine spirit and so make a case for their belief that the changeable is not begotten by the Changeless[3]." Other fragments give his own opinions. "The soul of Jesus is rational and consubstantial with the souls of men, even as the flesh born of Mary is consubstantial with the flesh of men[4]." It is this human Jesus, not the eternal Wisdom or Logos, that suffered and was raised and glorified: all the texts which Arians employ against the Godhead of the Lord apply solely to the man: suffering and glorification are alike impossible for the divine[5]. He separates entirely the Anointing from the Anointed: the one is by nature God and the Son of God, the other is man who, although Himself "adorned

[1] *Dial.* i. ed. Schultze, IV. 56–8; ii. 134–6; iii. 233–8.

[2] XI. I (Migne, *P.L.* LXVII. 795–8): Facundus' quotations are unfortunately not always reliable.

[3] From the *De Anima* in Theodoret, *Dial.* iii, S. 233. The date of the book is unknown, and its objective may be either Arius or Eunomius.

[4] On Psalm xv. (Theodoret, *Dial.* i. 56).

[5] Cf. fragments of Sermon in Theodoret, *Dial.* iii., and Eustathius' comments on Matt. xi. 27, xix. 28, and xxiv. 36, and on Psalm ix. 7 and ciii. 19 in Facundus.

with righteousness[1]," has received in addition "an acquired virtue[2]" owing to the indwelling in Him of the divine[3], and thus "progresses in dignity towards a better state[4]." "Not in appearance or supposition but in very reality God was clothed with a whole man, assuming him completely[5]." So distinct are the two that this man Jesus remains, even when united to the Word, in complete ignorance of such matters as the date of the Second Advent[6]. All the Gospel accounts of the glory prepared for Christ are spoken of this man, who is thus often treated, as Facundus demonstrates, as an independent subject, a separate personality[7].

Of the theologians of Antioch between the banishment of Eustathius and the rise of Diodore we know very little. It seems probable that the main features of the School were not confined to the Eustathian party, but that even their opponents adopted a Christology of a markedly "Antiochene" type. Diodore himself was never a Eustathian, and we know of no direct connection between the two men: for Diodore, although, in Basil's phrase, "the nurseling of the blessed Silvanus[8]," was certainly trained, if Jerome[9] may be

[1] Facundus, *l.c.*, quoting Eustathius, *Adv. Arian.* vi.

[2] ἐπίκτητον ἀρετήν, representing the "accidentes virtutes" of Facundus' third extract, is a phrase specially attacked by Apollinarius. Cf. Gregory Naz., *Ep.* 202; Gregory Nyss., *Antirrh.* 17.

[3] On Psalm xcii. *ap.* Theodoret, *Dial.* i. 58.

[4] *Ad meliora dignitate procedens.* Facundus' third extract.

[5] In Gelasius, *De duab. Nat.* (Migne, *P.G.* XVIII. 693).

[6] Facundus' first extract, quoting Matt. xxiv. 36.

[7] Facundus declares that Eustathius had openly taught that for which Theodore was condemned: *arguitur unum Christum in duos dominos divisisse*: desiring to prove this, Facundus may give a one-sided impression by his extracts.

[8] *Ep.* 244.

[9] *De Vir. Illustr.* 119.

trusted, by the heretic Eusebius of Emesa. This Eusebius, though an Arian and an intimate friend of Apollinarius' enemy, George the Arian bishop of Laodicea, had adopted a curious compromise in his view of the Incarnation. Like other Arians he speaks always of Christ's manhood as flesh or body; at the same time he treats it as in some sense possessed of a personal centre of its own, and refuses to attribute to the Logos or indwelling divine power any direct share in the sufferings and weakness of the flesh. The power is impassible: nails which cannot even pierce a soul certainly cannot pierce it: yet, though not pierced, it is pained; for the pains which actually affect only the bodily element are transferred and ascribed to the indwelling Godhead[1]. How far Diodore was in sympathy with Eusebius' doctrinal position is uncertain. There are indications in the fragments of his work that he was distinctly more deistic in his thought than Theodore, and this may well be due to the influence of his Arian master. But in later life he was a vigorous opponent of Arianism[2] and a follower of Meletius, and was received along with him into communion with the orthodox, although even then he was perhaps infected for a time with Macedonian heresy[3]. Nevertheless, he was undoubtedly a man of great piety and learning, and took a leading part in the Christian life of Antioch during the years between the formation of the Meletian

[1] Quoted by Theodoret, *Dial.* iii., ed. Schultze, IV. 259, to prove that Eusebius taught the impassibility of Christ's Godhead.

[2] So Facundus, *Def. Tri. Cap.* iv. 2, quoting Chrysostom; and Narses' Homily in *Journal Asiatique*, 1900, p. 481: "Diodore combatted Arians and Eunomians and revealed their deceit."

[3] So Cyril Alex., *Ep.* xlv: the charge, coming from him, may be slander: but it is borne out by Pseudo-Justin, Q. 129, and may account for Apollinarius' references to the Spirit.

party and his own transference to the see of Tarsus[1], being in charge of a church in the old part of the town. After his consecration he still kept a close connection with Antioch, visiting the city as late as 392 A.D. when Chrysostom describes him as infirm with age but still eloquent and influential[2]. His eminence is perhaps best proved by the fact that he was the teacher of the greatest scholar and the most famous saint of the Eastern Church in the persons of Theodore of Mopsuestia and John Chrysostom.

Of his works all have perished unless we follow Harnack[3] in assigning to him the authorship of four treatises of the Pseudo-Justin[4], three of which form a work arranged as a dialogue and certainly written about this time[5]. As this deals with Trinitarian not Christological doctrine, it is only indirectly of value for our

[1] The date is uncertain. Silvanus of Tarsus was deposed by the Homoeans in 360, but was alive in 365, although, apparently, dead by the time of Basil, *Ep.* 244, *i.e.* about 376. If the letter of Athanasius, greeting Diodore as bishop, quoted by Facundus, *l.c.* IV. 2, were genuine, it would date Silvanus' death before 373.

[2] Facundus also declares that he died full of years and honours (Migne, *P.L.* LXVII. 619). Leontius, *Adv. Nest. et Eutych.* iii. 9, tells a story of Theodore's attempt to intrude at Tarsus after Diodore's death: if so, Diodore must have died after 393 A.D., the year of Theodore's consecration to Mopsuestia.

[3] *Texte und Unters.* N.F. VI. 4 (1901). The theory was first proposed by La Croze.

[4] Printed in Otto, *Justin*, IV. and V. The *Confutatio Dogmatum Aristotelis* is unlike the others and much less likely to be by Diodore.

[5] Harnack's case is strong and on this point convincing. Evidence not quoted by him can be found from Q. 139, where the analogy of Three Persons of Trinity to three human beings is exactly parallel to Basil, *Ep.* 38, and Gregory Nyss., *Ad Ablab.*, and must be contemporary. Q. 112, containing a vigorous attack on the Chiliastic views which the author states that some hold, must surely refer to Apollinarius, who alone at this time maintained this antiquated opinion (cf. Basil, *Ep.* 263 and 265; Gregory Naz., *Ep.* 102); and Apollinarius was Diodore's chief opponent.

present purpose. Tradition and the extracts from his writings on the Incarnation agree in proving him the father of Nestorianism. Leontius collected a series of passages from his work against the Synusiasts[1] to prove that "ideas which originated with Paul of Samosata were handed down in succession and descended upon Diodore who became Theodore's guide along these evil ways[2]." To translate the selections by which he tries to establish this would only be to give a scrappy anticipation of Theodore's theology: they are too brief to give ground for an adequate treatment of Antiochene doctrine at its best, and are naturally so similar to those subsequently quoted from Theodore as to demonstrate nothing except their resemblance. Leontius had no desire to examine Diodore's position in itself: if in any important respects he differed from his pupil, mention of it would defeat Leontius' object. It is obvious from the title of this book and from the works of Apollinarius that there was acute controversy between the School of Antioch and the bishop of Laodicea: but as Theodore inherited not only the feud but, as Leontius shows, the general argument and position of Diodore, we may well defer the full statement of their case until we have considered Apollinarius' teaching and can use the fuller material supplied by Theodore's own writings. Suffice it to notice that Diodore laid great stress on the complete

[1] *συνουσιώμενος* is a word used to describe the relation of the Godhead and manhood in Christ by Apollinarius: cf. Lietzmann, Fr. 116. The title was bestowed upon the Monophysite section of the followers of Apollinarius who exaggerated his teaching by insisting that the flesh of Christ became in consequence of the union of one *οὐσία* with the Godhead. Polemon was the leader of the sect.

[2] Leontius, *Adv. Nest. et Eutych.* iii. 37 (Migne, *P.G.* LXXXVI. i. 1376).

separation of the Godhead from the manhood. "The man born of Mary is Son by act of grace; the divine Logos is Son by nature[1]." Each is perfect; yet there are not two Sons: the perfect Son of God has assumed and been pleased to dwell in the perfect Son of David. Only by an abuse of language can the one be called by the title of the other, and in so speaking we must guard carefully against any idea of commingling of natures or confusion of attributes. Their combination is a harmony of two essentially distinct entities not a physical union. Thus there is no great fundamental difference between the Christology of Paul and that of his successors. Although in accepting belief in the personal pre-existence of the Logos they escaped the necessity of representing Christ's personality as human, they none the less took this tenet of Paul's as their starting-point, and interpreted the Incarnation as an agreement and unification of two independent beings, effected by a complete harmony and coincidence of will, developed through the period of Christ's childhood and ratified by the announcement at His baptism.

Yet although the four treatises and the fragments do not enable us to give a more satisfactory account of Diodore's opinions, there remains one brief clause quoted from him, which is not only unique in directness of statement but casts a new light on the wider aspect of the coming controversy. This is the last extract in Leontius, and in it Diodore definitely claims that the Incarnation is ultimately due to mankind, since, if there had been no Fall of man the constraining cause

[1] From *C. Synus*. i. Fr. 2 (Migne, *l.c.* 1388). The opposition between χάρις and φύσις is thoroughly characteristic of the Antiochenes.

of Christ's coming would have been lacking. It is an admission that can be paralleled from Irenaeus[1] but perhaps from no other early writer. Certainly all the Platonists who, like Origen and Apollinarius, tried to represent the Incarnation as the manifestation in time of an eternal inclination of the divine nature towards man, would have unhesitatingly rejected it[2]. The later Antiochenes, though they might have been driven to admit it as a logical consequence of their anthropology and Christology, shrank from repeating Diodore's bald statement. At the time the matter was not further discussed. But it is interesting to find the issue which in Scholastic times separated the stricter Aristotelians or Thomists from the platonising or mystical Scotists, already raised in the conflict between Diodore and Apollinarius. It is, indeed, symbolic of the difference between them. And if Diodore, perhaps owing to his Arian teacher, is more distinctly deistic and Pelagian than his successors, his attitude is thoroughly characteristic of his School. Narses, the Nestorian, is no doubt right when, after repudiating the views of Paul of Samosata, he insists with all emphasis that between the "three righteous men," Diodore, Theodore and Nestorius, there was no vital difference since each alike proclaimed "one invincible doctrine[3]."

[1] *E.g. Haer.* iii. 21.

[2] Even Augustine, as Thomas Aquinas reluctantly admits, refuses to confine the scope of the Incarnation to the reparation of the Fall.

[3] His homily on the three Nestorian doctors was published in the *Journal Asiatique*, 1900, pp. 446 *seq.* by Abbé F. Martin.

CHAPTER IV

APOLLINARIUS OF LAODICEA: HIS LIFE AND WORKS

We have already seen that the Christology of the Antiochenes had aroused the suspicions of Athanasius and called forth a mild protest from him. It was left to an abler theologian to challenge their doctrines specifically by developing against them a full and precise statement of the characteristic Greek position, and by so doing to commence the great controversy which, after three campaigns, finally rent the Church in twain. Apollinarius of Laodicea[1] is perhaps the most remarkable, as he is certainly the last, of the great

[1] In addition to the general histories of doctrine there are three important monographs: J. Dräseke, *Apollinarios von Laodicea, sein Leben und seine Schriften* (Texte und Unters. VII. 3 and 4), 1892; G. Voisin, *L'Apollinarisme: Étude historique littéraire et dogmatique sur le début des Controverses Christologiques*, 1901; H. Lietzmann, *Apollinaris von Laodicea und seine Schule*, 1904. Dräseke is concerned chiefly with the chronology and reconstruction of Apollinarius' writings and attempts to ascribe to him various pseudepigraphic treatises: his arguments are ingenious and often suggestive, though generally unconvincing and always verbose: his conjectures have been rejected by most scholars: he says little about doctrine. Voisin's book is careful and complete: his survey of the history and teaching of Apollinarius is generally accurate and fair: but the attempt to reach a preconceived conclusion is painfully obvious and drives him into contradictions and special pleading: he must make the facts fit the theory, and the theory is wrong. Lietzmann has given us an admirable critical edition of the fragments, and his introduction, though incomplete, and on the doctrinal side very slight, contains valuable material: for the sources and text of the Apollinarian literature his book is indispensable. Quotations from Apollinarius are given with the page or number in his collection.

Hellenic students and thinkers who devoted their lives with all the intellectual eagerness of their race to the pursuit of truth, who were ready to grapple with problems however abstruse rather than evade the task under cover of a self-raised cloud of paradoxes and legalisms, whose results, however audacious and insecure, reflected at least their author's sincere conviction and neither contemplated secular favour and ecclesiastical advancement nor were dictated by political motives and personal prejudice. From the little that we know of his life it is plain that Apollinarius, like Origen, was a man of learning rather than of affairs. Despite the troublous times and his own enthusiasm for the Nicene faith, he was left undisturbed to pursue his enquiries in theology during a long life and to produce a noble list of long-perished works, a list in which those devoted to the heresy called by his name supply but a small proportion of the total.

The outline of his uneventful existence can be gathered from the disconnected tales of the Church historians[1], and from the scanty references of his contemporaries. Pieced together, the result is the barest sketch. His father, Apollinarius also, was by race a man of Alexandria, who after leaving his native town had

[1] Socrates, *H.E.* ii. 36, iii. 14; Sozomen, *H.E.* v. 17, vi. 25, 27; a brief notice in Suidas with a quotation from Philostorgius, *Lex.* I. 615; Photius, a passage in Rufinus, *H.E.* ii. 20; Jerome, *De Vir. Illustr.*; documents in Theodoret, *H.E.* v. 10, 11.

Dräseke, *l.c.* p. 4, conjectures that Timothy of Berytus, whose history of Apollinarius was known till the time of Leontius, was used by Philostorgius and that Sozomen and Socrates drew from Philostorgius. Lietzmann, *l.c.* pp. 43–7, indicates Timothy as the source of most of our knowledge; but treats Philostorgius and Sozomen as independently indebted to him. For Rufinus, see below, pp. 174, 175.

settled at Berytus as schoolmaster, and thence had moved up the coast of Syria to Laodicea. Here he married and his son was born. The first incident recorded of them arose out of their friendship with Epiphanius, the sophist. This man, like Libanius Apollinarius' friend in later life[1], was one of those professors of literature and philosophy, whose names remind us that this century was the St Luke's summer of Greek thought. Following on the revival of Platonism by Plotinus, the Eastern world was for three or four generations illuminated by the last flicker of the torch which Athens had kindled and passed on to other centres of culture and education. The settled rule of Diocletian had given an opportunity to the arts of peace: Maximin Daza's policy shows that pagan learning still flourished: Julian's edict demonstrates that the teaching profession was still a monopoly in the hands of the Greeks. Men of real learning if of little originality were numerous and influential; and the popularity of Arianism is testimony to the power of heathen schoolmasters. For, with the establishment of Christianity, a more tolerant spirit had arisen, and it was no longer a scandal, as it had been in Origen's time, for the faithful to sit at the feet of unconverted lecturers. The scholars of the Church had been trained at the universities: her writers had learnt to embellish their style in the fashion of the day: her preachers were skilled in all the arts of the professor of rhetoric[2]. Culture like wealth was one of

[1] So Suidas, *Lexicon*, I. 615. Of the letters of Libanius to Apollinarius it is unlikely that any except *Ep.* 449 refer to the Bishop of Laodicea: cf. Voisin, *l.c.* p. 34, note, where the problem is well discussed. Fabricius, *Bibl. Graec.* VII. 586, and Dräseke, *l.c.* p. 14, accept the letters as written to our Apollinarius.

[2] John Chrysostom, for example, was destined to succeed Libanius until the Christians captured him.

the fruits of her victory over rival religions. Apollinarius the elder was obviously a type of the new age. He had certainly been a Christian for many years, if not born in the faith: for he was ordained priest at Laodicea, and his son is never taunted with pagan ancestry. Yet, even if he is not the Apollinarius of the Greek anthology, he was a man widely read in classical literature, and determined to give his son the best education of the time.

So he went with the young man to the lectures of Epiphanius along with many of his fellow-believers; and with them was one day present at the recital of a hymn in honour of Bacchus[1]. This came to the ears of Theodotus, then bishop of Laodicea, who decided that though laymen might attend such performances without harm it was intolerable that the clergy should do so[2]. The younger Apollinarius was at this time already in orders as a Reader; and both were in consequence suspended from communion until after a period of penance. The story is unimportant except as furnishing a clue to the date of Apollinarius' birth. Theodotus died in 335 A.D., and as he restored the penitents before his death the event cannot have happened before 333. Readers were usually lads of not less than eighteen, and we may therefore assume that Apollinarius was born between 312 and 315, a time which fits in well with the other indications of his age. His father must have been about thirty when he married: for he could hardly have been schoolmaster at Berytus at any very youthful age, and appears to have been alive and full of intellectual

[1] The story is in Sozomen, *H.E.* vi. 25.

[2] Lietzmann, *l.c.* p. 2, notes that Theodotus was an Arian, and the Apollinarii were Nicenes.

vigour in 361[1]. This makes an earlier date for his son's birth hardly possible: and a later one would be incompatible with the story of Theodotus and with Epiphanius' allusion to Apollinarius as "aged and venerable" in 377 when his book against the heresies was written.

The next recorded episode is the first meeting of Apollinarius with Athanasius. In 346 when Gregory of Alexandria died and Constantius allowed the exile to return to his see, he went to Antioch and from there to Caesarea, being entertained by Apollinarius on his way. George the bishop of Laodicea was a staunch Arian, and not only refused to communicate with Athanasius[2] but excommunicated Apollinarius for his insubordination and in spite of his petitions never afterwards readmitted him. The meeting is important, partly because it proves that the Laodicea in question was the town on the coast south-west of Antioch[3], not that on the head-waters of the Orontes from which the province Laodicene draws its name; but much more because it initiated a lifelong friendship which was of the greatest importance to the future heresiarch. We know of no other occasion on which the two actually met[4]; but there is plain proof of their intimacy and of the regularity of the correspondence between them[5].

[1] This is the obvious inference from Socrates, *H.E.* iii. 14: possibly his works were published posthumously in 361.

[2] Dräseke, *l.c.* pp. 9, 10, points out that George, who had been degraded from the priesthood at Alexandria, had no cause to love Athanasius.

[3] Athanasius came so far by the *Cursus publicus* and thence by sea.

[4] Dräseke, *l.c.* p. 22, on the evidence of the Pseudo-Justin Λόγος παραινετικός, which he conjectures to be by Apollinarius, assumes that he visited Alexandria frequently.

[5] Timothy of Berytus is said to have based his history on the "countless" letters from Athanasius to Apollinarius: Sozomen,

Until after George's removal from Laodicea in 360 we hear nothing of Apollinarius[1]. From the fame of his championship of the Nicene position it is possible that after his excommunication he continued to minister to a congregation of the faithful who would not accept their Arian bishop, much as Paulinus was doing at Antioch. He may even have been consecrated bishop, an office which he certainly attained[2], during this period. But it is more likely that he had little to do except study and write and teach. For his literary activities were so numerous that he could hardly have combined them with great practical activity. Three groups among those into which his writings may be divided must have been produced during these years—his commentaries on Scripture, his philosophical books and his controversial treatises. In the first group come the books on the Psalms, Isaiah, Jeremiah, Ezekiel, Daniel, Hosea and Proverbs, on the Gospels of St Matthew and St John and the Epistles to the Romans, Galatians and Ephesians[3]; in the second, the thirty volumes against Porphyry with whose work he was intimately acquainted[4]; in the third the criticisms of Origen, of Marcellus and of Eunomius. It is more than likely that the bulk of these were produced as material for lectures and that he was at this time already in the habit of teaching regularly at

H.E. ii. 17, quotes Apollinarius' account of the summons to Athanasius by Alexander on his deathbed—an intimate detail implying close acquaintance.

[1] It is possible that he was actually exiled for a time and during it visited Italy: cf. Libanius, *Ep.* 449, and Dräseke, *l.c.* p. 19.

[2] So Basil, *Ep.* 265; Jerome, *De Vir. Illustr.* 104; Timothy of Berytus, *ap.* Leontius, *Fraud.* 138; and, plainest of all, Athanasius, *Tom. ad Antioch.* 9.

[3] This list is based upon the quotations in the *Catenae* and the references in Jerome.

[4] Cf. Jerome, *Pref. in Daniel*, etc.

9—2

Antioch as he certainly did later[1]. For Jerome, who attended his classes there in 373[2], tells us that his commentaries were very brief, resembling headings for a speech or notes of points to be expanded rather than complete exegeses[3]. From the fragments of his work that have survived it is clear that he was gifted with a brilliant and versatile intellect; from the references to him by his contemporaries that he had won a great reputation as a scholar and in a sphere outside ordinary clerical duties[4]; from his friendship with Libanius, the most famous sophist of the day and a man of high renown, that he was a prominent person in the cultured world of Antioch; and from his complete disagreement with the dominant theology of the city that he held an independent position there. All the indications point to his having been engaged in educational rather than in ministerial work, and during these years the bulk of his time may well have been given to it. But no doubt questions of doctrine absorbed his attention already. He was certainly deeply interested not only in the Arian controversy, but in the efforts of the Nicenes to consolidate their party and to work out the details of their faith. And it is probable that Christology had also begun to attract him: for though his earliest writing on the subject that can be accurately dated falls outside this period, its quality proves that he was familiar with the subject and had already formulated at least in out-

[1] Cf. Dräseke, *l.c*, p. 14.

[2] *Ep*. 84: "I heard Apollinarius regularly at Antioch and made a friend of him."

[3] *Pref. in Isaiam. Non tam commentarios quam indices capitulorum*; and *Pref. in Hoseam*: "In his youth he had composed brief *commentarioli*."

[4] *E.g*. Basil's criticism in *Ep*. 265 indicates that he did little pastoral work—a point supported by Basil's whole attitude to him.

line his characteristic opinions. Possibly the dispute with Diodore should be assigned to these years[1], and the composition of his book "in chapters" against him may well be early. The only clear evidence on the point is the letter of Gregory Nazianzen written about 382, in which he states that Apollinarius has been preaching his heresy for thirty years[2]. From the context it is evident that Gregory is speaking in round numbers and under circumstances conducive to exaggeration, but there may well have been some event about 352 which gave point to his assertion.

In any case, it is certain that during this time Apollinarius had won for himself a position of great eminence as an expert in theological questions. We have already seen that Athanasius referred to him the draft of his letter to Epictetus; and the four letters[3] that passed between him and Basil apparently in the year 362 confirm the belief that he was generally recognised as a consultant in the solution of difficult problems. In the first of these Basil, who was then moving towards what came to be known as the New Nicene position, consults Apollinarius as to the propriety of the *ὁμοούσιον* and admits that he himself prefers the Lucianic phrase, *ἀπαραλλάκτως ὅμοιον*[4]. Apollinarius' reply contains an elaborate justification of the orthodox belief, and is

[1] Dräseke, *l.c.* p. 38, dates the book against Diodore not earlier than 373 on the strength of Basil's letter to Meletius (*Ep.* 129) in that year which shows no knowledge of such a controversy.

[2] *Ep.* 102. Lietzmann, *Apollinaris*, p. 74, accepts this as substantially accurate, but Gregory's statement in the same letter that Christ has been preached for almost four centuries shakes our confidence.

[3] *Ep.* 361–4.

[4] In *Ep.* 9, written about 360, Basil accepts *ἀπαραλλάκτως ὅμοιον κατ' οὐσίαν* as equivalent to *ὁμοούσιον*. *Ep.* 7 proves that at this time he was perplexed over theological language.

similar in many respects to the passage with which Eustathius of Sebasteia afterwards taunted Basil[1]. The second letter is simply an expression of gratitude coupled with a request to be allowed to submit similar problems to one whose advice was so admirably convincing. Apollinarius, in answering, reinforces his previous letter by alluding to the Council of Alexandria and its restatement of the Nicene faith. These letters, which are naturally regarded with suspicion by Catholic scholars, who are unwilling to admit that a saint could ever have had doubts about the Nicene Creed or gone for help to a heresiarch, are now recognised by most students[2] as genuine and important. Dräseke[3] has shown how admirably they harmonise with what we know of the two men: for it is clear that Basil and the party of which he was the leader understood the *ὁμοούσιον* in a sense definitely more tritheistic than that which it bore to Athanasius or Apollinarius[4], and the famous extract upon which Eustathius based his charge of Sabellianism is no doubt a genuine presentation of the older doctrine. Voisin[5], who tries to controvert Dräseke's arguments, succeeds only in supporting them.

[1] The text of this passage is given in Basil, *Ep.* 129. The controversy over it is the subject of *Eps.* 131, 223, 224, 226.

[2] *E.g.* by Lietzmann, *l.c.* p. 21, where the whole problem of Basil's relations with Apollinarius is discussed. Bethune-Baker, *Texts and Studies*, VII. 1, pp. 39–40, admits that all the evidence internal and external is in favour of their authenticity except Basil's later letters. Robertson, *Athanasius*, p. xxxii, accepts them.

[3] *Apollinarios*, pp. 100–21.

[4] In spite of Bethune-Baker, *The Meaning of* 'Ομοούσιος, *Texts and Studies*, VII. 1, the New Nicene position represented something in the nature of a compromise with the Semi-Arians; a growing stress upon the personal differentiation within the unity is characteristic of the later orthodoxy, as is the accusation of Sabellianism brought by the New Nicenes against Old Nicenes like Paulinus and Apollinarius.

[5] *L'Apollinarisme*, pp. 237–42.

For he bases his whole case upon the letters of Basil in 376[1] when the struggle with the Eustathians was at its zenith, and these letters admit that the saint had corresponded with Apollinarius, that the extract on the Trinity is probably his, and that garbled versions of it had been circulated. It is true that Basil states the time of his correspondence as twenty or in another letter twenty-five years ago[2]—a discrepancy which proves either that his dates are wholly unreliable or that he is capable of exaggeration; and that he declares that the letters were few and such as a layman might write to a layman—that is, that they were not official communications[3]. But Basil was writing from his sick-bed and at a time of crisis when acknowledged intimacy with the bishop of Laodicea, who was by that time suspect of heresy, would have been disastrous to him[4]; and the petulance of his tone, when every allowance is made for his difficulties and irritation, creates the belief that his conscience was not quite at ease[5]. Moreover,

[1] *Eps.* 129, 131, 223, 224, 244.

[2] *Eps.* 223 and 226, twenty; 224, twenty-five. The MSS. may be in error over the numerals: Voisin suggests κ for κε in 224, Dräseke ιε for κ.

[3] This interpretation of the phrase "as layman to layman" has been challenged. The words cannot be taken literally, for whenever we date the letters Apollinarius was certainly a priest and, by 362, a bishop.

[4] As his treatment of Gregory Nazianzen in the matter of Sasima proves, Basil never allowed friendship to stand in the way of policy.

[5] His statements about the Sabellian extract are curiously disingenuous. He sends it to Meletius, stating that the Eustathians are not clever enough to have forged it and accusing Apollinarius (*Ep.* 129): he then states that he is ignorant of its authorship, but recognises that parts of it are by Apollinarius, though these he has not read (*Ep.* 131). So, too, of his correspondence with Apollinarius he writes: "one single document...twenty years ago" (*Ep.* 223); "the letter written now five and twenty years ago" (*Ep.* 224); "letters written twenty years ago" (*Ep.* 226).

Voisin's final argument that the letter circulated by the Eustathians and printed by Sebastiani[1] and Loofs[2], which is admittedly a garbled version, proves that the other four letters are also Eustathian forgeries, is singularly inept; for Basil himself declares that such a forgery was in existence and that it ascribed to him the Sabellian document which he declares to be by Apollinarius[3]. The facts beyond dispute are that Basil had written to Apollinarius, that his letters were afterwards used as the basis for a charge of Sabellianism, that he declared the charge to be false, since the Sabellian tendency was in his correspondent not himself and was only imputed to him by a falsification of the documents. All these facts exactly fit the letters which have been preserved: in the four genuine ones Apollinarius combats Basil's dread of Sabellianism by arguments not inconsistent with the ascription to him of Eustathius' extract; in the forgery we have a reversal of the position, Apollinarius being made to criticise the ὁμοούσιον and Basil to reply in a Sabellian strain—a reversal contrary to all that is known of the two men and justifying Basil's furious protestations. Basil's own statement of the date is the sole point in Voisin's favour, and under the circumstances such an error is intelligible: ill-temper and ill-health are not favourable to the strictest accuracy.

Apart from this we have no knowledge of him or his father until 360, when the emperor Julian published his famous edict forbidding Christians to give teaching in Greek literature or at pagan schools[4]. This was a shrewd

[1] In 1796 at Rome.
[2] *Eustathius v. Sebaste*, p. 72.
[3] *Ep.* 224, *Ad Genethlium*, and 129 *Ad Meletium*.
[4] *Ep.* 42.

blow, and the Church strove at once to meet it. The two Apollinarii, recognising that Christians had no educational apparatus of their own, set themselves to remedy the defect. Socrates[1] and Sozomen[2], the latter of whom is the better authority for Apollinarius, both narrate the story of the Christianised classics then issued at Laodicea, Socrates assigning the poetry to the father and the prose to the son[3], Sozomen mentioning the son only. Their output was enormous—an epic in twenty-four books covering the narratives of the Old Testament down to the death of Saul, comedies in the style of Menander, tragedies in that of Euripides, and lyrics like those of Pindar dealing with episodes in Jewish history[4], and in prose renderings of the Gospels and Apostolic writings in the form of Platonic dialogues. And all these, if Sozomen may be trusted, were of great elegance and at least equal to the originals! Obviously so large a literature, whatever its quality, could not have been produced during the one year in which the edict was enforced. Probably both father and son, who were certainly highly gifted and appreciated the value of classical learning, had learnt from their own unpleasant experience the disadvantage of the pagan monopoly, and had devoted their leisure to exercises of this kind. Julian gave them an opportunity to publish what else

[1] *H.E.* iii. 16.

[2] *H.E.* v. 18. He shows much fuller knowledge of the facts and some acquaintance with Apollinarius' writings: cf. *H.E.* ii. 17. Lietzmann surmises that Sozomen drew his material from Timothy of Berytus' history of Apollinarius.

[3] Lietzmann, *l.c.* p. 45, points out that this must be a reversal of the truth.

[4] The version of the Psalter in hexameters of the Homeric type may also have been published at this time: cf. Zonaras, *Hist. Epit.* XIII. 12, and below, pp. 154, 155.

might never have seen the light; and they were able to supply material for a complete course of training. Apollinarius added at this time to his other efforts the writing of a book, *In Defence of the Truth*, addressed to the emperor and refuting his position by arguments based solely upon secular grounds and without reference to Scripture[1].

It is in the next reign that we have the first Christological fragment that can be dated with certainty, the letter and confession of faith addressed to the emperor Jovian. This is preserved under the name and in the manuscripts of Athanasius; and as it contains the famous phrase *μία φύσις τοῦ Λόγου σεσαρκωμένη* which was accepted as Athanasian by Cyril of Alexandria, was probably regarded as genuinely his at an early date. The orthodox writers who first developed the theory that the Apollinarians circulated their master's writings pseudonymously, were largely influenced by the conviction that Athanasius could not have given expression to such doctrines[2]—a conviction which we have seen to be groundless. But in the present case the letter is quoted as Apollinarian by his follower Polemon, and is eminently characteristic of the style and method of Apollinarius. On linguistic grounds alone it is clearly not Athanasian: and the parallelism between it and

[1] Sozomen, *H.E.* v. 18. He states that this book was also ascribed to Basil: but Basil, *Ep.* 263, seems to allude to it as by Apollinarius. Julian's reply was the famous *ἀνέγνων, ἔγνων, κατέγνων*. Dräseke, *l.c.* pp. 19 and 83–99, claims to have discovered this book in the Λόγος παραινετικὸς πρὸς Ἕλληνας preserved among the works of Justin.

[2] Voisin, *l.c.* pp. 159, 160, admits this. The *Adversus Fraudes*, ascribed to Leontius, but probably not by him (cf. Loofs, *Leontius von Byzanz*. pp. 89 ff.), is the earliest work to discuss the question critically.

undisputed writings of the heresiarch confirms the identification.

During the next ten years there is evidence of continued activity on his part, and towards their close signs that he was becoming an object of suspicion. He had by this time been consecrated a bishop, possibly when the Arian Pelagius succeeded George at Laodicea[1], and had been recognised as such at Rome[2]. But Basil makes it plain that he had little opportunity for exercising his functions, and he seems to have kept up his close connection with Antioch, and to have carried on his teaching work independent of the struggle between the followers of Paulinus and of Meletius. Jerome, who was always jealous of his reputation for orthodoxy, attended Apollinarius' lectures in 373–4, a fact which proves conclusively that at least until those years he was under no suspicion of heterodoxy or irregularity[3]. To this period may perhaps be assigned a number of his smaller Christological writings and the commencement of his friendship with Vitalis, who was the direct cause of his severance from the Church, and the chief organiser of the sect[4]. It is exceedingly difficult to disentangle the true position of affairs there[5], and the references to the status of Vitalis and his connection with Apollinarianism are very confused. But it is evident that he was for some years a priest of the Meletian party[6] along with Diodore

[1] So Lietzmann, *l.c.* p. 5.

[2] So Leontius, *Fraud.* 151, and Facundus, *Def. Tri. Cap.* VII. 3.

[3] *Ep.* 84.

[4] Sozomen, *H.E.* vi. 25, says that they were still called Vitalians in Antioch when he was writing.

[5] Lietzmann gives a very clear account, but hardly reconciles it with the facts: *e.g.* he treats Vitalis as an "Old Nicene" and the natural ally of Paulinus, disregarding the evidence of Vitalis' connection with Meletius.

[6] Sozomen, *H.E.* vi. 25.

and Flavian, perhaps succeeding the former when he became bishop of Tarsus. Whether he quarrelled with Meletius and joined the party of Paulinus, as Duchesne[1] supposes, or, after coming under the influence of Apollinarius and thus disagreeing with Diodore and his friends, took up an independent position, as Epiphanius' references to the affairs of Antioch when he was there in 374–5 would lead us to suppose[2], it is impossible to decide. In any case, whichever bishop he recognised, there is no doubt that before 375 he had accused Paulinus of Sabellianism and had himself been charged with holding erroneous views of the Incarnation. Epiphanius, who speaks of those who teach that the human nature of Christ was imperfect, in his book, the *Ancoratus*[3], written apparently in 374, and who visited Antioch shortly after[4], then regarded Vitalis as the chief exponent and founder of the heresy: and no doubt he had been for some time propagating Apollinarius' opinions. In 375[5] he went to Rome either on his own

[1] *Hist. ancienne de l'Église*, II. p. 598. He bases this on the supposition that Vitalis went to Rome as a supporter of Paulinus, *i.e.* before Epiphanius' visit to Antioch.

[2] Dräseke, on the evidence of Epiphanius, *Ancor.* 75, represents Vitalis as already a bishop at the time of its composition. But in *Ancor.* Vitalis is nowhere mentioned. He is described as bishop in *Haer.* lxxvii. 20, and, apparently, as holding the office when Epiphanius was in Antioch. Sozomen's story that he joined Apollinarius in consequence of a slight from Flavian, his fellow-presbyter (*H.E.* vi. 25), may have this much truth in it that intercourse with Apollinarius would certainly involve a quarrel with Flavian.

[3] 75–80.

[4] Lietzmann, *l.c.* pp. 15–17, gives an elaborate account of his visit and efforts to unite Vitalis and Paulinus and to persuade Basil to throw over Meletius. Cf. also Dräseke, *l.c.* pp. 53, 54.

[5] Voisin, *l.c.* pp. 81–2, makes a strong case for placing Vitalis' visit to Rome in this year. Duchesne, *l.c.* places it before Vitalis

initiative or at the bidding of Paulinus in order that the double charge might be investigated. Paulinus, who was unpopular with the New Nicenes and is accused in a formal letter by Basil of favouring the error of Marcellus, but who was recognised in the West as the legitimate successor of Eustathius, must have been responsible for this appeal to the pope: in his very difficult position he hoped to strengthen himself by securing an official acknowledgment of his own orthodoxy and a censure upon one whom the Roman Church with its stricter ideas of discipline would regard as a schismatic. So he sent to Rome a confession of faith anathematising Sabellius, and a request that Vitalis should be examined on the lines suggested by the Conciliar Letter of the Council of Alexandria in 362 which he had personally signed. Damasus called a synod, accepted his confession and also one presented by Vitalis[1], and sent him a letter *Per filium meum Vitalem*[2] containing the two propositions, first that Christ assumed a complete man, body, soul and sense, but without sin, and, secondly, that Christ is one both before and after the Incarnation—this letter being intended for use as a test of right doctrine. Vitalis, whose confession of faith is quoted by Cyril of Alexandria[3], like his master Apollinarius, was prepared to sign the formula in the *Tomus ad Antiochenos*, and Paulinus was therefore unable to take further steps against him. After this incident Vitalis seems to have definitely thrown in his lot with Apol-

split with Paulinus and as due to Vitalis' desire to get Paulinus recognised at Rome—*i.e.* before 375.

[1] This Confession is probably that mentioned by Gregory Naz., *Ep.* 102. Both he and Damasus accepted it at this time as orthodox.

[2] Mansi, *Conc.* III. c. 425.

[3] *De recta Fide ad Reg.* 10; Lietzmann, *l.c.* p. 273. Vitalis quotes the *Tom.* and anathematises those who reject it.

linarius and to have formed an Apollinarian party in Antioch, perhaps in consequence of a later letter from Damasus[1] which he was unable to sign.

At about the same time[2] another event occurred which showed that the bishop of Laodicea was already breaking off communion with those who disagreed with his Christology and forming a group of disciples. In 373 there had been an outbreak of persecution under Valens in Egypt. Peter, the successor of Athanasius, had fled to Rome, and certain Egyptian bishops had been exiled to Diocaesarea. To these exiles Apollinarius had sent letters of greeting, and receiving no answer followed up his action by a brief statement of his views[3], inviting the bishops if they agreed with him to enter into communion. He bases his plea upon the fact that "the blessed Athanasius knew that we were in complete sympathy with his doctrinal position and yielded him support in all things," quotes with his own explanation the relevant clauses of the *Tomus*, and definitely states that he has no communion with those who think otherwise. The exiles had been approached in similar fashion by many other bishops, and after considerable hesitation refused to recognise Apollinarius on the ground that he was not in communion with Paulinus whom they accepted as the orthodox bishop of Antioch[4]. Basil's comment upon their action[5] proves that Apollinarianism had now become a definite schism; for though he professes to have no special knowledge of the Christological issues, he writes with bitter indigna-

[1] In Mansi, *Conc.* III. c. 425: so Voisin, *l.c.* p. 83.

[2] Dräseke, *l.c.* p. 45, dates this letter in 377.

[3] *Ad. Dioc.*, Lietzmann, pp. 255–6.

[4] The exiles describe their action in a letter to the monks of Nitria, *ap.* Facundus, *Def. Tri. Cap.* IV. 2.

[5] *Ep.* 265.

tion of the sectarian spirit of the bishop of Laodicea, a subject on which, as Lietzmann sagely remarks, he "would stand no nonsense[1]."

It is indeed apparent that the condemnation of Apollinarius by the official verdict of the Church was due rather to ecclesiastical than to doctrinal grounds. In addition to Vitalis, who was by this time certainly a bishop and the head of an Apollinarian congregation in Antioch, Timothy, another pupil of Apollinarius, had broken off communion with several of the Eastern bishops[2] and had himself been consecrated to the see of Berytus[3]. He was a man of vigour and ability, as well as, like Vitalis, of marked asceticism and piety; and his version of his master's teaching which exaggerated the Monophysite tendency in it[4], created much discussion and unrest. Jerome's pathetic appeals to Damasus[5] for guidance describe the three orthodox parties at Antioch and his own uncertainty as to which he should recognise; and throughout the East the position was one of the gravest disunion. In addition to recognised heretics like the Eunomians and the Photinians, there were almost innumerable diversities of doctrine, Arians and Semi-Arians, Old Nicenes and New Nicenes, Macedonians and Marcellians: every centre of Church-life had its schisms. Syrian bishops were split up into tiny cliques, and regarded all their

[1] *L.c.* p. 22.

[2] Cf. Peter Alex., *Ad Diocaes. ap.* Facundus, *l.c.* IV. 2. He mentions Basil, Paulinus, Epiphanius and Diodore.

[3] Possibly by Apollinarius: cf. Basil, *Ep.* 265: but Timothy's was probably an orthodox consecration, since he appears at Constantinople in 381.

[4] Cf. Valentinus, *Cap. Apol.* (Lietzmann, *l.c.* pp. 287–91).

[5] *Eps.* 15 and 16, written from his seclusion in the desert of Syrian Chalcis in 376 or 377.

neighbours with suspicion. Faction was everywhere, and any prominent man seemed to introduce a new complication. And in face of all this chaos there was still an Arian emperor, bent on forcing his views upon the Church. It is small wonder that the champions of unity were driven almost to distraction, or that Basil wore himself to death in a desperate effort after more effective organisation, or that when Apollinarius showed himself obdurate in his opinions drastic action should have been taken against him.

It is not surprising under the circumstances that from his sick-bed Basil should have appealed to the West[1]. In the famous letter[2] which was the immediate cause of Apollinarius' condemnation he implored the pope to deal with the three who were especially the centres of disturbance, Eustathius of Sebaste, Apollinarius, and Paulinus of Antioch. Arianism he regarded as sufficiently notorious to be incapable of much further harm: but these wolves in sheep's clothing, whose error is the more dangerous because unrecognised, must be denounced publicly and compelled either to stop their sectarian activities or to break off from the society of the faithful. His accusation against Apollinarius is noteworthy; for he bases it upon the chiliasm of the Laodicene, merely adding that his teaching on the Incarnation has given rise to much confusion among the brethren—a confusion in which Basil, as his other letters at this time show, evidently shares[3]. This letter produced an unexpected response. A synod, presided

[1] Basil had written in 371 (*Ep.* 66) to Athanasius that the "safety of the churches of the East depends on the sympathy of the West": and an appeal to Rome was always in his mind.

[2] *Ep.* 263, sent by Dorotheus.

[3] Cf. below, pp. 253–6.

over by Damasus and Peter of Alexandria, was held at Rome in 377[1]. Timothy of Berytus, perhaps sent thither by his teacher[2], was present; and both he and Apollinarius were expressly anathematised, not as sectarians but for doctrinal error[3]. We know nothing of the procedure, but it is plain from the various anathemas[4] that either then or soon after an attempt was made to suppress sectarianism, though by no means along the lines which Basil had suggested. Arius, Eunomius, Macedonius, Photinus and certain other leaders of heterodoxy were condemned, and sentence was also passed upon those who said that the Logos took the place of rational soul in Christ instead of assuming a perfect but sinless manhood. Peter joined in the sentence and wrote to the bishops at Diocaesarea to announce it to them.

This verdict of the Western Church, although a full and official condemnation, does not seem to have had much influence; for Timothy of Berytus was present despite it at the Council of Constantinople in 381, and as we see from the case of Meletius, Roman influence

[1] Hefele, *History of the Councils*, pp. 288–91, following Mansi, supposes there to have been three councils at Rome, one in 374, at which Apollinarius was condemned on the strength of Basil's letter; a second in 376, where Timothy, whom he calls Apollinarian bishop of Alexandria, and Vitalis were condemned also; a third in 380, when anathemas were issued. The dates given here follow Rade, *Damasus*, and the recent monographs.

[2] Leontius, *Adv. Fraud.* 151.

[3] Cf. the letter of Damasus to the Eastern bishops in Theodoret, *H.E.* v. 10. The Latin fragments, *Illud sane miramur* and *Non nobis quidquam* (Mansi, *Conc.* III. c. 461), perhaps belong here also: cf. Lietzmann, *l.c.* p. 60.

[4] Quoted by Theodoret, *H.E.* v. 11, with the heading "to Paulinus in Macedonia who was at Thessalonica." This visit of Paulinus to Thessalonica seems to have been in 382: they may belong to the Roman Council of 377 or to that of 381.

was still unimportant in the East. Far more influential was the publication, probably in the same year, of Epiphanius' great work against the heresies[1]. The chapter on the Dimoeritae in this is the first open attack upon the new heresy, and reflects the amazement and regret with which the East learnt that "the venerable old man, ever beloved by us, by the blessed pope Athanasius and by all the orthodox," had fallen into error. Epiphanius had indeed been the first bishop to realise and repudiate the teaching of Apollinarius, and though his criticism of it can hardly be regarded as honest[2], it was effective in arousing the Church to the knowledge that the Apollinarians were offenders not only against ecclesiastical order, a trivial matter at such a time of chaos, but against the content of the faith. Although he could only do this by insinuating against them errors which on his own showing none of their recognised leaders accepted[3], the East took alarm at his voice. A synod of 153 bishops was held at Antioch in

[1] The date of publication was apparently 377. The chapter on Manichaeism was written in 376 (lxvi. 20): but that on Apollinarius was probably among the latest. Epiphanius states that a Council had been convened on account of the unrest over Christology, and that certain errors had been condemned; this may refer to the synod of 377: but, as it is mentioned in the portion of the chapter (lxxvii. 2) in which Epiphanius is dealing with crude Gnostic ideas and next to his citation of the *Ad Epict.* he probably alludes to the Council of Alexandria in 362.

[2] Cf. above, p. 101, note. He attacks a variety of errors, some of which he supposed at first to emanate from Apollinarius. When he met Vitalis he discovered the true doctrine of Apollinarius. Yet he allows the previous misinterpretations to appear in his work.

[3] It is due to the influence of Epiphanius and of Ambrose that Church historians have accused Apollinarius of creating the elementary heresies which treat the body of Christ as composed of the substance of the Logos, etc. Epiphanius himself admits that these came from teachers outside the Church (ἀλλότριοι) and were akin to the beliefs of Valentinus, Marcion and Manes (lxxvii. 15).

October, 379, at which Apollinarianism was formally condemned. This was endorsed in the first canon of the Council of Constantinople in 381[1], although, as Ambrose pointed out, the sentence was inadequate to exclude them—the ambiguity being, as Lietzmann has demonstrated[2], no doubt deliberate and aimed at making their return to communion as easy as possible. In September, 383, Theodosius declared the heresy illegal, and in 388, under pressure from Gregory of Nazianzus, strong measures were initiated against it.

Of Apollinarius himself we know little more. He set to work upon a full exposition and vindication of his views in his most finished Christological work, the *Apodeixis*, from which Gregory of Nyssa has quoted numerous extracts in his criticism, the *Antirrheticus*. Dräseke, who makes the publication of the *Apodeixis* the cause for the condemnation of Apollinarius, is constrained in consequence to place its composition in 375, and to represent Gregory's reply as written in the next year[3]. This is neither necessary nor, in view of the character of the *Apodeixis*, which presupposes a break with the orthodox, probable: and it may have been published any time between 381 and 385. In 378 the Apollinarians certainly held a synod at which their leader presided[4], and there are indications of a second meeting later[5]. Otherwise the verdict of the Church seems to have

[1] Mansi, *Conc.* III. 461 and 557.

[2] *L.c.* p. 31.

[3] *L.c.* pp. 44, 45. It is very difficult to believe that the *Antirrh.* was written before the *C. Eunom.*, *i.e.* before 382: for the *C. Eunom.* contains many distinctly Apollinarian arguments and phrases, and makes no reference to the heresiarch.

[4] Cf. Gregory Naz., *Carmen de Vita sua* 609–51.

[5] At least two synodal utterances, the *De Fid. et Inc.* and the *Tom. Synod.*, are included in the Apollinarian writings.

affected the bishop of Laodicea very little. His life's work had been that of a scholar and teacher. He had formed certain conclusions which he held with tenacity and sincerity, and for which long before his condemnation he had begun to withdraw from communion with his opponents. This detachment from practical affairs was hardly disturbed by the sentences passed upon him: for the organisation of Apollinarian churches was in the hands of his followers. His own death may well have taken place soon after the publication of the *Antirrheticus*[1], and in any case happened before the year 392 when Jerome wrote his *De Viris Illustribus*[2]. Nilus testifies that his old age was spent in a fashion as wise as it was reverend[3].

It is unnecessary for our purpose and in view of Lietzmann's very adequate treatment of the subject[4], to enter at length into the subsequent history of the sect. For the first few years after its condemnation progress was rapid, and Apollinarian congregations appeared in a number of Asiatic towns. The sanctity of life which was so characteristic of its chief supporters, the similarity of their belief to the traditional tenets of Greek Christendom, and the general prevalence of schism, combined to give them a favourable opportunity. But their success was short-lived. After the Council of Constantinople the cause of Church unity, for which

[1] Apollinarius had certainly been condemned; for Gregory writes with violence and bitterness of him. The verdicts of Councils against him are not mentioned: which makes it likely that the book was composed when their result was notorious—*i.e.* after 383.

[2] Jerome states that he died in the reign of Theodosius (§ 104). Voisin, *l.c.* pp. 112–3, suggests that he was dead in 384: but his evidence is weak.

[3] *Ep.* 257.

[4] *L.c.* pp. 32–42.

Basil had so heroically laboured, speedily triumphed, less, it must be admitted, from the growth of a spirit of tolerance than from the pressure of the emperor and the work of men like Jerome and Epiphanius who dreaded speculation and made a fetish of doctrinal and ecclesiastical uniformity. A judicious combination of episcopal leniency in readmitting Apollinarians to communion without requiring them to change their opinions[1], and of imperial severity towards the obstinate, brought back the majority of them into the Church long before their beliefs were restated by Cyril in his quarrel with Nestorius. This process was hastened by disputes between the leaders. Timothy had definitely overstepped his master's teaching in the emphasis which he laid upon the consubstantiality of the flesh of Christ with His Godhead as a consequence of their complete union. Polemon, who appears to have been a later recruit to the school, and who was a violent sectarian in temper, still further encouraged the movement towards Monophysitism, quarrelling with Timothy and founding a party of his own, the Synusiasts or Polemianists[2]. These extremists were bitterly attacked by the more moderate followers of the Laodicene, like Homonius and Valentinus, the latter of whom has left a statement of his case against them based upon the appeal to his master's own words[3]. Even in Apollinarius' lifetime the synodal utterances of the sect and the

[1] As was definitely done by Theodotus of Antioch between 410 and 415.

[2] Theodoret, *Haer. Fab.* iv. 9, etc.

[3] *Capita Apologiae* (Lietzmann, pp. 287–91), *ap.* Leontius, *Adv. Fraud.* (Migne, *P.G.* LXXXVI. 2, 1947–75), where Timothy's letter to Homonius, quoting another series of passages to prove that Apollinarius agreed with him, is also preserved.

letters of its leader show that the formation of a left wing had attracted attention. For the heresiarch repeatedly renews his condemnation of those who say that the flesh of Christ was consubstantial with His Godhead. After his death schism became open. The moderates returned to communion: some of them had perhaps never left the Church. The Polemianists formed groups of small congregations in various centres and may even have survived until the Eutychian heresy and the rending of Eastern Christendom. The general uncertainty in the Greek world on matters of Christology, which was so characteristic of the fourth century, prevailed throughout the fifth also, and is reflected in the sordid intrigues and tergiversations of the whole Two-Natures controversy. Apollinarius had been lucid and consistent: his orthodox opponents, no less than his followers, were only able to fasten upon phrases and quibble over their meaning. Like Origen he had opened up and surveyed a new tract of country: his successors were content to divide up and quarrel over their portions of his bequest. Much of it was absorbed by the diplomacy of Cyril into the domain of the Church Catholic: much of it was claimed by the Monophysites. If Origen was, by his discovery of the eternal generation of the Son, the spiritual sire of the Eastern Nicenes, and by his subordinationist language the ancestor of Arianism, Apollinarius may equally claim to be at once the source of the doctrine of the impersonal humanity and of belief in the one nature of the Incarnate. Smaller men catalogue and classify: the genius creates. Diversity of offspring is the prerogative of a creator.

Of Apollinarius' personality and character we know as little as of his life: but that little is an amazing testimony to his worth. At a time when it was customary to associate unconventional opinions with moral obliquity and when the defamation of a heretic was almost a religious duty, Apollinarius alone stands out unassailed. Epiphanius[1] and Jerome[2], whose saintliness did not include the bridling of the tongue and who never allowed personal feelings to mitigate their castigation of doctrinal error, unite in paying tributes of affection and reverence to the heresiarch of Laodicea. Philostorgius the Arian[3], who cannot indeed equal their pungency of speech, but seldom speaks well of a Nicene and had no special cause to love Apollinarius, is not less warm in his admiration. Basil[4], bitterly as he regretted a connection which had given his enemies an opportunity to blaspheme him, cannot withhold a grudging testimony to his quality. Nilus[5] frankly appeals to his memory as an example to one of his monks. Only Gregory of Nyssa[6] descends to a piece of gossip about him, and this, as even Tillemont remarks, does small credit to its author. Apollinarius stands unblemished, a man of the loftiest ideals, of stainless honour and devoted piety, with the scholar's passion for truth and the saint's confidence in righteousness, beloved by his friends, admired by his opponents, reverenced by all, fit to take his place with Origen as a type of the noblest product of Greek Christendom.

And his intellect was on a level with his character.

[1] *Haer.* lxxvii. 24.
[2] *Ep.* 84, etc.
[3] *Ap.* Suidas, *Lex.* I. 615, 616.
[4] *Ep.* 244: "I have never regarded him as an enemy, and in some respects look upon him with reverence."
[5] *Ad Diocletianum Ep.* 257.
[6] *Paneg. in S. Ephrem.*: cf. Voisin, *l.c.* p. 40.

Athanasius and Basil, as we have seen, recognised in him the leading expert of the day in matters of doctrine. Jerome brackets him with Didymus as his master in sacred studies[1]. Philostorgius reckons Apollinarius, Basil and Gregory of Nazianzus as by far the most prominent champions of the Nicene faith, excelling alike in secular literature and knowledge of Holy Writ, and accounts him the greatest of the three by reason of his familiarity with Hebrew, of his scientific presentation of argument, of his fulness and strength of expression[2]. Vincent of Lerins, singling him out as an example of fallen greatness, gives him the palm for insight, for unremitting labour and massive learning[3]. But in this case we need not rely solely on the testimony of others; for sufficient of his own works have survived to support by first hand evidence what has been written in his praise. And before we consider his Christology in detail it will be well to consider his earlier works, so as to estimate the scope and quality of his mind.

The first point that strikes a student is the volume and variety of his output. Songs and poems, translations into Homeric verse and religious dramas, commentaries upon Scripture, treatises against pagan philosophy and Christian heterodoxy, expositions of Trinitarian and Christological doctrine, confessions of faith and letters to a large circle of correspondents—rarely can one man have covered so wide a field. Basil[4] may well taunt him with having filled the world with his books; and in an age remarkable for its literary productivity his record

[1] *Ep.* 84.

[2] *Ap.* Suidas, *l.c.* He has an interesting comparison of the style of the three.

[3] *Commonit.* XI. (ed. Moxon, pp. 43, 44).

[4] *Ep.* 263: cf. also *Ep.* 244.

stands unequalled. His doctrine of the Incarnation, the crowning labour of his life, was at least not undertaken lightly or unadvisedly nor without adequate preparation. Like Origen he is equipped at every point for his task as a theologian: like him he combines in himself all that is best in the culture of his time.

We have seen that the groundwork of his studies was supplied by a rigorous classical education, and that, as his activities under Julian demonstrate, he had trained himself in the most exacting of studies, the art of translation into the language of another time. Of his skill as a poet and writer of songs we know only that his enemies ascribed the spread of his opinions not least to his merit in this respect. Men at work and over their cups, women at the loom, on holidays and festivals, in all the affairs of life, his were the hymns that they sang to the glory of God[1]: and so great was their vogue that Gregory Nazianzen[2] felt himself called to furbish up his classics and save the faithful from chanting themselves into heresy.

Of his dramas all have perished: for the *Christus Patiens*, upon which Mrs Browning wastes so much good satire at the heresiarch's expense[3], is certainly not by him or indeed of his century[4]. Nor does his reputation lose by its removal; for it is a poor thing, a mere cento of tags from Euripides, a bad parody of the *Medea* rather than a translation or an original work.

[1] Sozomen, *H.E.* vi. 25.

[2] *Ep.* 101.

[3] In the essay on the Greek Christian Poets, printed in her collected works.

[4] The words Μήτηρ τοῦ διφύους (line 1792) are sufficient to exonerate both Apollinarius and Gregory Nazianzen from responsibility for its authorship; and the exaggerated Mariolatry of the whole play is certain proof that it is not of their age.

The translation of the Psalter is very much more likely to be genuine. Ludwich, who has recently edited it[1] and who formerly rejected its Apollinarian authorship, now declares himself convinced that it is certainly his, and produces strong arguments in favour of that belief. It is certain from the testimony of Gregory Nazianzen[2], who speaks scornfully of the "new psalters rivalling and perhaps contradicting those of David," and of Zonaras[3] that Apollinarius had published such a version; and in the introductory prelude the author claims that his is the first attempt at a metrical translation since Ptolemy and the Seventy cared for the sense but not the form. So, too, the prelude presupposes a heathen and possibly hostile environment[4], a condition appropriate to the fourth but to no later century. The introduction into the version of the Fourteenth Psalm[5] of the verses from the third chapter of the Epistle to the Romans[6] which might seem to favour a later date is indecisive: for this interpolation was already familiar when Origen composed his Hexapla. Moreover, the style of the translation is strongly in favour of its ascription to Apollinarius: for the rendering is simple and very close to the Septuagint[7], and there is a complete absence of glosses or of Christian additions or of any sign of allegorising: and the references to the Trinity and to the co-equal Godhead of the Spirit support his

[1] Teubner edition, 1912. Dräseke, *l.c.* pp. 63–80, reviews the earlier phases of Ludwich's opinion.

[2] *Ep.* 101.

[3] *Hist. Epit.* XIII. 12.

[4] Cf. especially: *ἐγείρομεν αὖτις ἀοιδὴν ἑξατόνοις ἐπέεσσιν ἵνα γνώωσι καὶ ἄλλοι γλῶσσ' ὅτι παντοίῃ Χριστὸν βασιλῆα βοήσει.*

[5] *Ps.* xiii (LXX), 8–15.

[6] *Rom.* iii. 13–18.

[7] Ludwich proves by a long list of passages that none of the existing MSS. exactly represent Apollinarius' original.

authorship[1]. The arguments against his authorship are based mainly upon the style, the prevalence of spondaic verses and the resemblance of certain words to those used by Nonnus[2]: but in the absence of any other examples of Apollinarius' verse it is difficult to give them much weight. The mention of Marcian in the Prelude is unimportant; for there is no indication that the reference is to the emperor of that name[3]. The translation is into Homeric dialect and hexameter verse; and if not great poetry avoids the faults of most of such exercises and gives us a high opinion of its author's literary skill and mastery of language. As regards its date Dräseke is probably right in view of the evidence of Sozomen and of Gregory Nazianzen in separating it from the works published by Apollinarius in Julian's reign, and ascribing it to the later years of his life. It must have been issued before 382, and in view of the striking allusion to the restoration of peace among the peoples in the Prelude may well have appeared shortly after Theodosius' pacification of the Goths in 378. No doubt the work had occupied its author for many years and the organisation of separate Apollinarian congregations gave him occasion to finish and issue it for their use.

Of his exegetical works a list has already been given, and we have seen that Jerome comments upon their brevity and excellence. Voisin, whose work is admirably

[1] Cf. Prelude, vv. 54–7, 102–4, and Dräseke, *l.c.* pp. 68–9.

[2] So Herman, quoted by Ludwich, p. viii, who argues that it is later than Christodorus and John of Gaza.

[3] Dräseke, *l.c.* p. 72, disposes effectively of the idea that he was the emperor: his suggestion that Marcian was the hermit of that name who lived at Chalcis in Syria in the reign of Valens (cf. Theodoret, *H.E.* iv. 28) is very plausible.

thorough, gives a full statement of the fragments that have been published by Mai[1], Cramer[2] and Faulhaber[3], and a general account of their character: but he dismisses them too briefly and has overlooked at least one important piece of evidence which they supply. From the fragments it is plain that Apollinarius adopted a method of his own. Hitherto Christian commentators had followed one of three lines in their attitude towards Scripture. Some few had taken the Old Testament literally; and like Marcion, failing to reconcile its teaching with that of Christ, had accounted for it by assigning its inspiration to a different and inferior deity. The majority had followed Philo's example and explained its meaning by the use of allegory: from the time of the Epistle of Barnabas, when the vagaries of ancient physiology had been introduced to explain why Israel was forbidden to eat the hare and the hyena[4], and the Greek use of letters for numerals had made Abraham's male servants a prediction of Jesus and the Cross[5], exegesis had consisted mainly of researches into symbolism: the Bible was verbally inerrant, but its language was a complicated cryptogram. Only among the Theodotians was the modern method of historical study undertaken; and their sole heir, so far as we know, was the Antiochene, Theodore of Mopsuestia. Apollinarius, though nearer to these than to the allegorisers, struck out a line of his own. He rejected wholly the methods of the Alexandrians, insisting that both Old and New

[1] *Nov. Patr. Biblioth.* VII. 2, on Isaiah, Ezek. and Prov. *Script. Vet. Nov. Coll.* I. on Daniel.

[2] *Cat. Graec. Patr. in N.T.*, especially on Matt., John and Romans.

[3] *Propheten-Cat. nach Röm. Handschr.*

[4] *Barnabas*, 10.

[5] *L.c.* 9. Three hundred and eighteen—10 = I, 8 H and 300 T.

Testaments must be taken in their simple and literal sense. At the same time he seems to have paid little attention to critical problems[1], making use of all the versions indiscriminately, taking a conservative view of the dating and authorship of the several books and devoting himself to the discovery of the meaning of their authors and to the moral lessons conveyed by them. His commentaries consist of short paraphrases emphasising the ethical and devotional element, making no parade of learning and striving simply to discover and explain the spiritual value of the text. His own deeply religious nature, his sincerity, austerity and earnestness, are revealed in every line. Scripture is to him not an intellectual problem or a piece of literature: it is a guide to right living, an incentive to the practice of godliness. Like Athanasius and unlike the Christian Platonists, Christ is in his eyes primarily the Saviour: sin is not ignorance to be dispelled by *gnosis*, nor is it a disease to be cured by observance of the cultus; rather it is death, a separation from God, a condition of impotence in which man cannot save himself; and what is needed is a resurrection, a new life which only God can give. That is why he insists with a passionate and unfaltering confidence that neither the demi-god of Arianism nor the inspired man of the Antiochenes can do what Christ has done. The gospel is not a text-book of philosophy nor the record of a perfect life: it is a way of salvation for a world in direst need.

Of his generally conservative attitude and love of literalism in exegesis two striking examples are supplied by his treatment of the Book of Daniel. Porphyry, in

[1] Cf. Jerome, *Adv. Ruf.* ii. fin.: *Bono quidem studio sed non secundum scientiam.*

his work against the Christians, had argued with surprising modernity of outlook[1] that the book was pseudonymous and written in the time of Antiochus Epiphanes: he seems to have devoted much time and study to the subject; for he not only criticised the passage about the Abomination of Desolation quoted in the Gospels, but also drew attention to the play upon words in the story of Susannah, shrewdly deducing from it that the prophet, whenever he lived, at least was familiar with Greek. Apollinarius will have nothing to do with his aspersions upon the canonical book, devoting a whole volume of his treatise against Porphyry to its vindication[2]: but for Susannah he is less solicitous; for this, as he argued, was not written in Hebrew and therefore could not be regarded as authentically inspired[3]. So, too, in his interpretation of the prophecies in the ninth chapter of Daniel, Apollinarius took the eschatology literally and calculated from it a precise prediction of the end of the world—a prediction which, as Jerome justly remarks, those who live then may haply have to revise[4]. This acceptance of the apocalyptic element in Scripture *au pied de la lettre* caused Apollinarius to reproduce the chiliastic beliefs which had been so prominent in Papias and had so strongly excited the anger of Eusebius of Caesarea[5]. In his refusal to

[1] Porphyry also anticipated the views of the Tübingen school in his view of the relation between St Peter and St Paul: cf. Jerome, *Pref. in Ep. ad Galat.* I.

[2] Vol. 26. So Jerome, *Pref. in Daniel.*

[3] Jerome, *l.c.*

[4] *Comm. in Daniel*, 9. 24.

[5] His chiliasm apparently led him to compose two books against Dionysius Alex., who had written ridiculing belief in the literal fulfilment of the Apocalypse (cf. Jerome, *Pref. in lib. xviii Comm. in Isaeam*). His views, set out in these books, influenced, so Jerome declares, not only his own sect but the orthodox of the East, and are described in Epiphanius, *Haer.* lxxvii. 26–8.

allegorise the bishop of Laodicea was at least consistent[1].

It is a great misfortune that these references to Daniel represent all that we know of what was undoubtedly the most highly esteemed[2] of all the works of Apollinarius, the thirty volumes against Porphyry. Plotinus' successor had made of Neo-platonism a religion which, without losing its attractiveness for philosophers and mystics, had found room for the mythologies, the allegorisings, the spiritualism, the magic and the ceremonies of the time. A synthetic system such as this which claimed to explain and include all the faiths and had the sanction of the sacred name of Plato and the active support of the emperor Julian (whose character after all compares very favourably with those of his Christian predecessors), was a serious rival to a Church torn with factions over niceties of dogmatic. To attack it with any fulness or hope of success was a task worthy of a great Christian scholar, and calculated to extend him to the uttermost. If Apollinarius' monumental work had been preserved, we might be possessed of a worthy rival to the *Contra Celsum*. Having been deprived of it, we can only be sure that the heresiarch, whom it is the fashion to treat as an Aristotelian, had at least made himself acquainted with the latest and in some respects the most important heir of the Platonic tradition.

Further proof of his interest in Platonism is to be found in his book against Origen. As we have seen, he

[1] A similar instance of literalism is to be found, unless Epiphanius, *Haer*. lxxvii. 36, and lxxviii. 1, is libelling him, in his belief that Mary became the wife of Joseph after the birth of Jesus—after all a natural inference from Matt. i. 25 and the mention of His brethren.

[2] It is warmly praised not only by Jerome, *Ep*. 84, and as above cited, but by Vincent of Lerins, *Commonit*. 31.

utterly eschewed the allegorical method of exegesis, and also the indulgence in unscriptural speculation. On these grounds he would have found much material for criticism in the great Alexandrian. Indeed it is probable that his commentaries on the Bible were largely undertaken, as were Theodore's after him[1], in order to free the Church from dependence upon the scholarship of the Christian Platonists. But if he objected to them on this account, it by no means follows that he belonged to the rival school of philosophy; and in this respect many of his critics have done him an injustice. On the strength of his books against Porphyry, Origen and Dionysius, and of his fondness for syllogisms and for certain antitheses such as that between the mover and the moved, and of his geographical connection with Antioch, he has often been described as a follower of Aristotle[2]—a description which is wholly misleading. He undoubtedly adopted certain of the methods characteristic of the Antiochene theology: but his bent of mind is thoroughly Platonist, and he stands with Athanasius in the direct line of those typically Greek Christian thinkers who were idealists through and through. By temperament as well as by birthright he was a man of Alexandria. We shall see, when we examine Apollinarius' Christology in detail, how close is his general outlook to that of Origen. Like him, his thought starts not from the human but from the universal and the divine: like him, he must see the Incarnation not merely as a fact

[1] Cf. below, pp. 277–9.

[2] *E.g.* Voisin, *l.c.* pp. 57, 58, says that Aristotelianism is the only philosophy to which he is in any way indebted. Fritzsche, *De Theod. Mops. Vita et Scr.*, p. 96, is much more correct when he writes: "*Ille* [Apollinarius] *optimus Platonicus, hic* [Theodore] *non satis acutus Aristotelicus.*"

in time, but as an eternal condition of the nature of God: like him, he finds difficulty in explaining the proofs of human growth and limitation in Jesus: like him, he has recourse to a theory of kenosis for their interpretation. The resemblance between them goes far deeper than any differences of method: it is of the very stuff and substance of their intellectual lives. And, fortunately, it is clinched for us by the curious chance that among the relatively scanty fragments of Apollinarius' writings[1] there is at least one indisputable citation from Origen[2], when he borrows the simile of iron plunged in fire and taking into itself the properties of heat and light to explain the union of Godhead and manhood in Christ. This spiritual kinship is of primary importance for an understanding of the Bishop of Laodicea. The accident of his birthplace brought him into contact with Syrian Christianity in its stronghold. He spent his life among the followers of Eustathius and the friends of Diodore. And all the Greek within him rose in revolt against them. If this was Christianity, then he would be content to go out into the wilderness with such followers as might be willing to share his excommunication. At least he would proclaim the faith that was in him, the faith which had given the Church a succession of its most brilliant champions, the faith of Justin and Athenagoras, of Clement and Origen, of Dionysius and of Athanasius. And in him speaks in its clearest and most uncompromising tones the voice of Hellenic Christendom, in him its latest and in some respects its greatest representative.

Of the book against Marcellus we know nothing

[1] *Ap*. Theodoret, *Dial*. i.
[2] *De Princ*. II. vi. 6.

except the name[1], though the pseudepigraphic Κατὰ Μέρος Πίστις, which is certainly Apollinarian, contains sections[2] definitely dealing with this heterodoxy, and possibly reproducing the arguments of the larger work. Our ignorance of it is the more to be regretted because Marcellus is one of the most interesting figures of the time, and a man whose theory obviously exercised much influence upon Apollinarius. The Bishop of Ancyra represents a line of attack upon Arianism not otherwise developed, and is possibly an example of genuine Sabellianism[3]. He saw that the emphasis upon the title Son favoured tritheistic and subordinationist conceptions of the Godhead, and therefore reverted to the language of the Logos-theology, treating the Logos as the active principle in the deity and as operative in connection with creation and revelation. God, according to his teaching, was eternally changeless and impassible: in relation to the cosmic process certain limitations and differentiations within the divine nature were manifested: these culminated in the Incarnation which involved for the Logos circumscription within the bounds of personal and fleshly existence[4]. He seems to have accepted the Arian contention that as incarnate the Logos was passible and capable of change, but to have insisted that this humiliation was only temporary

[1] Jerome, *De Vir. Illustr.* 86.

[2] §§ 13–26. Dräseke, *l.c.* p. 40, perhaps rightly treats these sections as Apollinarius' reply to Basil's charge of Sabellianism.

[3] We know almost nothing of the real Sabellius or his teaching, most of the accounts of him in ancient and modern times being coloured by what is known of Marcellus: for Marcellus cf. Zahn, *Marc. von Ancyra*, and fragments in Rettburg, *Marcelliana*.

[4] Marcellus did not succeed in solving the problem of the Person of the Incarnate. Certainly the manhood was not personal: but neither was the pre-incarnate Logos. Apparently the Logos became personal by limitation or union with the flesh.

and a necessary part of the whole divine purpose of self-revelation, and therefore furnished no proof of the inferiority of the Logos except for the brief space of His sojourn upon earth. His theory was thus a refined version of the doctrine of the Apologists: and its strength was due to the moral lessons drawn from it of the infinite condescension of God and the need for a similar self-surrender on the part of mankind. Apollinarius, who was a thorough-going Trinitarian although, as the charge of Sabellianism made against him by Basil proves, by no means a tritheist[1], insisted that the differentiation of Persons[2] is not due to a process of expansion and contraction for the sake of creation but constitutes an eternal condition of the existence of God[3]. And he repudiates utterly all acceptance of the belief that Incarnation involves change and limitation in the Son's eternal nature. Marcellus had treated the whole cosmic process as on its divine side an act of kenosis: Apollinarius confines the kenosis to the actual union of the Godhead with the flesh. His Christology was elaborated in opposition to two beliefs to which he objected: on the one hand, he attacks the Antiochenes who seemed to him to save the impassibility of the Son by regarding His Incarnation as a close alliance with a deified man; on the other, he avoids and criticises the Marcellan theory which, while accepting a real union of the Godhead with the flesh, saw in it only a temporary theophany wherein the passibility of the Logos was

[1] The opposite charge of teaching gradations within the Trinity was also brought against him by Gregory Naz., *Ep.* 101, and *Carm.* 30: but is wholly groundless: cf. below pp. 260, 261.

[2] The use of πρόσωπον instead of ὑπόστασις in the K.M.Π. may indicate that it is earlier than the Council of Alexandria in 362.

[3] K.M.Π. *l.c.* It is probable that the general line of his larger book resembled that in Athanasius, *Or. c. Ar.* iv. 15–24.

admitted at the cost of denying the eternity of the Trinity. His repeated emphasis upon the changelessness of Christ, and his stress upon the sameness of the Son both before and after His Incarnation, demonstrate his desire to safeguard himself against the peculiarities of Marcellus.

This insistence upon the immutability of the Godhead is no doubt due also to Apollinarius' hostility to Arianism, a hostility expressed in his work against Eunomius. This is especially interesting on account of Dräseke's claim[1] to have recovered it in the fourth and fifth volumes of the *Antirrheticus* of Basil which are universally acknowledged to be by some other hand. His hypothesis is that Basil wrote the treatise in three volumes, that Eunomius answered with an *Apologeticus*, and that to this Apollinarius replied[2], his work being in consequence circulated along with Basil's. Funk[3] has demonstrated that this is incorrect, and both Voisin[4] and Lietzmann[5] pour contempt upon the identification, the former in common with Funk declaring that the style is wholly unlike that of Apollinarius[6]. While admitting that Dräseke's discoveries are often based on precarious evidence[7], and that in this case Philostorgius' account hardly corresponds with these

[1] *Apollinarios*, pp. 122–38.

[2] He bases this conjecture upon Photius' citation from Philostorgius.

[3] *Kirchengesch. Abhandl. und Unters.* II. 291–329, deals with the subject.

[4] *L.c.* pp. 243–5.

[5] *L.c.* p. viii.

[6] Garnier, *ap.* Migne, *P.G.* XXIX. pp. 231 ff., had already commented on the defective style, and strained and often almost incoherent reasoning.

[7] *E.g.* his ascription to Apollinarius of the shorter version of Pseudo-Justin, Ἔκθεσις Πίστεως—a ridiculous piece of critical perversity.

Pseudo-Basilian books, we cannot regard the question as settled. For the detailed arguments based on the use of texts by Apollinarius and this author, upon which Funk and Voisin lay great stress[1], are singularly unconvincing, and since their time Lietzmann has recovered a genuinely Apollinarian writing which in its strained argument and syllogistic form is exactly parallel to the books of Pseudo-Basil. This work, the *Anacephalaeosis*, as Lietzmann calls it, is found in the fifth dialogue on the Trinity, usually printed as Pseudo-Athanasian[2], but ascribed by Caspari and Harnack to Maximus the Confessor. Four verses of it are quoted by Theodoret[3] and printed by Dräseke[4], and the whole treatise represents the arguments of an Apollinarian to which Maximus gives orthodox replies. If Lietzmann is correct in ascribing these arguments to Apollinarius, and Theodoret's quotation seems conclusive, we have here in all probability an appendix of syllogisms added to the great book against Diodore[5] as a summary and similar in intention and style to the appendices which Theodoret himself adds to his own *Dialogus*[6]. Its discovery over-

[1] *E.g.* Voisin quotes John v. 9 as cited differently by them: but one part of the verse is used by Pseudo-Basil (Dräseke, *l.c.* p. 206) and totally different words by Apollinarius (Lietzmann, Fr. 131). Voisin's second example, Matt. xxvi. 39, is used without perceptible difference by them both.

[2] In Migne, *P.G.* XXVIII. pp. 1265 ff.

[3] *Dial.* iii, ed. Schultze, IV. 256. He quotes *Anac.* 17, 20, 29, 18 consecutively.

[4] *L.c.* p. 367, printed as part of the *C. Diodorum*.

[5] Theodoret, *l.c.* quotes it as "another book following upon the 'Book of Chapters'"—as Theodoret calls the *C. Diod.* One quotation from Apollinarius in Leontius *Adv. Fraud.* (Migne, *P.G.* LXXXVI. 2. 1968), is labelled as from the *Anacephalaeosis* of the *C. Diod.*: it is not found in Lietzmann's *Anac.*: but is cast in exactly similar syllogistic form.

[6] The custom of adding a brief and epigrammatic recapitulation seems to have been not unusual.

throws the argument that the style of Pseudo-Basil makes it impossible to ascribe these books to Apollinarius, and suggests that they may be the syllogistic summaries of his lost work against Eunomius[1]. This suggestion is borne out by their character. There is in them a close resemblance of thought and expression to the genuine confessions of Apollinarius, both in regard to Trinitarian[2] and to Christological[3] doctrine. There is a very frequent and exactly parallel use of biblical texts and the exegesis is always literal and close to the original meaning. Photinus[4] is the only heretic mentioned, and there are two striking references to the writings of Athanasius[5]. The provenance of the books is thus thoroughly Apollinarian.

These exegetical and controversial writings, interesting as is the light which they throw upon his mind, are of infinitely less importance than the treatises and letters on Christology. Lietzmann[6] has discussed and edited these so admirably that there is no need for full surveys of them in detail. Students of the subject will find in his *Apollinaris* all the material that can be collected from

[1] The earlier portion of Pseudo-Basil exactly corresponds in style to the *Anac.*: the later consists mainly of proof-texts from Scripture.

[2] *E.g.* the emphasis on the divine impassibility (*C. Eunom.* 291 E); the use of Aristotelian antitheses (*C. Eunom.* 296 E, which is almost identical with Apollinarius, *De Unione*, 11); the treatment of the inner mystery of the Trinity (*C. Eunom.* 314, 315, etc.: cf. the so-called Sabellian passage in Basil, *Ep.* 129); the doctrine of the Holy Spirit (*C. Eunom.* 303 C, a thoroughly Apollinarian passage).

[3] References in the *C. Eunom.* are naturally not many, but are very characteristic: cf. the explanation of John xvii. 5 in *l.c.* 292 C, and in Lietzmann, Fr. 5; the belief that Christ cannot have been "part of the world," 293 B and *Anac.* 1; the saying "Christ suffered in the flesh," 293 D and *Ad Jov.* 2; and the quotation of Phil. ii. 9, 289 A and *Anac.* 14.

[4] *C. Eunom.* 292 B.

[5] *C. Eunom.* 291 B and *De Sent. Dion.* 10; and *C. Eunom.* 281 C and *De Sent. Dion.* 17.

[6] Dräseke's very full discussion of their dates is full of interest and ingenuity, but the proofs are highly precarious.

quotations as well as all the pseudepigraphic works that can safely be assigned to him. The two most important are the *Contra Diodorum*, which Theodoret quotes extensively in order to prove that its author was not a Monophysite and always calls the "Book arranged in Chapters" perhaps because of his reverence for Diodore, and the *Apodeixis*, of which Gregory of Nyssa in his *Antirrheticus* has preserved long extracts and a clear general outline. In addition, there are many fragments of pamphlets or letters quoted chiefly by Leontius from Timothy and Valentinus or in the Doctrina; a confession of faith, the Κατὰ Μέρος Πίστις, traditionally ascribed to Gregory Thaumaturgus; a book or books, the *De Unione* and the *De Fide et Incarnatione*; and the letter to Dionysius ascribed to Pope Julius; and the letter to Jovian ascribed to Athanasius: these are certainly by Apollinarius. Other Pseudo-Athanasian writings are more doubtfully his; for the tendency to bestow his name upon any writing of the great Alexandrian which conflicted with later orthodoxy cannot be forgotten. Lietzmann refuses to assign certainly to him the *De Incarnatione* which Voisin accounts undoubtedly Apollinarian, and the *Quod unus sit Christus* of which he is less confident, and also the *Encyclion* and third letter attributed to Julius, and the fragments of Julius and Felix[1].

[1] Voisin, *l.c.* pp. 152–67, 408, who refuses, as a Catholic, to admit that the Christology of Apollinarius was only a precise and formulated development of the general Greek opinion and who has therefore to explain the wide prevalence of Monophysitism, lays exaggerated stress on these "frauds," and makes them responsible for the whole Eutychian heresy. Thus Apollinarius becomes the sole source of the great schism of 451. Voisin does not realise that the fact that these books could be circulated without arousing suspicion proves that the general tradition of the East was already favourable to Monophysitism.

It is surprising, considering how scanty is our material and that most of it has been selected for us by his enemies, that we can gain any adequate idea of Apollinarius' teaching. Few theologians have written so carefully that a judicious opponent or a mistaken disciple could not select passages from their works which when divorced from their context and placed in the most unfavourable light would not be susceptible of an heretical meaning. And in the long struggle with the Monophysites the orthodox searched with a meticulous enthusiasm for any scrap of evidence that would establish a precedent for their condemnation. Certainly if a book like Gregory of Nyssa's *Antirrheticus* had been treated in this fashion, we should have a poor opinion both of the intelligence and of the orthodoxy of its author. It is perhaps the highest testimony to Apollinarius' unequivocal sincerity, clearness of understanding and consistency of utterance that his foes although often libelling him through perversity or ignorance have hardly been able to find in his own works a single saying to support their misunderstanding or to contradict the plain meaning of his belief. Facundus and Leontius, from their opposite standpoints in the matter of the Three Chapters, have both cited extracts from him; and yet from the patchwork we can rediscover without much difficulty the details of his original design. Mistaken he may have been: obscure or elusive or dishonest he certainly never was[1].

[1] Neither he nor probably his immediate followers can be blamed for the circulation of his writings under the names of others. The origin of these "frauds" is obscure. Leontius, or the anonymous critic, whose *Adv. Fraud. Apoll.* is preserved as his, states that "certain of the heresy of Apollinarius or of Eutyches or Dioscurus have ascribed books by Apollinarius to Gregory Thaum., Atha-

Nevertheless, there is one such charge against him which cannot be neglected. Rufinus[1] declares that Apollinarius began by teaching that Christ "assumed only a body and not a soul at all," but that being controverted by such passages as "I lay down my soul that I may take it again[2]" and "My soul is sad even unto death[3]," "he changed his opinion, and to disguise his change and conceal his discomfiture said that He did indeed possess a soul but only on its animating and not on its rational side, and that to supply the place of a rational soul there was the Word of God." This account is copied by Socrates[4] and by Augustine[5]; and Lietzmann[6] suggests that it is supported by Epiphanius on the strength of his statement that these two theories were held by different people who may or may not have been pupils of Apollinarius. Dräseke[7], Voisin and Lietzmann accept the story, attempting to prove from it that Apollinarius was a "dichotomite" before his condemnation, or at least that there are two distinct

nasius or Julius": but as he proves this by quoting the Apollinarians Timothy and Valentinus, in whose writings these "frauds" are quoted as by Apollinarius, it is clear that they had not been perpetrated in Valentinus' time. We first trace them in Cyril Alex. who defended the *μία φύσις τοῦ Λόγου σεσαρκωμένη* of Apollinarius, *Ad Jov.*, as Athanasian. Presumably, therefore, they were initiated in the first half of the fifth century, though most of them may be Monophysite. Forgery of all sorts became prevalent during the later phases of the Two Natures controversy.

[1] *H.E.* ii. 20. [2] John x. 18. [3] John xii. 27.

[4] *H.E.* ii. 46. Socrates, although copying from Rufinus, admits that he is by no means reliable, *H.E.* ii. 1.

[5] *De Dono Persev.* 67. Lietzmann regards this as copied from Rufinus, *l.c.* p. 4.

[6] *L.c.* p. 5.

[7] *L.c.* p. 26. He takes the *Ad Jovian.* as typical of the earlier use and assigns all similar passages to the year 363: but admits that so able a teacher as Apollinarius may have adapted his psychological language to the understanding of his readers!

phases in his teaching, and using it as a guide in the dating of the fragments. The final belief of the heresiarch was certainly that Christ possessed human body (σῶμα or σάρξ) and soul (ψυχή) but that the highest element in His nature, His mind (νοῦς) or spirit (πνεῦμα) was divine. Was this only an elaborate afterthought[1]?

In view of the concurrence of the three monographs whose authors speak with the greatest authority, it may be rash to maintain that Rufinus and they with him are doing Apollinarius a grave injustice. But the arguments against their view are very strong; and, as the matter is important, must be fully stated.

In the first place, the principle that the earlier books are likely to be less technical and that in them soul may sometimes be found used in a general and popular sense, may be readily admitted as plausible. For Apollinarius developed his theory out of the current conception held by his friend Athanasius and his predecessors that the Logos in the Incarnation took upon Himself our flesh. Moreover, the early books are controversial, and their author would necessarily accept the ordinary usage: he was attacking the Antiochene doctrine of an inspired man, not setting out his own faith in detailed terms, and to provoke a discussion on psychology would have been beside the mark. But, as a matter of fact, even in these earlier books there is remarkably little evidence that he used "soul" in a different sense from that which it bore in the *Apodeixis*.

Furthermore, if we set aside his Christological

[1] The only parallel to Rufinus' charge is to be found in the Pseudo-Athanasian *Sermo c. Omn. Haer.* 11 (Migne, *P.G.* XXVIII. pp. 520 ff.), where Apollinarius is represented as denying a ψυχή to Christ, and John xii. 27 is quoted against him. This book is certainly a forgery, and wholly valueless.

writings, there is conclusive proof that his psychology from first to last was based upon a triple division of man's nature. It is the universal testimony of antiquity and of the fragments that he was a traducian. Jerome[1] and Nemesius[2] definitely state that he believed that souls were generated from souls even as bodies were from bodies. The words of the *De Unione*[3], which Voisin and Lietzmann declare to be dichotomite and early, "From the will of the flesh and the will of man ordinary human beings receive souls and life[4]," prove that this was his opinion at the time when he first wrote of Christology. It is on general grounds exceedingly unlikely that he meant by soul what Tertullian, the other great traducianist, meant by *anima*: for no Greek ever believed in so lowly a source for man's intellectual and spiritual faculty. And in Apollinarius' case we know that he never did so from a series of passages quoted by Mai[5] from his commentary on Ezekiel. In them he maintains that the animating soul is an earthly element bound up with matter and transmitted by procreation: but in addition there is another element in man, natural to him indeed but specially bestowed by God, the mind and will. "The intellectual faculty is not from the world but from above": Voisin[6] quotes the saying, and refuses to recognise that it is fatal to his hypothesis. If he was a traducian, he was also a "trichotomite": and trichotomy supplied, as Nemesius tells us[7], the basis of his Christology.

[1] *Ep.* 82.

[2] *De Nat. Hom.* 47.

[3] § 13. The *De Unione* is the work in which "soul" is most plausibly said to be used in a popular or dichotomite fashion: cf. § 5 and perhaps 12.

[4] *De Unione*, 13.

[5] *Nov. Patr. Biblioth.* VII. 90.

[6] *L.c.* pp. 273–6.

[7] *De Nat. Hom.* 9.

Thirdly, the evidence on which the theory of a change depends is not only inconclusive but can be met by equally strong passages on the other side. Voisin relies principally upon an extract from the *De Unione*[1] and three sayings in the *Contra Diodorum*[2] in which Apollinarius uses the union of body and soul in man to illustrate the union of flesh and Godhead in Christ. In all of these the point is not any parallelism between the soul and the Godhead, but simply a comparison of the method by which the two combine without losing their peculiar attributes: as soul remains invisible, so Godhead remains divine. The words in the *De Unione* compare the union of God and man into one nature to the union of the "two imperfect parts of man" whereby soul and body become a single nature and are spoken of interchangeably, each being called the whole. There is nothing here to imply dichotomy; and the passage is explained by the first fragment of the *Contra Diodorum* which is fatal to a dichotomite interpretation. For in it Apollinarius argues that soul and body are of a common origin and growth[3] (that is, they both arise from procreation), and therefore might be expected to fuse together and lose their distinctive qualities, whereas Godhead and flesh are not of common origin and are less likely to do so. The allusion to his traducianism seems plain enough, and the two shorter passages can be explained in the light of it. There is a saying in the

[1] § 5.

[2] *Ap.* Theodoret, *Dial.* ii; Lietzmann, Frs. 129, 134, 135.

[3] *κατὰ συμφυίαν* and *συμφυής*. It is notable that though Godhead and manhood cannot be described as *συμφυής*, yet as united in Christ they are called *σύμφυτος* (cf. *Apod.*, Lietzmann, Fr. 36): and in one fragment where the unity is emphasised *σὰρξ ἁγία Θεότητι συμφυής* is found (Lietzmann, Fr. 155).

Apodeixis[1] which seems meant to apply to his whole use of the word "body": "The flesh is not soulless (or inanimate); for it is said to wage war with the spirit and against the law of the mind; and we speak of the bodies of irrational creatures as possessing soul." No doubt this passage from the latest of his works is inadmissible as direct evidence: but it draws attention to several earlier sayings which clearly imply trichotomy, such as that in the *Contra Diodorum*[2], in which he claims that "men are consubstantial with the irrational creatures according to the body which is irrational, but different in substance inasmuch as they are rational." We may also note that in no single passage early or late does Apollinarius say that Christ did not assume a human soul. Even in the earliest of his writings he is always careful to specify that it is His spirit or mind that is divine; and thus though he speaks of the human element by the terms body or flesh, he may fairly be assumed to include by implication the other lower or earthly element, especially as in one place he actually defines the flesh as "a living organ adapted by its affections for the divine purpose[3]"—words equivalent to those of the *Apodeixis*. Moreover, when we consider the circumstances under which these earlier works have been preserved, it becomes obvious that we cannot expect to find in them a developed psychology. For Theodoret quotes them in order to confute a Eutychian, and heretical passages would be irrelevant; and the pseudepigraphic documents could not have been unnoticed if they had contained the heresiarch's most characteristic

[1] *Ap. Antirrh.* 7, Lietzmann Fr. 22.
[2] Lietzmann, Fr. 126; cf. also Frs. 146 and 132.
[3] *Anac.* 29, etc.

definitions. Rufinus' statement is unsupported by the evidence of Apollinarius' own words: indeed, they show that the charge is unfounded.

And Rufinus, if not a liar, is at least gifted with an imperfect appreciation of the truth. As Gwatkin[1] has conclusively demonstrated, "his history contains a large element of mere romance." Where a heretic and an opponent of Origen is concerned, an unsubstantiated charge of fraud coming from such a quarter would need a large weight of corroborative evidence, and in the absence of this may safely be set aside. And the details of his story do not bear investigation. Apollinarius was one of the most learned biblical students of all time. His writings prove his intimate acquaintance with the whole range of Scripture, and in particular his absolute familiarity with the Fourth Gospel. And yet Rufinus has the insolence to suggest that he had overlooked two of the most obvious of all texts for students of Christology, two which had been quoted over and over again in the controversies of the Arian period[2]. No doubt certain of Apollinarius' hearers in the attempt to popularise his teaching may have missed the whole point of his belief, that it was only the innermost faculty in Christ which was not human, and especially when they came to translate his ideas into Latin may have used *anima* inaccurately. Voisin[3] is almost certainly wrong when he states that for one who has adopted trichotomy "the word ψυχή can never be taken to include a rational soul": for there existed, as we shall show later, the greatest vagueness upon questions of psychology.

[1] *Studies of Arianism*, p. 101.

[2] Apollinarius actually quotes one of the two texts in an extant fragment—John x. 18, in Lietzmann, Fr. 60.

[3] *L.c.* p. 172.

Rufinus, then, may have heard Apollinarists who were less accurate than their master: but if a teacher is to be condemned as holding the misbeliefs of his pupils, then Origen was an Arian and Cyril of Alexandria a Monophysite

Lietzmann[1] indeed, though he accepts the idea of a change of attitude, pays little attention to Rufinus' accusation, and treats the two phases of Apollinarianism as characterised not so much by a different psychology as by a change of emphasis from the words "one incarnate nature of the Logos" to the "heavenly man[2]." This evidently contemplates a less specialised alteration than that mentioned by Rufinus; and we shall await with interest the appearance of a fuller treatment of the subject.

Meanwhile we can only note that no quality in Apollinarius' work is so arresting as its uniformity and consistency. Different groups of extracts selected for different reasons naturally emphasise separate aspects of his thought: but each aspect plays a part in any reconstruction of his system, and the synthesis is easy to reach. To those of his critics who assume that he instigated all the errors of the letter to Epictetus, a change of psychology is no doubt a trivial matter: but those who study the fragments will find them singularly

[1] *L.c.* pp. 5, 6.

[2] Lietzmann seems to forget that the *Apodeixis* is only quoted when Gregory Nyss. is able to criticise it. Μία φύσις τοῦ Λόγου σεσαρκωμένη did not offend him: ἄνθρωπος ἐξ οὐράνου, the phrase with which the opening of the *Apod.* is concerned, savoured of Gnosticism. But in the rest of the book the ideas already developed in the *C. Diod.* appear—the criticism of ἄνθρωπος ἔνθεος (Fr. 51, etc.), the insistence on κένωσις (Fr. 71) and on the μία φύσις (Fr. 107). Almost every extract from the *Apod.* can be paralleled from the early writings.

free from even the appearance of contradiction. If we were not told the names of the books from which they came it would be impossible to arrange them in any certain sequence. Sayings from the earlier books often throw a flood of light upon difficulties in the language of the *Apodeixis*, and in some places this in turn supplies us with a deliberate explanation of debatable points in his previous work. In summarising his teaching it is impossible to treat it as a gradually expanding growth. Rather it stands as a complete and elaborate system of doctrine, to which all his writings make their contribution, the creation of a master spirit, the finest and most typical product of Christian Hellenism.

CHAPTER V

APOLLINARIUS OF LAODICEA: HIS CHRISTOLOGY

IT is sufficiently obvious, alike from the course of Christological development and from his life-story, that Apollinarius elaborated his doctrine of the Incarnation as a champion of the Origenist or typically Greek, against the Samosatene or Syrian, school of thought. He is the descendant of Malchion and the partner of Athanasius in the struggle against the Antiochene followers of Paul, and represents one side of the universal paradox, God and man, Gnostic and Ebionite, just as clearly as Diodore represents the other. Yet that his system was primarily directed against the Antiochenes has only recently been recognised. Most of the older historians of the early Church[1] agree in regarding Arianism and the doctrine of the mutability of Christ as his point of attack, laying stress on the passages in which he insists that if Christ be God in the flesh then His mind is changeless and incapable of suffering, save in so far as by union with the body there has taken place a transference of the human attributes to the Godhead. This is no doubt largely due to the neglect of the earlier Antiochenes and to failure to recognise the importance of Apollinarius' work against Diodore, a point naturally obscured by the fact that Theodoret the Antiochene quotes it under a different

[1] *E.g.* Dorner, *Person of Christ*, II. 352–99; Harnack, *H.D.* IV. 149–163; Gwatkin, *Studies of Arianism*, pp. 250–4.

title; and partly to the great reputation of Apollinarius as a defender of the Nicene cause. At the same time, though he employed it rather against the Adoptianism of Syrian Christology than against Eunomius' Subordinationism, this aspect of his theology, supplying as it does the basis of his doctrine of salvation, is fundamental; and his repeated emphasis upon it may well be caused by his vigilance in guarding against any suspicion of Arianising tendencies. Nevertheless Voisin's[1] theory that the school of Antioch was his chief objective is unquestionably more adequate as an explanation of his standpoint and of the circumstances and contents of his writings: it is an illuminating and incontrovertible discovery. Its author indeed goes too far when he asserts that Apollinarius did not know, and even unconsciously adopted, the Arian position; for when he says that the union in Christ was similarly interpreted by Apollinarius and by the Arians, he is overlooking the fact that the former denied to Christ a human spirit in order to secure His divine changelessness, while the latter rejected the idea of a human soul in order to prove Him changeable and less than perfect God. But the titles of his books are proof enough that Apollinarius had no intention of imitating Eustathius and the Antiochenes and attacking the Arian Christology directly. Had this been his object he could not have formulated a belief which bears so close a superficial resemblance to theirs without devoting far more attention to the small but vital differences between them and himself: nor would he have needed to spend so much time upon matters in which he and they are agreed.

[1] *L.c.* p. 25 and *passim*. Caspari, *Alte und Neue Quellen*, p. 76, had already pointed out Apollinarius' hostility to the Antiochenes.

No doubt, like Basil[1], he felt that Arianism had spent its force, and that the danger to the future of the Church came not from discredited heretics already reduced to dependence upon the emperor for their support, but from unrecognised heterodoxies within the ranks of her accepted teachers. At any rate, in his Christological writings, there are numerous references to Paul of Samosata and his successors, but not a single mention either by name or implication of Eunomius or any of those whose errors engaged the chief attention of Athanasius and the Cappadocians. The evidence seems to show plainly that all his early works on the subject were directed against the Syrian Christology, that his whole habit of mind made an Arian conclusion impossible to him, and that when he came to treat the doctrine in full he was careful to emphasise by laying special stress upon the heavenly nature of Christ the fact that even if a heretic he was still at least a Nicene.

His criticism of Diodore and the Antiochenes is everywhere from first to last the same. These "Paulianisers," as he calls them, have in an evil hour introduced a division into the nature of the one Lord. "These slaves of Paul of Samosata," he writes in the first letter to Dionysius[2], "say that the element from heaven which they acknowledge to be God is totally distinct from the man from the earth: they call the one uncreate, the other created; the one eternal, the other a thing of yesterday; the one master, the other slave: in either case they act impiously, whether in worshipping what they call slave and creature, or in not worshipping Him who redeemed us by His own blood....I hear that they speak of two natures, although John clearly showed that

[1] *Ep.* 265.

[2] §§ 1, 2. Lietzmann, pp. 256–7.

the Lord is one when he said 'The Word became flesh.'" That is Apollinarius' main objection and the text from the Fourth Gospel is the summary of his reply. Many passages might be quoted to prove how much he feared the consequences of such a duality: here are some from the *Anacephalaeosis* appended to the book against Diodore—"If God gives His energy to a man, the result is a prophet or apostle not the Saviour of the world[1]": "A man deriving energy from God is not God: but a body conjoined with God is God: so Christ is not a man receiving energy from God, but a body compacted with God[2]": "A man the yoke-fellow of God remains distinct from God in the impulses of his life, reason and emotions[3]." And these can be paralleled from the *Apodeixis*: "If the Lord is not incarnate, He would be wisdom illuminating the heart of a man: but this is present in all men[4]": "If he who receives God were very God, there would be many Gods, since many receive God[5]": "If God has been joined to man, the perfect to the perfect, there would be two, one by nature Son of God, the other added to Him[6]": "If He consist of two perfect elements, then He is neither man in that wherein He is God, nor God in that wherein He is man[7]." He evidently regards the Antiochene school as destroying the fundamental tenet of Christianity, the union of God and man in Christ. However close the juxtaposition of the two, however complete their harmony, yet to him

[1] § 1. [2] § 21. [3] § 29.

[4] Lietzmann, Fr. 70. [5] Lietzmann, Fr. 83.

[6] Lietzmann, Fr. 81, with which we may compare the aphorism "Two perfect units cannot become one," cited as Apollinarian in Pseudo-Athanasius, *C. Apoll.* i. 2.

[7] Lietzmann, Fr. 92.

nothing short of perfect union is enough, and if any vestige of separation be maintained the value of Christ's redemptive work is debased if not destroyed. "The death of a mere man does not do away with death[1]," and the resurrection is a proof that Christ was not man but God. The claim of the Church can only be justified if her Lord be not a God-inspired man but God Himself incarnate. "Even the very Greeks and Jews would accept it if we taught that He who was born was only an inspired man like Elijah[2]": "He who was born of Mary is by nature Son of God and very God, and that not by any mere gift or imparted grace[3]."

Thus Apollinarius grasps the point which Athanasius had already perceived, that in the interest of Christianity it is essential that there be no minimising of the reality of Christ's Godhead, no tampering with the conviction that only through the Incarnation of the deity can man be brought into atonement with His Maker, that only the very God can save sinners[4]. But it was easy enough to censure Paul of Samosata, or for that matter the Nestorians, for "dividing Christ": the difficulty arose when Churchmen, starting from a conception of God and man as opposites, tried to define the method of the necessary union and to localise the exact seat of Antiochene error. Apollinarius felt, as we have seen, that any duality of person was fatal: he asked himself what element in Diodore's Christ gave rise to this duality:

[1] *Apod.*, Lietzmann, Fr. 95.

[2] *Apod.*, Lietzmann, Fr. 51.

[3] *Ad Jovian.* 2 (Lietzmann, p. 251). The concluding words χάριτι καὶ μετουσίᾳ are characteristic of the Antiochenes and are regularly used by Theodore; cf. Swete, *Theod. Mops. on Minor Eps. of S. Paul*, II. pp. 298, 303, etc.

[4] Cf. *De Fid. et Inc.* 5 (Lietzmann, p. 196).

and he naturally concluded that it was the possession of a human will, mind, or spirit. Unlike most of his orthodox critics, he accepted the Antiochene estimate of the importance of the human mind and would not consent to empty it of meaning by representing it as present indeed but swallowed up in the divine like a drop of vinegar in the ocean[1]. His desire for real, that is, for organic and physical, union will not let him admit that such union is effected by the coincidence of human and divine in pursuit of a common goal: and his conception of mind will not allow belief in a distinction without a difference between two minds. In both respects he is a typical Greek, and as such, while shrinking from the Antiochene theology, he cannot quite accept the Cappadocian. To him a human mind implied "a self-determinating subject, impelled naturally by its own volition[2]" and supplying the motive power to the flesh which is purely passive[3]. It is this power of self-determination or freedom of will which to him constitutes the very essence of mind: without it mind ceases to be mind: "It is the destruction of a self-determinating creature to deprive it of its self-determination[4]": and this conception made it impossible for him to believe that two minds could coexist in a single person. "Two separate principles of mind and will cannot dwell together without one striving against the other[5]": "In one and the same subject two mutually

[1] This is the familiar metaphor employed by Gregory Nyss., *Ad Theophil.* 3, a passage more Monophysite than Apollinarius: and cf. *C. Eunom.* v. 5 (Migne, *P.G.* XLV. 708).

[2] *Ad Julian.* Lietzmann, Fr. 150. This letter to his pupil is the most important source for knowledge of his psychology.

[3] *Apod.*, Lietzmann, Fr. 107.

[4] *Apod.*, Lietzmann, Fr. 87.

[5] *De Unit.*, Lietzmann, Fr. 2.

opposed wills cannot exist side by side; for each of them achieves the object of its own will in accordance with a self-determined impulse[1]." And if in the abstract it is impossible for two minds thus defined to coexist, it is still less possible for this to have happened in the case of Christ. If it is against the Antiochenes that he urges the Aristotelian argument that mind and body are related as active to passive, "mover to moved," and that two independent agents or "movers" cannot coincide without the loss to one of them of its fundamental character, it may well be from his fear of Arianism that he introduces the further contention that coexistence in a single person is still more impossible for such eternal opposites as human and divine. Like Athanasius and unlike the earlier Greeks, he has a strong sense of sin; and this not only appears in his insistence that redemption cannot be secured unless Christ is very God, but supplies him with a further reason for denying His possession of a human mind; for a mind if truly human is sinful. This conviction of the taint of evil inherent in men separates him widely from the Pelagianism of the Antiochenes, and, as we shall see, involves him in difficulties: at the same time it proves him to have been a thinker who could rise above the rather shallow optimism of his race to the moral earnestness of St Paul and the "twice born." Emphasis upon this is characteristic of his whole position. We find it clearly stated in the letter to Julian[2], quoted above: "Those who speak of two minds in Christ failed even to comprehend this, though it is surely plain to everyone, that the divine mind is always self-impelled in the

[1] *Ad Julian.*, Lietzmann, Fr. 150.
[2] Lietzmann, Fr. 151.

same direction since it is changeless, while the human mind is self-impelled indeed but not always in the same direction since it is changeable, and that the changeable does not mingle with the changeless to constitute a single subject. For such a subject would be in a state of perpetual turmoil, distracted by the conflicting wishes of the elements of which it consists." It is in the light of this conviction that in his letter to the exiled bishops he can accept the definition of the Council of Alexandria: "Our confession is not that the Logos of God sojourned in a holy man as happened to the prophets: but that the very Logos became flesh, not assuming a human mind, a mind changeable and the prey of filthy thoughts but being Himself divine mind, changeless, heavenly[1]." And here, too, he appeals to soteriology for his justification: "If with the Godhead which is itself mind, there was in Christ also a human mind, the first purpose of the Incarnation which is the overthrow of sin is not accomplished by Him[2]." It is his insistence upon the sinlessness of the Saviour and his belief that such sinlessness is incompatible with the possession of a human and therefore sinful mind, that drives him to reject belief in the perfect manhood of Jesus. The Lord exists "not in two substances but in one[3]," "perfect indeed but with a true and divine perfection, not two natures nor two persons[4]." "There is no distinction in Holy Scripture between the Logos and His flesh: but He is one nature, one hypostasis, one energy, one person, at

[1] *Ad Diocaes.* 2, Lietzmann, p. 256.
[2] *Apod.*, Lietzmann, Fr. 74.
[3] Lietzmann, Fr. 158. For the use of οὐσία here cf. *Ad Heracl.* Lietzmann, Fr. 117.
[4] K.M.Π. 31, Lietzmann, p. 179.

once wholly God and wholly man[1]": "one incarnate nature of the Logos[2]."

This denial to Christ of a human mind or spirit is the sum of Apollinarius' heresy, and his own statements leave us in no doubt that he realised and intended such a mutilation. At the same time, in order to explain the harshness of the fact, Church historians have represented him as introducing at this point the defence that Christ, in whom the divine Logos took the place of a human mind, was not made thereby less perfect man—indeed, that only by this substitution could His manhood attain perfection. Dorner[3], who is responsible for this theory, writes, "He viewed the Logos in Christ as the eternal humanity, probably on the ground of His being the archetype of universal humanity": and, having read this notion into the pages of Apollinarius, is so pleased with it that he devotes several paragraphs to comment upon its deeper aspects. He has been followed by most English scholars[4], even by so recent a writer as Dr Relton[5]; and in view of the popularity of the idea it will be well to quote the passages upon which it depends before we go on to give their true explanation. There

[1] *De Fid. et Inc.* 6, Lietzmann, pp. 198–9. For the appeal to Scripture, cf. *Ad Dion.* I., Lietzmann, p. 258.

[2] *Ad Jovian.* I, Lietzmann, p. 251—the famous phrase which Cyril Alex. accepted as Athanasian; cf. φύσις θεικὴ σεσαρκωμένη, Apollinarius, *De Inc.*, Lietzmann, Fr. 9.

[3] *Person of Christ*, I, ii. 371–80. It should be added that Dorner's treatment of Apollinarius is in other respects judicious and accurate.

[4] *E.g.* Gwatkin, *Studies of Arianism*, p. 252; Mackintosh, *Person of Jesus Christ*, p. 199; Gore, *Belief in Christ*, p. 120: Bethune-Baker, *J.T.S.* VI. 619, showed this view to be untenable.

[5] *A Study in Christology*, pp. 12–19. Although published only in 1917, this book shows no acquaintance with the work of Voisin or Lietzmann, and very little with that of Apollinarius.

are two groups of sayings which if they stood alone might suggest a doctrine of archetypal manhood. The former consists of certain passages in the *Apodeixis*, in which the phrase "the man from heaven" predominates: "Christ, because He has Godhead as His Spirit, that is, as His mind, together with soul and body, is naturally called 'man from heaven[1]'": "If man consists of three elements and if, furthermore, the Lord is man, He also to be sure consists of three, spirit and soul and body: none the less He is a heavenly man and a life-giving spirit[2]": "If we consist of three and He of four, He is not man but 'Man-God[3].'" These three passages must be read in connection with another from the same book: "If the heavenly man consist of elements all of which are equal to those composing us earthly men, so that He possesses a spirit equal to the earthly, then is His manhood not heavenly but the receptacle of the heavenly Godhead[4]." Here, as elsewhere, he is using the words "heavenly" and "life-giving" to emphasise the contrast between the Apollinarian or divine and the Antiochene or human Christ: he is justifying, not without a touch of sophistry, his use of the word "man" on the ground that a threefold being can properly be so called, and ridiculing the Antiochenes for teaching that Christ is a monstrous compound or hybrid who has even less right to the title[5]. The second series are the passages which suggest the belief that Christ existed before the ages; and the full interpretation of them must be deferred. Here we may note that they nowhere indicate the idea of archetypal manhood, but are directed against

[1] Lietzmann, Fr. 25.
[2] Lietzmann, Fr. 89.
[3] Lietzmann, Fr. 91.
[4] Lietzmann, Fr. 90.
[5] Cf. *Anac.* 16, Lietzmann, p. 244.

Diodore's belief that the Incarnation involved a hasty change of plan on God's part, against which Apollinarius argues that it existed potentially from all eternity in the nature of the Son of God. Both groups of passages are difficult, and were fastened upon by the earliest critics of the heresy. But Dorner's explanation is not required by either of them, and is on other grounds wholly untenable.

As we have seen, the doctrine of archetypal manhood and of the analogy between the Logos in Christ and the "seeds of Logos" in ourselves can be found in the earliest efforts of Greek thought to formulate a Christology. In Apollinarius there is a complete absence of the traditional phrases of the Logos-theology which treat Christ as the Image of God and men as made after that image—phrases which appear in the *De Incarnatione*, but seldom later, and are characteristic of the Apologies. It is of course possible that the Bishop of Laodicea had recourse to them in his book against Julian: but in none of his extant writings is there a trace of their influence. And in addition there is abundant evidence that they were foreign to his thought. His whole criticism of Diodore is directed against the representation of Christ as differing only quantitatively from the prophets. He sees that if the divine is regarded as an inspiration then the distinction between Christ and mankind is endangered; and on this distinction his whole soteriology depends. Seeing this, he, like Athanasius, cannot accept a theory which in effect would mean the same thing; for the relationship of type to archetype implies a degree of resemblance which would expose him, inevitably if not quite justly, to the charge of teaching the very belief in a quantitative distinction against which he was specially protesting. The contrast between God and man as between the sinless and the sinful is fundamental to his position, and is inconsistent with Dorner's hypothesis. Very many passages can be quoted to prove his emphasis upon it: "If there be the same nature in Christ as in ourselves, He is but the old man, a living soul not a life-giving spirit: Christ gives life and is therefore not of our nature[1]": "God is consubstantial with men according to the flesh, different in substance as Logos and God[2]": and even more forcibly in the *Apodeixis*, the treatise from which support of the belief has been drawn, "He is not man though like man; for He is not consubstantial with man in the most important element[3]." His meaning is perhaps best summarised in the syllogism "God dwelling in man is not man; spirit united to flesh is man: Christ is man as has been said titularly, for He is divine spirit united to flesh[4]."

We are therefore driven to reject as contradictory to the course and expression of his thought the ingenious exposition of it which his modern admirers have so generously placed in his mouth, and to admit, albeit with reluctance, that when he said that Christ was not man he meant what he said. It is a pity that modern Apollinarians, who, like their master, believe in the impersonal humanity, are not equally honest. He, at least, was too fine a spirit to resort to subterfuge and quibbling in the statement of his convictions. He had worked out in the light of the best psychology of his time and of its

[1] *Anac.* 23, Lietzmann, pp. 244–5.
[2] *C. Diod.*, Lietzmann, Fr. 126.
[3] Lietzmann, Fr. 45.
[4] *Anac.* 16, Lietzmann, p. 244.

deepest Christian experience the significance of the Incarnation, and was not afraid to abide by the results of his work. There were certainly two alternative methods by which, without sinking to the level of Cyril and resorting to ambiguities of speech, he could have avoided the mutilation of Christ's perfect manhood. On the one hand, the Platonic concept of type and antitype which was implied in the Logos-theology and explicitly taught by Heracleon[1], and which Dorner assigns to him, would have saved him from it: on the other, if he had followed to its logical conclusion the belief in the heavenly origin of mind which appears, as we have seen, in his commentary on Ezekiel, he could have reached the doctrine according to which spirit only exists potentially in man and has no function except that of receiving and appropriating the divine—a doctrine similar to that of St Paul. The Greek belief that the mind of man and the mind of God are alike divine he rejects because in his attitude to sin he is thoroughly Pauline: the Pauline belief that spirit only exists at all in man when he is in relation with the Spirit of God he rejects because his estimate of mind is wholly Greek. An examination of his psychology will explain his reasons for doing so and clear up the significance of his heresy.

In his account of the nature of Christ, Apollinarius employs, as we have observed, two terms, "mind" and "spirit," as equally descriptive of the element in man which in the Incarnate was replaced by His Godhead. These two represent the two strains of influence to which a Greek Christian was exposed. The conception of mind as the highest constituent of humanity is

[1] So Origen, *In Joh.* ii. 14, who cites Heracleon's comment on John i. 3 as manifesting this belief.

essentially Hellenic. Both Plato[1] and Aristotle[2] are at one in ascribing to men the possession of a twofold nature. Inhabiting the visible and earthly body is the invisible and Godlike, if not actually divine, mind. There is for them no third intermediate element or animating principle, such as Apollinarius finds in ψυχή: but mind is capable of two kinds of activity, firstly, through sense-perceptions and the organs of the body, and, secondly, independently of the body and in its own purity. It is the task of philosophy, as Plato saw it, to free the mind from the fetters by which it is bound to the flesh and to lead it from the study of the objects of sense to the exercise of pure thought upon abstract concepts, from opinion to knowledge. So, too, in the later Greek philosophers man is always represented as composed of two elements, "soul," of which mind is merely the highest expression, and "body." Even Plotinus, from whom Nemesius[3] declares that Apollinarius derived his trichotomy, seems not to have departed from the Platonic psychology[4], although his mysticism tended

[1] Many writers (*e.g.* Bethune-Baker, *Introd. to Hist. of Christian Doctrine*, p. 242 n.) state that Apollinarius derived his trichotomy from Plato. Plato's division of the soul into three parts, ἡγεμονικόν, θυμοειδές and ἐπιθυμητικόν is of course very familiar: but for his belief in a three-fold nature in man the only possible evidence is *Timaeus*, 30 B, and *Philebus*, 30 C: and that they do not imply it, is proved by Archer-Hind's note in *Timaeus*, *ad loc.*

[2] For Aristotle cf. especially *De Anima*: while criticising the *Timaeus* for resolving body into terms of mind (*De An.* 407 B), he describes mind as concerned with knowables just as the perceptive faculty is with objects of sense-perception (429 A): sense-perception gives rise to imaginative concepts and these are the material of mental activity (432 A): sense-perceptions perish with the body, mind is an actual imperishable substance, somewhat divine and incapable of suffering (408 B).

[3] *De Nat. Hom.* p. 9.

[4] His cosmology as given in *Ennead*, v., certainly suggests a clear distinction between νοῦς and ψυχή: the super-essential One

to differentiate the function of the soul whereby man apprehends and enters into direct communion with the divine, from the mind which is concerned only with intellectual pursuits. He certainly divides soul into higher and lower, rational and irrational, the one peculiar to man, the other common to him and other animals[1], and in this respect comes close to certain sayings of Apollinarius[2]. But even so he does not contemplate any essential difference between them; "for," says he, "soul is or becomes mind in proportion as it escapes from the shackles of the body: it is divine in itself, and in the employment of its highest faculty, mind or soul undiluted, attains its greatest perfection[3]." Further, he definitely declares in several places[4] that man consists only of two parts, soul and body which is the vehicle of soul.

Nemesius, then, appears to have misrepresented Plotinus in his eagerness to accuse Apollinarius of deriving the basis of his theory from pagan sources. Many of the Fathers, and especially the more unscientific Latins, certainly considered the triple division to be unscriptural. Yet in spite of their opinion it is from Scripture that Apollinarius drew his trichotomy. Gregory of Nyssa[5] admits that it is to St Paul's use of "spirit, soul and body[6]" and to the Song of the Three

generates existence (οὐσία or νοῦς), and existence generates ψυχή, which "has a downward look towards the sensible world" (*Enn.* V. ix. 3), and ψυχή imposes its form upon matter; cf. Strong, *Journal of Theol. Studies*, III. 28.

[1] *Enn.* I. i. 10.

[2] *E.g. C. Diod.*, Lietzmann, Frs. 126, 146.

[3] *Enn.* V. i. 10.

[4] *E.g. Enn.* IV. vii. 1, and I. i. 3.

[5] *Antirrheticus*, 46.

[6] 1 Thess. v. 23: he appealed also to such passages as Rom. vii 23, where flesh is said to war against spirit.

Children, "O ye spirits and souls of the righteous[1]," that he appealed for justification: and, though in reality his psychology differs widely from that of the Bible, there is little doubt that in his use of terms he believed himself to be following its authority. To the Jew, life is a dualism not of mind and matter, but of God and the world. Man, through his body, is of the earth; he shares with other animals the breath of life, the breath of the nostrils: but he possesses also the breath of God, the breath of the mouth, the vehicle of speech and reason, an effluence of the divine spirit which raises him from the earthly sphere to the heavenly. Thus man consists of two lower elements, body and animating soul, and in some cases, though perhaps not in all, of a third, the direct gift of God, spirit[2]. How far this third is regarded as a necessary constituent of man as man, and in what respects, if so, it is to be distinguished from soul, are disputable points. Numerous passages prove that in St Paul this distinction is clearly marked; and it is from St Paul that Apollinarius has derived most of his thought and language. The Pauline psychology has of late years been the subject of keen discussion—Dr B. Weiss[3] and others maintaining that spirit is always used by him to mean divinely given or Holy Spirit, while Professor W. P. Dickson[4], following Wendt, supports the opposite view. It is outside our scope to enter into the question fully or to pretend to decide where doctors disagree. To unravel the difficulties and represent the Apostle's thought as a con-

[1] Song 64

[2] For a recent discussion of these words cf. M. Scott Fletcher, *The Psychology of the N.T.* pp. 23–71.

[3] *Biblical Theol. of the N.T.* I. 346–7.

[4] *St Paul's Use of the Terms Flesh and Spirit*, pp. 168–78.

sistent whole would take many volumes—and might, even so, be a task impossible of fulfilment. "Sometimes the word 'spirit' is used in such a way as to make it impossible to decide when the Apostle is speaking of God's Spirit or of the Divine Spirit subjectively appropriated by the faith of the believer[1]." Nor is it necessary for our purpose to reach a final decision. For even if Dickson be right, no one will deny that there is a mass of evidence showing that the Apostle, when speaking strictly, regarded spirit as the direct gift of God, and even if potentially present in the natural man, only called into activity or true existence by communion or even identification with the Spirit of Christ[2]. Throughout the Epistles there runs the idea of a warfare between the flesh whose guide is law and whose inclinations are evil and the spirit whose source is God and whose energy is the free gift of His grace[3]. The flesh has its centre in the lower or animating soul, and the man dominated by this soul cannot understand the things of God which are sought out and discerned by the spirit[4]. Besides these lines of thought and the *locus classicus* in the First Epistle to the Thessalonians[5], it is clear from other New Testament writers that language suggesting if not compelling a belief in trichotomy represents a common phase of Jewish thought on the subject[6]. We do not wish to assert for a moment that their complete psychology is to be interpreted in the light of these passages: a review of the whole evidence might give a

[1] Scott Fletcher, *l.c.* p. 264.

[2] *E.g.* Rom. viii. 9; 1 Cor. iii. 16; Gal. iv. 6, etc. Passages which support the view that spirit is proper to all men are Rom. viii. 16; 1 Cor. xiv. 14; xvi. 18, etc.

[3] *E.g.* Rom. viii. 1–4; 1 Cor. ii. 10.

[4] 1 Cor. ii. 10, 13, 14.

[5] 1 Thess. v. 23.

[6] *E.g.* Hebr. iv. 12; James iii. 15; Jude 19.

totally different result. But in any case whether we regard soul as distinct from spirit or as a debased form of it, the difference between them is quite clear: "Man as such *is* a soul, but he may *have* the fuller, richer life of the Spirit[1]." In St Paul and elsewhere there are sufficient grounds for maintaining as Apollinarius did, that the two terms when used technically represent separate entities, whether elements, functions or aspects matters little; that soul is common to all men as "the image of the earthly"; and that spirit, "the image of the heavenly[2]," is bestowed only when man is brought into relation with God, or at least is dependent for its existence solely upon the presence of the divine.

Whatever be the exact relation of spirit and soul, in any case the identification of spirit with mind is impossible for St Paul as it is for any Jew. Greeks might boast of wisdom[3]: they are "always learning and yet never able to come to the knowledge of the truth[4]." The knowledge of God is to be won by the spiritual not by "the wise of this world." The peace of God is above all mind[5]. The element which to the Greeks was man's highest and almost divine, was to the Jew only a faculty for the expression of character, an attribute like speech which can interpret but cannot originate, which is concerned only with the objects of sense-perception, which is part of man's earthly birthright not of his heavenly treasure.

Now it is clear that this is not Apollinarius' position. If he had simply followed the Scriptures, he could not have spoken of mind and spirit as identical and as

[1] Scott Fletcher, *l.c.* p. 65.
[2] 1 Cor. xv. 43 ff.
[3] 1 Cor. i. 19; Eph. iv. 17.
[4] 2 Tim. iii. 7.
[5] Phil. iv. 7; cf. Col. i. 9, etc.

wholly different from soul. The triple division of man on which his psychology is based is due neither to Greek nor to Jewish thought but to a fusion of the two, a fusion commenced as soon as the religious ideas of Jews and Christians were expressed in the language of the philosophies of Greece. We have already seen what a prominent part the term Logos played in the history of this process; and as in dealing with the Godhead the Greek substituted the Logos for the Holy Spirit, so in dealing with man he used Logos, the intellectual element of the Stoics, as the synonym of the spiritual element of the Christians. In each case the result was to produce an exaggerated intellectualism in his concept of God and of religion—a tendency to which he was already liable. Instead of being regarded as a divine gift external to man and attainable only by God's grace, the identification with reason and mind necessarily transformed it into a natural part of man's normal equipment, a third division of his person, shared alike by all independently of divine inspiration. Spirit was to St Paul the privilege of the saints; mind was obviously the possession of saints and sinners alike.

The attempt to harmonise and unify the Greek "mind" and the Jewish "spirit" can be traced in all those religious thinkers who tried to interpret the Scriptures into the language of Hellenism[1]. Philo, for

[1] In Irenaeus we find a psychology much closer to St Paul than in most of the Greeks. In *Haer*. v. 6 he quotes 1 Thess. v. 23, and states that in the perfect man the three elements are all present. "When spirit mingled with soul is united with body (*plasma*), by the outpouring of spirit man is made spiritual and perfect: and this is he who is made after the image and likeness of God." He speaks of the spirit of man as distinct from the Spirit of God, but seems to regard it as a special and divine gift. Cf. Harnack, *H.D.* II. 269, note.

example, divides soul into two, "the animal whereby we live, and the rational whereby we possess reason[1]." "Irrational creatures," he continues, "share the former with us, the latter they do not share, but God is its source. The animal soul has as its essence blood: but that which is derived from the source of all reason has as its essence spirit. This is not a mere current of air [a hit at Stoicism] but an imprint of the divine power which Moses nobly calls a likeness." Spirit is apparently regarded by him much as it is by St Paul, as a gift of God: "For God extends His power to its object through the mediation of spirit...how could the soul be conscious of God unless in accordance with His power He had inspired and come into contact with it[2]?" It is to Origen, rather than to Philo, that we must look for an explanation of Apollinarius' theory; and although his thought is difficult to systematise, he discusses the various opinions of his own time with some fulness. When dealing with the origin of sin[3], he states that there are three different ideas of the nature of man, first that man has two souls "one more divine and heavenly, the other lower," secondly, that soul and body constitute man and that sin arises from the conflict between them and is therefore due to corporeal existence, and, thirdly, the Greek view which he states but dismisses as unscriptural. He then proceeds to describe at length the two former. Of the threefold division he writes that the higher soul is regarded as the medium of revelation and is the gift of God; the lower is procreated "a material spirit not subject to the law of God, by reason of its earthly wishes and corporeal yearnings,"

[1] Philo, *Quod det. pot. ins.* (ed. Mangey, I. 206–7).

[2] *Leg. alleg.* i. 13 (Mangey, I. 49). For Philo's psychology, cf. Drummond, *Philo Judaeus*, II. 274–324.

[3] *De Princ.* III. iv.

and is hence called "the flesh": the will of this lower soul is a mean between body and spirit and can attach itself to either as it chooses, and thus make men carnal or spiritual. He then expounds the arguments for a twofold division; and invites his readers to choose between them. This discussion leaves undecided the question how far he regards spirit as a necessary part of every human being. But the commentaries on Scripture[1] make it plain that he usually treats it as an individual possession equivalent to the rational element or mind: for he argues that the spirits of all men, even of the bad, return to God, being accompanied in the case of the good by the lower soul[2]; and in a passage in which he claims to have searched the whole Bible in order to discover its teaching he states that the spirit of man is unable to receive evil influences, since the fruits of the spirit are those not of the Holy Spirit but of the spirit in each of us, and that "the soul is a mean, receptive both of good and bad[3]." In his treatment of the Incarnation[4] this distinction and the identification of spirit and mind come out very clearly. For he is always careful to attach the human experiences of Christ to His soul, the divine to His spirit[5]: and after citing various texts he declares that mind is the original and divine condition, that soul is the result of the shrinking away of this divine mind from its perfect state[6], and

[1] Cf. *Comm. in Rom.* i. 5, in addition to passages here cited, where he argues that St Paul, knowing that soul is intermediate between spirit and body, makes no reference to it.

[2] *In Math. Comm. Series*, 57 and 62.

[3] *In Joh.* xxxii. 11.

[4] *De Princ.* II. viii.

[5] *E.g.* he cites *Tristis est anima mea* and contrasts it with *In manus tuas commendo spiritum meum*.

[6] He supports this by quotations from 1 Cor. ii. 14, xiv. 15, and xv. 44, compared with 1 Peter i. 9: and derives ψυχή from ψύχεσθαι.

that human souls become incarnate by reason of this fall, being restored to their primal state and becoming again mind if they act well. In this passage he does not mention spirit: but presumably mind is used to denote the Godlike element which is capable of becoming individualised, spirit is the divine efflatus which stimulates the fallen mind to its return to God. Probably we may regard him as using the two terms to describe the same element viewed respectively from above and from below. In any case we have in him a preference for trichotomy, a concept of mind much higher than in St Paul, and a tendency to identify mind and spirit and to regard both as a natural part of every human being. The syncretism between Jewish and Greek thought has led him to introduce a third element into his concept of personality.

It is evident from the quotations already given that Apollinarius held a similar belief. Mankind is endowed with three elements in its nature. The lowest is the body or *σῶμα*, the material structure through which the invisible is revealed and expressed: to this the term flesh (*σάρξ*) is often applied, though *σάρξ* is freely personified and used to denote both body and lower soul. Higher than the body but still an earthly element comes this lower soul (*ψυχή*); and the term when strictly employed is always used for that which man shares with the animal creation: but where *σάρξ* is used of the living body, it is natural that *ψυχὴ* should be contrasted with it, and should signify the whole non-material part of personality —this being of course its popular meaning. Highest of all comes the heavenly element, which St Paul calls the spirit (*πνεῦμα*), but which Apollinarius regularly identifies with the mind (*νοῦς*), and which in consequence he regards not as the special prerogative of the saints, but as belonging to all men "by nature," and as constituting the centre of personality. Epiphanius' account of his argument at Antioch with the Vitalians makes this perfectly clear[1]. He fastened upon this very problem, and asked them if the mind is "the underlying reality (ὑπόστασις) in man," and if so how they explained the saying of St Paul, "I will sing with the spirit and will sing also with the mind[2]"—a saying which lays bare the difference between St Paul and Apollinarius. When being unable to reply, some of them said that mind was not the ὑπόστασις, Epiphanius then asked "If mind is not the centre of our personality but only a faculty or impulse of the underlying reality in us, and if Christ took the place of mind thus defined, surely His personality has no centre and His sojourn on earth is nominal and docetic?" It is obvious that this second opinion does not represent their master's belief. To him mind signifies the seat of personality, the ego or true self, that which thinks and wills, that which separates man from the brutes and enables him to have communion with his Maker. It is in a special sense divinely imparted, but as individualised in mankind has fallen and become tainted with sin; and in this condition, despite its heavenly origin, is sharply distinguished from the perfect mind which took its place in the case of Christ. Indeed so far has the human mind forfeited its divine character that it is only through the Incarnation that "we who share in the justification by faith are

[1] *Haer.* lxxvii. 23 and 24. Epiphanius' own view, as given in § 34, is that mind is an "energy" of which Christ or the ego in us is the hypostasis.

[2] 1 Cor. xiv. 15. In the fragments of Apollinarius this text is nowhere quoted.

saved and set in the likeness of the heavenly[1]" when "Christ gives a share of His spotless virtue to every mind that is subject to Him, to all those who are being made like Him in mind and not unlike after the flesh[2]."

Yet to mutilate the perfect manhood of Christ by treating the centre of His personality as divine, while it safeguards His power to save and is at once more logical in itself and more in keeping with the traditions of Greek theology than the Antiochene Christology, is obviously open to grave objections. It is in his manner of meeting these rather than in the bald fact for which he was condemned that Apollinarius displays the ingenuity and originality which justify his reputation. In his belief that Christ was the Logos made flesh, there was nothing new. In expanding the phrase he used language less ambiguous and therefore less safe than Athanasius or the Cappadocians or Cyril or those moderns who have adopted the formula "impersonal humanity" as an orthodox substitute for his denial of a human mind, but fundamentally he does not differ from them or make an important contribution to theology. It is in the detailed explanation of the mode and scope of the union, by which he forestalled and answered criticism, that he breaks fresh ground and shows himself not only a master of uncompromising definitions but also a speculative thinker of profound and daring genius. He has a firm grasp of difficulties that had been evaded by all previous enquirers, difficulties to which his contemporaries were as much exposed as he and which have to be faced in some form by all believers in

[1] *Tomus Synod.*, Lietzmann, p. 263.
[2] *Apodeixis*, Lietzmann, Fr. 80.

an Incarnation; and he suggests solutions for them which had never before been propounded and have been given a permanent place in the orthodoxy of Christendom.

The first of these is the fundamental question, if the Godhead be changeless, how can God become incarnate at all: does not Incarnation, if it affects the Godhead in any way, imply change? In its widest aspect this is the same old problem of the relationship of the one to the many, the static to the kinetic, the eternal to the temporal, which had occupied Greek thought from its beginning, and which every Theist must admit and explain. Christians had tried to solve it by the dualistic Logos-theology: but this had led them straight to Arianism; and Eunomius' criticism had forced them to think out the issue afresh. Whether Apollinarius ever treated it on broad general lines is outside our knowledge: in his work on the Trinity he must surely have done so. His strong superficial resemblance to Arianism compelled him to deal with it in his Christology: for the Eunomians who, like him, denied to Christ a complete manhood were eagerly pressing the conclusions which seemed to them to follow from it. The Antiochenes, although the theory of a dual nature as conceived by them rather evades than answers the difficulty, were to some extent protected; for they could use the human nature as the receptacle of all those elements which conflicted with the divine changelessness, and so, albeit at the expense of the unity of Christ and the simple meaning of Incarnation, save the dignity of the Godhead. Apollinarius, with his insistence upon the one nature and personal divinity of the Incarnate, could not escape attack. For him there could be no substitute, no human scapegoat to bear the blemishes which would disfigure the deity. The "one incarnate nature of the Logos," Godhead, soul and body, must Himself partake of all His experiences, even those of ignorance and suffering. Apollinarius as a typical Greek, with his strongly physical conception of deity and his dread of tampering with the divine attributes, had here an almost insoluble problem. He was too devoutly Christian to accept the Arian answer and see in Christ a subordinate to the Father, or to imitate the early Gnostics and to assign to a phantasmal Jesus what could not touch the impassible Christ. Nor would his biblical scholarship allow him to follow Athanasius and expurgate from the Gospels the marks of the Lord's humanity. How otherwise could he secure both the unity and the divinity of the Incarnate? That was his difficulty.

He met it by a theory derived from the words of his favourite St Paul, words now so familiar in this connection that we may easily do less than justice to him for his use of them[1]. "He emptied Himself of His glory and assumed the form of a servant" was a text that had already been employed by Origen to explain the infancy and growth of Christ; and it is possible that Apollinarius may have had it suggested to him from his study of his great predecessor. But, if so, the theory which he based upon it is very different from that of Origen and represents a notable discovery in dogmatic theology. To Origen the kenosis had been a single act of submission to a state of temporary ignorance: to Apollinarius it was identical with the whole condition of Christ's life

[1] Harnack, *H.D.* IV. 154–5, though rightly laying stress upon Apollinarius' indebtedness to St Paul and the N.T., strangely neglects all notice of his doctrine of kenosis.

upon earth, a continuous process of voluntary renunciation. "Incarnation is self-emptying," he writes in the *Contra Diodorum*[1], "and the self-emptying revealed Him who emptied Himself to be not man but Son of Man, by way of limitation not of change." He even urges the words of St Paul in a syllogism against the Antiochene Christology[2]: "If God dwelt in a man, He was not limited: but He who was in the form of God was limited by receiving the form of a servant: He did not therefore dwell in a man": and repeats the argument in the *Apodeixis*[3]: "If the Logos was not mind incarnate but only wisdom in the mind, the Lord did not descend nor limit Himself."

The effect of this wilful self-limitation is to make a distinction between Christ's divine nature as co-essential with the Father and that same nature as subject to the conditions of the Incarnation: and this distinction is clearly expressed in the *De Unione*[4] where Christ is described as "God invisible changed in form by His visible body, God uncreate made manifest by a created limitation, self-limited in assuming the form of a servant, unlimited, unaltered, unimpaired in His divine essence." The Son of God has to this extent renounced His Godhead and assumed a position of inferiority to and even alienation from His true splendour. The contrast between His two states is emphatically marked in such sayings as "If He who came to suffering and the Cross was an equal sharer in the Father's essence, how was it that in agony He prayed that the cup might pass by Him and that not His will but the Father's should

[1] Lietzmann, Fr. 124.
[2] *Anac.* 15, Lietzmann, pp. 243–4.
[3] Lietzmann, Fr. 71.
[4] § 6, Lietzmann, pp. 187–8.

be done? How can we describe His will when He thus prayed except as out of harmony with and opposed to God's[1]?" And he explains it on this theory of separate spheres of action, limited and limitless, in the one Christ: "The emphasis lies not on the separate wills in disagreement with one another but on the fact that, though one and the same, His will put forth power in its divine aspect, but in its incarnate aspect shrank from death: yet He who uttered the words was God wearing flesh, with no distinction in the exercise of His will[2]." It is in virtue of this contrast between the Godhead and the Incarnate that Apollinarius can speak of Christ as "a mean between God and man, neither wholly man nor wholly God, but a combination of God and man[3]," as "a nature compacted and intermediate between God and man[4]," as "a new creation and a wondrous mixture: God and flesh have constituted one nature[5]," and that he adopts "commixture" (σύγκρασις) as a fitting description for the method of the Incarnation instead of the familiar "indwelling" (ἐνοίκησις) which he criticised[6]. The fullest statement of his thought upon the kenosis and its results is to be found in two passages which the author's habit of expressing his profoundest thought in the tersest and most idiomatic language renders particularly difficult to translate adequately. The first is in the *Contra Diodorum*[7]: "The qualities of the two when commingled mingle but are not lost: a certain distinction

[1] *De Manif.*, Lietzmann, Fr. 110.
[2] *De Manif.*, Lietzmann, Fr. 109.
[3] *Syllog.*, Lietzmann, Fr. 113.
[4] Lietzmann, Fr. 111.
[5] *De Inc.*, Lietzmann, Fr. 10. Most of these extracts in which the idea of mixture occurs come from Justinian, *C. Monoph.*
[6] Compare *Mari. Enc.*, Lietzmann, Fr. 11, with *Anac.* 28.
[7] Lietzmann, Fr. 127.

remains between them in spite of the commingling, as it does between wine and water. The commixture is not with the body nor like that of one body with another" (*i.e.* is more complete) "but none the less it preserves the character of being unmingled (as well as mingled), so that the energy of the Godhead acts on each occasion either separately or in combination (with the self-limited or mingled) as is necessary. This happened in the case of our Lord's fasting. When the Godhead, with its capacity for superiority to want, acted in combination, His hunger was appeased: when it did not employ its capacity to resist the feeling of want, His hunger increased." The second is a fragment of his commentary on St John[1], "Evidently it depends upon His heavenly will whether Christ suffers or not, just as it depends on the presence or absence of light whether man sees or not. It follows that, in so far as His heavenly and divine will repels it, suffering cannot affect Christ: it only appears in proportion to the restraint and withdrawal of the divine will."

It is by substituting this very ingenious distinction between the unlimited and the self-limited aspects of His Godhead for the more orthodox difference between His divine and His human nature, that Apollinarius was able to account for the growth, affections and death of Christ and attach them directly to His divine personality, while preserving the Godhead of the Son unimpaired. Christ while incarnate and by the fact of His Incarnation becomes to that extent inferior to Himself. "If in speaking of Christ anyone takes the saying 'What He sees the Father doing, He also does' as applying to His Godhead and not to the flesh wherein

[1] Cramer, *l.c.* II. 315.

the Incarnate is separate from the non-incarnate Father, he is dividing the divine energy into two: they are not so divided: He is not therefore referring to His Godhead[1]." A dual mode of action is made possible, and the crude blasphemies of the later Monophysites, as well as the absurdities which his critics, ancient and modern, have ascribed to him, are avoided. Misunderstandings of his position, numerous as they have been, arise almost wholly from failure to appreciate this phase of his thought. Not only was the idea a novelty; for the Greek Fathers had always accounted for the humanity of Christ by merging it in His Godhead[2]. But the language in which he expressed it is involved, epigrammatic and liable to distortion; the use of the metaphor of mixture gave general offence; and the insistence that the human sufferings belong to the Godhead incarnate was exposed to much misinterpretation. Yet although its metaphysical conceptions are very far from our own, although there is to some of us a painful unreality about such notions as the withdrawal and reappearance of the divine attributes, this discovery that the self-limitation consisted not in a series of self-conscious and pedagogic acts of special renunciation

[1] *C. Diod.*, Lietzmann, Fr. 131. This quotation comes near to the traditional distribution into human and divine of the sayings and doings of Christ—a distribution condemned by Cyril Alex. in his anathemas against Nestorius, but sanctioned by Leo in his Tome. Cf. for a similar distinction, *De Unione*, 14, 15 (Lietzmann, pp. 191–2); *De Inc.*, Lietzmann, Frs. 3, 4, 5.

[2] The famous passage in Irenaeus, iii. 20. 3, quoted by Theodoret, *Dial.* iii (ed. Schultz, IV. 232), might seem to contradict this. Theodoret's version *συγγινομένου τῷ ἀνθρώπῳ* is remarkably like this saying of Apollinarius. But the Latin gives *absorpto homine*; and it seems certain that Theodoret has substituted *συγγινομένου* for some word like *καταποθέντος* (so Stieren, *ad loc.*) which would fully justify our assertion.

but in the assumption of a condition involving the necessary absence of the divine attributes, is one of the greatest importance. Whatever its faults, and they spring from the fundamental weakness of all Greek theology, it is vastly preferable to the amazing theories of alternate action between two distinct wills supplanting one another in the fashion of Box and Cox, which are to be found in Tertullian and Leo. Indeed, the chief respect in which it differs from the kenotic doctrines of to-day is that Apollinarius did not venture to represent the self-emptying as complete. To him, Christ, although consenting to all the experiences of humanity, yet keeps the consciousness of His deity throughout. He may hold His power in reserve: but it is always at His command. As he says in several places, "The conjunction with the body does not involve the circumscription of the Logos, so as to leave Him nothing beyond corporeal existence[1]": "The invisible when compacted with a visible body remains at the same time invisible; moreover, it remains uncompacted inasmuch as it is not contained within the limits of the body[2]": "While dwelling in human semblance on earth the Logos of God maintained likewise His divine presence in all things, at once permeating all things and being in a peculiar sense commingled with the flesh[3]." Such language, though in accordance with strictly orthodox opinion on the subject, seems doubtless to give an unnatural and artificial meaning to the portrait of Christ, and is quite rightly deprecated by

[1] *C. Diod.*, Lietzmann, Fr. 138. [2] *C. Diod.*, Lietzmann, Fr. 133.

[3] K.M.Π. 11, Lietzmann, p. 171. This passage immediately precedes the sections dealing with Sabellianism and may probably owe its emphasis to the desire to oppose Marcellus' belief that Incarnation involved the circumscription of the Logos. Cf. above, p. 163.

most modern theologians[1]: but to a Greek of that time it was inevitable. Any belief in a more complete limitation would have seemed equivalent either to a total denial of Christ's divinity or to a view of His Incarnation similar to that of Marcellus. Apollinarius could only employ the thought and speech of his time, and his use of them deserves admiration rather than criticism.

Having thus avoided making the Godhead of Christ the seat of His human weaknesses, Apollinarius was at once confronted by a second objection, from the side of his opponents at Antioch. His insistence upon the need for a real union, and his use of words like "mixture" and "combination" to express it, laid him open to the charge, later deservedly brought against the Monophysites, of confusing together human and divine. In his book against Diodore he draws express attention to this criticism, quoting what may well be an actual saying of his opponent: "The union of God to the flesh was an event remarkable, wondrous, unique, never to be repeated. You and the predecessors who led you to this impious and unchristian misbelief do not in the least recognise this. You make a mock of the perfect union and say 'If there be a union, the attributes of God and the attributes of the flesh no longer remain distinct'; and you urge that the perfect union is dissolved if we confess a perfect union according to the flesh which is of David's seed[2]." Such an argument is unjust as against the kenotic theory; for nothing in it suggested a confusion, except the injudicious language which compared the self-limited Christ to other inter-

[1] *E.g.* very strongly by Bishop Weston, *The One Christ*, p. 157.

[2] Lietzmann, Fr. 140. Diodore's objection is exactly similar to that afterwards restated by Theodore: cf. below, pp. 291–3.

mediates, the mule, the colour grey, and the season of spring, and spoke of Him as neither man only nor God only but a mixture between them[1]. But it was very necessary for Apollinarius to make the point more clear; and to do so he had only to turn the kenotic theory round and show that what was from the one side a process of self-emptying was, from the other, a transference of the human attributes to the Godhead. His great definition, "Incarnation is self-emptying," implies his response to the Antiochenes. Christ's limitation consists in the assumption of the conditions of human existence. Christ incarnate takes up the manhood into God: the flesh by union in Christ receives the qualities of deity. The whole is explained when it is realised that the kenosis is the union, and that the union is a *Communicatio Idiomatum*. The two terms are only complementary descriptions of the single fact that in the one Christ God and man are one[2].

His statement of the argument can be seen most clearly in the fragments of the *Contra Diodorum*, and was evidently a constituent part of his Christology from the beginning. He first justifies his use of mixture by a vigorous affirmation of the entire distinctness of the body and the Godhead, in the course of which he quotes Origen's illustration of the red-hot iron[3]: "If the com-

[1] *Syllog.*, Lietzmann, Fr. 113, quoted above.

[2] The doctrine of the *Communicatio Idiomatum* is not a discovery of Apollinarius and had already been widely used against the Arians *e.g.* by Athanasius, *Or. c. Arian.* ii and iii: but no one before Apollinarius had seen that it involved a kenosis. Athanasius, for example, while maintaining the transference of human attributes to the Godhead had deprived them of all reality and come near to simple docetism, cf. above, pp. 92, 93 and *Or. c. Arian.* iii. 51.

[3] *De Princ.* II. vi. 6. This similitude became very familiar in the Monophysite controversy: cf. Leontius, *Adv. Nestor.* i. 49, and *C. Monoph.* (Migne, *P.G.* LXXXVI. 2. 1869 C).

bination of iron (with fire) makes the iron itself look like fire and enables it to work all the works of fire and yet does not change its nature, so the union of God to the body causes no change in the body, although the body offers to those who can touch it the energy of the Godhead[1]." Such a saying ought to acquit Apollinarius of the monstrous insinuation of his ancient and modern opponents that he taught the consubstantiality of the flesh and the Godhead; and in the same book he supports it by a series of arguments in which he uses the union of soul and body wherein there is no confusion in spite of their common origin[2]—"the commingling does not make the soul visible, nor change it into the other qualities of the body so that it can be pierced or mutilated[3]"—to prove that *a fortiori* there will be no confusion between Godhead and body which are not of common origin. This is, however, only by way of safeguard. The doctrine of transference is summed up in a single sentence which is a definite reply to Diodore's accusation, "If the body of the Lord has become one with the Lord, the attributes of the body have become His attributes on account of the body[4]"; and this is expanded in the same book, "The properties of God and the body are united in Him: He is eternally Creator, object of worship, Wisdom, Power; these He derives from His Godhead: Son of Mary, born in this last time, a worshipper of God, progressing in wisdom, growing stronger in power; these from His body[5]." In the one person the two series of qualities are fully and perfectly

[1] Lietzmann, Fr. 128.

[2] This is the passage which Voisin uses to prove that he was a "dichotomite," in spite of συμφυής! Cf. above, p. 172.

[3] Lietzmann, Fr. 134.

[4] Lietzmann, Fr. 137.

[5] Lietzmann, Fr. 125.

united, so that Apollinarius in the exposition of his teaching to Dionysius can summarise it in the words: "We maintain both of these, that the whole is from heaven because of the Godhead, and the whole from a woman because of the flesh: we recognise no distinction in the one person, nor do we divide the earthly from the heavenly, nor the heavenly from the earthly: such division is impious[1]." In view of subsequent history perhaps the most interesting of the results which follow from the use of this principle of transference is the bestowal upon the Blessed Virgin of the title θεοτόκος or Mother of God. In the confession of faith called the *De Fide et Incarnatione*[2] Apollinarius and his synod protest that neither they nor any sane persons speak of the flesh as consubstantial with God in itself, but only as indivisibly united with the Logos to form "one person, one hypostasis, wholly man, wholly God," and urge that in consequence of this inseparable union and not of any divinity of the body apart from such union the Virgin is θεοτόκος, and that if this belief in the reality and results of the union be rejected "she will no longer be believed to be θεοτόκος which would be an act of injustice and impiety foreign to every reverent soul"—words which, when taken in connection with the special allusions of Theodore to the subject[3], intimate that the title had already become a topic of party strife.

It is likely that the terms in which Apollinarius

[1] § 7, Lietzmann, p. 259.

[2] § 5, Lietzmann, p. 196. θεοτόκος occurs three times, always with emphasis: it occurs also in *Ad Jovian.* 1.

[3] Cf. below, p. 294. The title had been used by Athanasius, *Or. c. Arian.* iii. 33, and Alexander of Alexandria, *Ep. ad Alex. Byz.* (Theodoret, *H.E.* i. 3).

described the consequences of the *Communicatio* may have first led his enemies to the idea that he taught either the consubstantiality of the Godhead and the body or at least that the body was from heaven. Such a belief was certainly accepted and taught by one of his pupils Polemon[1] and with less clearness by his companion in misfortune, Timothy of Berytus. But Apollinarius himself expressly anathematised it with an emphasis which leaves no room for doubt in his letter to Jovian[2] and in the *Tomus Synodalis*[3], and denied it in the second letter to Dionysius[4] and elsewhere[5]. He is repeatedly at pains to explain that such phrases can only be used, if used at all, on account of the completeness of the union; and from the whole tenour of his theology it is obvious that a "heavenly flesh" would vitiate all the deeper aspects of his thought. Yet there is unquestionably a certain amount of language in the *Apodeixis* which countenanced the second if not the first of these beliefs: and as this gave occasion to his enemies to assume that he was reviving the Gnosticism of Valentinus, and also to regard the *Ad Epictetum* and

[1] Other Apollinarians attacked Polemon vigorously for misrepresenting their master. *E.g.* Valentinus, in his *Capita Apolog.*, Lietzmann, pp. 287–91, accuses Timothy of following not Apollinarius but Polemon whom he always calls πολέμιος—a pun parallel to the use of σκοτεινός for Photinus and ὁ μανείς for Manes. Timothy himself in his letter to Homonius quoted by Leontius, *Adv. Fraud.* (Migne, *P.G.* LXXXVI. 2. 1947–75) and by Lietzmann, pp. 277–8, quotes many passages to prove that Apollinarius taught this—but is singularly unsuccessful. His failure is convincing evidence that this was never Apollinarius' belief.

[2] *Ad Jovian.* 3, Lietzmann, p. 253.

[3] Lietzmann, p. 263.

[4] Lietzmann, Fr. 164.

[5] *Syllog.*, Lietzmann, Fr. 112; *Ad Serap.*, Lietzmann, Fr. 159; *Ad Terent.*, Lietzmann Fr. 162.

similar documents as directed against him, it is advisable to examine it in some detail[1].

The most striking and most familiar statement of this accusation is to be found in the letter of Gregory of Nazianzus to Nectarius of Constantinople[2] in which Gregory declares that a pamphlet of Apollinarius has fallen into his hands and quotes from it the words "The flesh was not acquired (ἐπίκτητος) by the only-begotten Son for the purpose of His sojourn on earth or assumed in order to change the rudiments of our nature, but from the beginning this flesh-like nature existed in the Son." Gregory continues: "Further he puts forward a phrase in the Gospel perverting it so as to make it testify to this folly: the words are 'No one has ascended into heaven except He who came down from heaven, the Son of Man': so that even before He descended He was Son of Man, and He descended bringing with Him the flesh which He always had in heaven pre-existent and united (συνουσιωμένη) with Him." This passage deserves especial notice because part of it is exactly what Apollinarius could and did say, and can be paralleled in passages quoted by Gregory of Nyssa from the *Apodeixis*. The first is, "The man Christ is pre-existent: the spirit—that is, God—does not exist as distinct from Him, but the Lord is the divine spirit in the nature of the God-man[3]"; and from it Gregory[4] infers that "the very Godhead of the Son is from the beginning man" and that "He has made the nature of God and man one." The second is, "The

[1] This subject is admirably treated by Voisin, *l.c.* pp. 297–301. He proves that the language of the *Apodeixis* does not imply the pre-existence of the flesh of Christ but is used in virtue of his theory of *Communicatio Idiomatum*.

[2] *Ep.* 202. [3] Lietzmann, Fr. 32. [4] *Antirrh.* 13.

divine Incarnation did not take its beginning from the Virgin, but was before Abraham and before all creation[1]"; Gregory comments: "So it always was what it appeared to the disciples to be, solid and a model of our own, furnished with flesh and bones[2]." The third is, "The flesh was not acquired by the Godhead for our benefit, but was united into a single personality and has grown into one with it (*συνουσιωμένη καὶ σύμφυτος*)[3]"; which Gregory contrasts with his own view that "the glory veils itself for the purpose of a sojourn on our earth[4]." The fourth is, "The God in flesh[5] existent before the ages was afterwards born of a woman and came by the necessity of His nature to the test of suffering[6]."

These quotations and criticisms are obviously similar in character to the passage in the *Ad Nectarium* and make it highly probable that the sentence from the pamphlet is genuinely Apollinarian. The quotation from St John is also doubtless correct; for it is used twice in the *De Unione*, first to prove that "there was a descent from heaven not merely a birth from a woman," and, secondly, to prove that "though He has descended yet He is called heavenly man lest anyone deny the attachment to the Godhead of a body from earth." The final clause quoted from the letter, although printed by Lietzmann as a quotation from Apollinarius, is obviously Gregory Nazianzen's deduction from the previous

[1] Lietzmann, Fr. 34.
[2] *Antirrh.* 15.
[3] Lietzmann, Fr. 36.
[4] *Antirrh.* 17.
[5] Θεὸς ἔνσαρκος is a strong phrase: but it is the obvious counterpart of the ἄνθρωπος ἔνθεος of Antioch, criticised in the next fragment, and as such is used as a title. Here the sentence does not mean "God, who was in flesh before the ages."
[6] Lietzmann, Fr. 50.

quotation. We have, therefore, five sentences from the heretic which were supposed by the two Cappadocians to imply Valentinian teaching. Is the charge just?

The first quotation from the *Apodeixis* taken by itself does not do more than assert that the divine spirit of Christ pre-existed and was the same spirit which with earthly soul and body constituted the Incarnate. With the second we may compare two brief remarks from other fragments, "Wherefore He who was before Abraham, Son of God, was no other than He who was after Abraham, but He is one, perfect, the only-begotten of God," and "How is that which is from Abraham before Abraham? By being united to that which was before Abraham." The two earliest quotations from the *Apodeixis* seem, therefore, to be both assertions that the Godhead of the eternal Son was verily and indeed the same as that which became flesh, and that the potentiality of Incarnation was always a characteristic of His nature[1]. The third quotation, which is almost identical with the words in the *Ad Nectarium*, reveals Apollinarius' true meaning and intention by its use of the term "acquired"—ἐπίκτητος. This had been a word specially employed by the Arians to describe the Godhead of the Son as an addition made later in time to that of the Father. As such it is attacked by Apollinarius in his confession of faith. But ἐπίκτητος had been used in the same sense and as a regular part of their technical theology by Eustathius and Diodore[2], the latter of whom had applied it to the Incarnation as

[1] This second consideration, emphasised by Dorner, *Person of Christ*, I. ii. 372, Voisin rejects, because he refuses to acknowledge any Platonism in Apollinarius. But it seems probable that both this idea and the *Commun. Idiom.* influenced him.

[2] Cf. above, p. 120.

a remedy specially devised by God in consequence of the Fall. According to Diodore, God's original purpose had been thwarted by man's sin, and therefore in order to repair the disaster an additional and acquired manhood had to be assumed by the Son of God. Apollinarius felt that this unforeseen alliance between a man and God involved the idea of mutability, not perhaps in the Incarnate, but in the Creator: the Eternal could not be thus treated as a bungling workman who had to adopt a sudden change of method: the Incarnation in time and space must be the expression and sacrament of a potentiality inherent in the very nature of deity, a condition of the life of God. Like Origen, Apollinarius is not content solely with history; the appearance of Christ on earth must illuminate the whole attitude of God towards His creatures. In the attempt to interpret his thought he was driven to the use of crude and questionable language: for the difference between abstract and concrete, potential and actual, was always difficult for a Greek with his limited vocabulary to express. But when he speaks of the nature of God as always incarnate, and says that it is following the necessity of His nature that He accepts the Cross, these phrases, taken in connection with his attack upon the Antiochene doctrine and with his repeated denial of the idea that Christ's body is of itself heavenly, ought never to have been so misunderstood. He has realised and is stating that although the actual union took place only in the womb of the Virgin-mother, such union was the fulfilment in history of an eternal yearning for men, a yearning characteristic of the inmost essence of the divine. He has transcended, for a moment, his traditionally Greek conception of God as the Absolute Power and unqualified Being, and risen to the nobler and more Christian belief of St John, "God so loved the world that He gave His only-begotten Son."

To prove that this was Apollinarius' position we need only refer to the specific disavowals of belief in the "heavenly flesh." "We condemn the utter madness of those who say that the flesh is consubstantial with God[1]" had been his comment in 359 upon the Gnosticism attacked in Athanasius' letter to Epictetus. In 363 he appended certain anathemas to his own letter to Jovian[2] in which the Antiochene and the Gnostic position are alike repudiated, "If anyone teach contrary to this from the Holy Scriptures, and say that the Son of God is one and the man from Mary, adopted Son by grace as we are, is another, so that there are two Sons, one by nature Son of God who is from God, and the other by grace, the man from Mary; or if any say that the flesh of our Lord is from above and not from the Virgin Mary, or that the Godhead has been changed or confused or altered into flesh, or that the Godhead of the Son is passible, or that the flesh of our Lord as being the flesh of a man must not be worshipped instead of saying that it must be worshipped as the flesh of Him who is Lord and God; such persons the Catholic Church anathematises obeying the Apostle's words 'If any preach to you a gospel contrary to that which ye have received, let him be anathema.'" In spite of this express statement he has to return to the same subject in both his letters to Dionysius, protesting against those who "blaspheme us as if we said that the flesh was from heaven, when we read the words of Scripture which speak of Him who

[1] *Ad Serap.*, Lietzmann, Fr. 159.
[2] § 3, Lietzmann, p. 253.

is from heaven as Son of Man[1]," and claiming that "it is manifest from what we have always written that no one can bring against us these charges that are made against some: for we do not say that the flesh of the Saviour was from heaven, nor that His flesh is consubstantial with God inasmuch as it is flesh and not God, but only God in so far as it has been united into one person with God[2]." And in his letter to Terentius[3], who came as Comes to Antioch in 375, he again anathematises "anyone who says that the Son is two persons, or that His flesh is consubstantial with God and not with ours, or that it has come down from heaven and not that it has been assumed by Him who is from heaven." Evidently by this time there were some who assumed that the crude errors condemned in the *Ad Epictetum* were derived from Apollinarius, and the principle of the transference of attributes was being misinterpreted as it was by the Gregories. Polemon had already begun to develop the exaggerated Monophysite doctrine which led him into conflict with the Apollinarians, and to the formation of a separate sect. And so in the formal confession of the Apollinarian Synod[4], which is perhaps the last writing of the Bishop of Laodicea, he returns to the anathema of the letter to Jovian, and closes his life's work with the words: "Flesh consubstantial with our flesh, has the living Logos assumed from Mary in union with the

[1] § 7, Lietzmann, p. 259. [2] Lietzmann, Fr. 164.
[3] Lietzmann, Fr. 163.
[4] *Tom. Synod.*, Lietzmann, pp. 262–3. The *De Fid. et Inc.*, also apparently a synodal confession, contains a similar statement, denying that the body is in itself consubstantial and that the flesh is from heaven, § 3, Lietzmann, p. 194. Either of these, but clearly not both, may emanate from the Synod which Gregory Naz., *Carmen de Vita sua*, mentions as held in 378 or 379.

Godhead from His first conception by the Virgin; and so He became man....Anathema therefore be he who denies that the flesh is from Mary and says that it is of the uncreated nature and consubstantial with God; and also he who says that the Godhead is passible and that the sufferings which come from the soul (τὰ πάθη τὰ ψυχικά) come from it."

And if his own words are not enough we have the testimony of one who was a member of the Antiochene party and a supporter of Nestorius, Theodoret the critic of Cyril and the enemy of Eutychianism, a man who had the best of reasons for disliking Apollinarius and for seeking to prove that the Monophysites were repeating his heresy. If there had been any truth in the charges made by the Gregories, Theodoret would have found them an invaluable weapon against the errors of his own generation. We should expect to find him setting out a catena of passages to prove that the arch-heretic of Laodicea had been the fount from which Eutyches had drawn his venom. Instead we find him quoting saying after saying from the *Contra Diodorum* to demonstrate not that the Eutychians are Apollinarists, but that Apollinarius himself condemns them. Although a man of no great brilliance, the Bishop of Cyrrhus was a careful and honest student: unlike the Cappadocians, he had read Apollinarius, and was quick to recognise and employ the truths that he found so well expressed by him. In consequence, when he undertakes in his *Dialogue* to prove that the divine nature of Christ is immutable, unconfused, and impassible, his proof is supported in every case by a string of quotations from the very man who is commonly regarded as the father of Monophysitism.

How far he can be justly given this title is a matter perhaps hardly worthy of discussion: for, as we have seen already and shall see yet more plainly when we come to consider his orthodox critics, he differs from them not in his insistence upon the unity of Christ but in his mode of interpreting that unity; and in any case, although, like them, he will have nothing to do with a duality of will in the Incarnate, he provides by his theory of kenosis for a duality of sphere of action. Any doctrine which merges the human in the divine, such as is to be found in the true Monophysites, would render meaningless his emphasis upon the self-limitation of the Son of God and upon the transference of attributes, both of which are introduced in order to guard against such confusion while preserving the real union.

Probably it is his repeated use of the term "one nature" that differentiates him from his Greek contemporaries and makes him appear more Monophysite than they. Critics, ancient and modern, noting its frequent occurrence, have assumed that he used it in its later technical sense, and have therefore classed him with the Eutychians. It is, of course, grossly unfair to do so—as unfair as it would be to call St Paul an Arian because he designates Christ "the firstborn of all creation." But before we close our account of his Christology it will be well to consider briefly some of the words which he employed, *οὐσία*, *ὑπόστασις*, *πρόσωπον*, and, most important of all, *φύσις*: for during the fourth century there was great confusion over them, and misunderstanding may foster a wholly unjust appreciation of his teaching. Few subjects are more interesting than the study of the process by which words like these, used at first in a wide and general sense, were given in the course of doctrinal history a highly specialised meaning: and few mistakes are more common than to read the work of an early thinker as if he possessed a prophetic understanding of technicalities invented long after his death. In Apollinarius' time this process with regard to Trinitarian doctrine was nearing its completion, though the uncertainty about *ὑπόστασις* was not yet removed even in the East, and between East and West, as Jerome's experience shows, it was still a stumbling-block. In Christology terminology was still vague and unscientific.

For the study of Apollinarius the term *οὐσία* and its compounds are of great importance; for not only do the Antiochenes use Synusiasts as a title for his followers, but he deliberately chooses *συνουσιώμενος* as his substitute for Diodore's *ἐπίκτητος*. Hence it is necessary to ask whether he employs it for Christology in the same sense in which it had now come to be used in speaking of the Godhead. There are, as we have seen, two original meanings of *οὐσία*[1]. It signifies, of course, the underlying reality, that which makes a thing what it is: but in this sense it can be applied either to a particular person or thing to denote its true self, or to the common element shared by a number of particulars. To the Greek theologians, as was made clear in the case of Paul of Samosata, it was at first used in the former meaning, and was equivalent to personality, *ὁμοούσιον* being forbidden because it implied "unipersonal." At Nicea the Easterns, almost without exception, disliked it, but accepted it from the West under the influence of Hosius of Cordova, as the translation of the Latin *substantia*,

[1] Cf. above, pp. 63–5.

a word regularly used since Tertullian's time to denote the essential quality shared by the three Persons. Even Athanasius took some years to get used to this meaning, and hardly employs ὁμοούσιον until after his first exile and visit to Rome: and in the East generally it was for a generation regarded as Sabellian, that is, as implying that God was one not in essence but in person. That this did in fact represent the earlier Nicene position would be an exaggerated statement. But it is very noticeable that the most orthodox Easterns during the early years of the controversy prefer to compare the Trinity to the Sun, its light, and rays, and never use the comparison to three men which is so common in the writings of the Cappadocians[1]. By the time of Apollinarius οὐσία in Trinitarian doctrine had wholly lost its application to personality, and the Bishop of Laodicea regularly uses it of the Godhead which the Three share: ὁμοούσιον is explained in his Confession as "possessing by nature His Father's divinity[2]." In his Christology also ὁμοούσιον has always this meaning, but his use of οὐσία is much less certain; and there is some evidence that he still employed it frequently to mean not "substance" but "person," especially perhaps in the earlier period of his work. The most striking passage is that in the *Ad Heracleum*[3] where he writes "The instrument (*i.e.* the body) and that which moves it naturally constitute a single 'energy' (ἐνέργεια): if the energy be one, the οὐσία also is one: so there is a single οὐσία of the Logos and His instrument." Now ἐνέργεια is a favourite word and is twice[4] employed as

[1] *E.g.* Basil, *Ep.* 38. [2] K.M.Π. 27 (Lietzmann, p. 176).
[3] Lietzmann, Fr. 117. This is the passage paraphrased by Ambrose, *De Inc.* 51: cf. above, p. 100, note.
[4] *De Un.*, Lietzmann, Fr. 2; *Ad Julian.*, Lietzmann, Fr. 151.

synonym for "will" (θέλησις) and once, in the *De Fide et Incarnatione*[1], for "person" (ὑπόστασις and πρόσωπον). Apollinarius constantly protests against the division of the energy of Christ into human and divine[2], since in every case it is the one Christ who acts[3]. Ἐνέργεια obviously denotes the activity by which a personality manifests itself, the fulfilment of volition in action. And this being so it is difficult not to believe that here at least οὐσία has the sense of entity or person. And this meaning is strongly confirmed in another fragment of the same book[4], where he says, "God and man are not two separate οὐσίαι, but one owing to the combination of God with a human body." Seeing that he repeatedly maintains that Godhead and manhood are distinct οὐσίαι, when he uses the word in its meaning of essence[5], and that here he uses θεός and ἄνθρωπος, not the abstract terms, it seems clear that "person" is a more adequate translation. And this is similarly the case in the fragment quoted by Justinian[6] "not in two οὐσίαι, but in one." And, finally, a sentence in the *De Incarnatione*[7] where οὐσία and πρόσωπον are used side by side and apparently as almost synonymous—"one in very reality according to His one οὐσία, not two in πρόσωπα existent according to their separate spheres and dignities"—proves that though οὐσία denotes a deeper and more permanent element than πρόσωπον, which never quite lost its meaning of mask, yet it is applied to a particular entity or person, in quite a different sense from that in

1 § 6, Lietzmann, p. 199.

2 *E.g. Apod.*, Lietzmann, Frs. 59, 60.

3 K.M.Π. 30 (Lietzmann, p. 178).

4 Lietzmann, Fr. 119.

5 *E.g.* K.M.Π. 25, 26 (Lietzmann, p. 176).

6 Lietzmann, Fr. 158.

7 Lietzmann, Fr. 9. The meaning in *De Fid. et Inc.* 7 (Lietzmann, p. 199) is obscure.

which it can translate *substantia*. His use of the compounds οὐσιώδης and συνουσιώμενος, both of which we saw employed in the sense of "person" in the disputation with Paul of Samosata[1], bears this out. In the *Encomium Mariae*[2] there is a sentence exactly recalling Malchion's classic definition: "Do you not suppose what has been inseparably conjoined to God and has become the same as He on account of personal union (διὰ τὴν ἕνωσιν τὴν οὐσιώδη) to be divine or God?" And his use of συνουσιώμενος must surely resemble this: for it obviously cannot mean "united in essence," since this would be equivalent to ὁμοούσιος, which, as we have seen, he anathematises. "United into a single entity or personality" is the term which he would naturally employ as against the Antiochene doctrine of juxtaposition which he regarded as a teaching of "two Christs": συνουσιώμενος has exactly that sense of vital and perfect union which is so fundamental to his Christology. And at the same time his use of it at a stage when it was being given a specialised significance may well have been responsible for the misunderstanding that compelled him so often to refute the charge that he considered Godhead and manhood to be ὁμοούσια.

The two next words, ὑπόστασις and πρόσωπον, are less important. The former, which was to become the orthodox term in the definition of the Incarnation as "one person, two natures," he very seldom employs, but on the two or three occasions where it appears it bears its "correct" significance, both when applied to the Persons of the Trinity[3] and to the Person of Christ[4].

[1] Cf. above, pp. 63–5.
[2] Lietzmann, Fr. 12.
[3] K.M.Π. 1, Lietzmann, p. 168.
[4] *De Fid. et Inc.* 3 and 6 (Lietzmann, pp. 194, 199). In both cases he explains it by adding πρόσωπον.

But in both doctrines he prefers πρόσωπον, which is after all the natural Greek equivalent of *persona*. It is indeed very noteworthy that even in his Confession, where he is combating Sabellianism, he uses the word which the Sabellians are supposed to have brought into disrepute. Probably he was well aware of the confusion which still enveloped ὑπόστασις, and which even the Council of 362 did not immediately remove. The Old Nicenes, who were familiar with it as an equivalent to οὐσία in the anathemas of their Creed, may well have been slow to welcome what must have seemed to them a concession to Tritheism, especially as the use of ὑπόστασις for *persona* created confusion between East and West.

Of the four words φύσις is the most interesting both for an understanding of Apollinarius, and because of the great part which it played in the long Monophysite controversy. Fifty years after the condemnation of the Bishop of Laodicea φύσις, which by that time had become one of the recognised technicalities, was still employed in two different meanings, being applied either to the "nature" or sum total of the attributes of a substance, or else to the "person" to whom those attributes belonged. Cyril's success against Nestorius was due not least to the skill with which he played upon the ambiguities of the formula ἕνωσις φυσική, which seemed to the Antiochenes sheer heresy, but which he was ready to explain in the sense of "hypostatic union." Even in the time of Severus the word had not yet been finally restricted, and cases can still be found in which it is identified with ὑπόστασις. In Apollinarius' generation φύσις had hardly a technical meaning at all, and the heresiarch himself uses it as the natural term to describe the characteristic quality either of Godhead and manhood or of God and man and Christ. Unfortunately, in later centuries, when it had been more precisely defined, the Apollinarian writings were ransacked by controversialists who wished to prove a case against him, and who read back into his words the meaning and implications of their own days: they were willing enough to glose over the irregularities of Cyril's usage; they dragged to light every phrase of his predecessor which could prove him the father of Monophysitism. And it is difficult to judge his meaning without bias on the basis of extracts from his work preserved not in order to discover his intention but to convict him of error. Nevertheless it is plain that he employs it freely in both the senses afterwards contrasted. There is a large group of quotations in which his use is that of later orthodoxy: a saying from the *Contra Diodorum*[1] may be quoted as typical: "Just as a man's body remains in its own proper nature and is not changed by possessing soul, so the mingling of Godhead with the body of Christ does not in any way alter it from being body." At the same time there are even more cases in which he identifies it with "energy" or "will[2]," "hypostasis" or "person[3]"; and it is these to which Justinian and Leontius draw special attention. At a time when *μία φύσις* and *ἕνωσις φυσική* had become the hallmarks of heresy, his emphasis upon them was enough to colour their whole attitude towards his doctrine: he spoke the language of Monophysitism—what further proof was needed? And yet his meaning is not that of later heretics.

[1] Lietzmann, Fr. 134.

[2] *Ad Julian.*, Lietzmann, Frs. 151, 152.

[3] K.M.Π. 31 (Lietzmann, p. 179); *De Fid. et Inc.* 6 (Lietzmann, p. 199); *Ad Dion.* i. 2 (Lietzmann, p. 257).

They used "one nature" to mean that the attributes proper to Godhead and manhood belonged without distinction to the one Christ: they "confused the natures." Apollinarius, like Cyril, applies φύσις in this sense not to the attributes but to the person, not to Godhead and manhood but to the hypostasis of the Incarnate; he never uses it of Christ in the sense given to it by the Monophysites; and though superficially his language is open to criticism it is as orthodox as Cyril's[1]. It is unnecessary to quote a string of passages: one from the first letter to Dionysius fairly represents them all: "Christ is one nature; for one person cannot be divided into two, and under the conditions of Incarnation the body is not a separate (ἰδία) nature, nor is the Godhead[2]: just as man is one nature, so is Christ who is in the likeness of man." φύσις here, as usually when the word is spoken of the Incarnate, refers not to the constituent elements but to the whole composed by their union. His emphasis is upon the unity of the Master and the reality of a divine Incarnation: "His nature is one, His generation is twofold[3]"; "we speak

[1] Voisin's attempt to contrast the two (*l.c.* p. 407), "Cyrille comprenait dans le sens orthodoxe de μία ὑπόστασις l'expression μία φύσις employée dans un sens hétérodoxe par l'hérésiarque," though repeatedly stated by him and by other Catholic historians, is unsupported by evidence of any kind except the argument that Apollinarius was condemned and Cyril canonised! And Voisin himself, on p. 278, says: "L'hérésiarque considère comme corrélatifs les termes: 'être un,' être vivant,' 'personne,' 'hypostase,' 'nature'": and on p. 290 admits again that "nature" and "person" are correlatives and quotes many passages which prove that they are identical: in the body of his book he proves that Apollinarius and Cyril are exactly alike in their use of the two terms, and in his summary denies it.

[2] Cf. *Ad Dion.* I. 8 (Lietzmann, p. 259): "The body is not by itself a φύσις since it is not life-giving nor can be separated from the life-giving Logos."

[3] *C. Diod.*, Lietzmann, Fr. 142.

of the Lord as in φύσις God and in φύσις man, but in a single combined φύσις fleshly and divine[1]." There is no confusion between manhood and Godhead save that which results from the perfection of their union in the *Communicatio Idiomatum*. Nowhere is his orthodoxy in this respect more plainly shown than in the concluding sentence of the *De Unione*: "The man who cannot understand what is peculiar to each in these united but still distinct elements will fall into utter perplexity: he who recognises the peculiarities and preserves the union will neither mistake the nature of the elements nor ignore their union." Chalcedon itself does not insist more clearly on the necessity for balance and on the twofold aspect of the truth.

In considering his terminology we must not forget that he was a pioneer, investigating a subject which had not yet received any scientific treatment, and interpreting his results in formulae for which there was no precedent to guide him. He found the Christological doctrine of the Church in a state of chaos. The Arians, accepting the general position of the Origenists and of Greek orthodoxy that Christ was the Logos made flesh, had shown that this naturally led, as Eusebius of Caesarea had admitted, to the belief that He was a second and inferior deity. Their opponents were being driven either to the Adoptianism of Antioch which saved the divinity of Christ at the expense of impugning the unity of His person, or to the Gnosticism of Athanasius' Orations against them, which saved it by explaining away the reality of His human experiences. Meanwhile, a variety of crude and incoherent speculations was flourishing unchecked. Apollinarius set himself to the creation of

[1] *Ad Petr.*, Lietzmann, Fr. 149.

a clear-cut and logical theory which should express in definite form the convictions of his compatriots and of the Christian conscience. He accepted as axiomatic the principle that Christ was Saviour and therefore God, that He was one single person possessing both unbroken communion with His Father and also a full human life on earth, and that, therefore, however it might be defined, the very God had entered into and shared the sufferings and limitation proper to humanity. That he also started from the conviction that God and man were naturally opposites and that their relationship could best be described in a series of antitheses, a conviction from which, in spite of his devotion to the Fourth Gospel, he was never able to escape, made his task infinitely difficult, if not in the long run impossible. But in fulfilling it by his theories of kenosis and of the transference of attributes he laid down the lines along which Catholic Christendom has been content to find a solution ever since his time. The centre of personality in Christ was divine not human: yet by a voluntary act of humiliation He took upon Himself our flesh and all the experiences of manhood: there is no confusion between God and man, although in the Incarnate they are verily one: by the completeness of this union man is redeemed and made at one with God. That was his faith. In defining it he emphasised especially the points on which he felt that the Antiochenes were mistaken, employing terms *οὐσία* and *φύσις*, which subsequent ages regarded as inappropriate, in his desire to enforce the unity of person, and giving too great a precision to his belief that the manhood of Christ was impersonal by his doctrine of the "heavenly mind." In this respect his fate was the opposite of that of Tertullian, the phrase-maker of

Christendom: legal training, unhampered by profundity of thought or interest in philosophy, enabled the Carthaginian to do what the Laodicene with his far greater spirituality and intellectual power failed to do. Like Origen, Apollinarius did all the research and provided all the material for a dogmatic formula: like Origen, he made possible a new epoch in theology: like Origen, he was a prophet and received a prophet's usual reward, while his work was surreptitiously absorbed into the fabric of orthodox dogmatic.

Even so the inadequacy of his formula was not the cause of his condemnation. Unlike Origen, he lived in an age when the Church had become an important factor in imperial politics, and when the ecclesiastical statesman was becoming more prominent than the thinker or the saint. Basil in the East and the papacy in the West saw that if the Church was to influence the state she must be outwardly united, even if union meant compromise and the sacrifice of principles. In their efforts they had the hearty support of the Emperor and his court, men who were straining every nerve to check the disintegration of their world. Apollinarius cared little for politics and would rather see the Church disunited than false to truth. He refused to ally himself in the interest of statescraft with men who seemed to him to be destroying the faith. He preferred to sacrifice position and privileges, and, like Athanasius before him, to stand alone, if need be, against dominant error. We may call it the sectarian temper or loyalty to conviction, uncompromising obstinacy or the martyr spirit, but whichever it be Athanasius, when he refused to communicate with the Arians, and Apollinarius, when he broke away from the Antiochenes, have an equal right to the title. Had Apollinarius been a young man, he too, like Athanasius, might have endured a brief exile[1] and been received back in triumph, when his belief prevailed over the Nestorians in 431. Had he lived until the Pelagian controversy, he might have renewed his quarrel with Antioch alongside of Augustine, and learned that true freedom does not consist in a mere power of capricious choice and that, therefore, a sinless humanity is not a contradiction in terms—knowledge which would have enabled him to grant to Christ not indeed "a mind like ours sinful and the prey of filthy thoughts" but a manhood perfect because without sin, a mind truly human and truly free because living in perfect harmony with the divine. As it was, he died a heretic; and it was left to Cyril the Alexandrian intriguer, the Apollinarian who was too clever to acknowledge his master, to bring back his doctrine into the Church by a deft concession in phraseology, a concession not greater than that which Athanasius had made to the New Nicenes.

We have seen that Apollinarius is orthodox enough in his doctrines of kenosis, of the *Communicatio Idiomatum* and of the eternal aspect of the Incarnation. His theology in these respects was accepted. It is not so generally recognised that his belief in the divine personality of Christ has also become part of the Catholic tradition, and that its acceptance has been the cause of no small embarrassment to those who in loyalty to that tradition are bound to condemn him as a heretic, while endorsing and maintaining the very belief for which he was cast out. Yet a brief study of the treatment of

[1] His followers were restored to full communion at Antioch, without any change of opinion on their part, by Theodotus in 410–5.

Apollinarius by Catholic scholars reveals the dilemma in which they find themselves. Very strikingly does this appear in the writings of such a learned and orthodox historian as the late Dr Bright. In his *Later Treatises of St Athanasius*, where page after page the Bishop of Laodicea is vilified and traduced, it is admitted in a footnote that "We must own that in Christ humanity is not a complete thing in the sense in which it is complete in each of us, inasmuch as it is not personal, it is taken into union with a Personality, an Ego, which is divine[1]." If translated into the language of a Greek of the fourth century, such a sentence could only be expressed in words like those of Apollinarius: "He is human, but not a man, since He is not consubstantial with man in His most important element[2]," or "Instead of a human centre of personality such as there is in us, there was in Christ a heavenly mind[3]." If Apollinarius was justly condemned, Athanasius and Cyril and Dr Bright should be condemned with him.

[1] *L.c.* p. 85. From first to last of his writings Bright's treatment of Apollinarius is inaccurate and unjust: cf. *e.g. Age of the Fathers*, I. 327, where he himself admits that Apollinarius is right in denying a human centre to Christ, for otherwise His temptations would have been real: but attacks his denial of a human mind because this makes His surprise, disappointment, anxiety and suffering also unreal! He then calls Apollinarianism paradoxical.

[2] *Apod.*, Lietzmann, Fr. 45.

[3] Pseudo-Athanasius, *C. Apoll.* i. 2—almost certainly a genuine quotation from Apollinarius.

CHAPTER VI

THE ORTHODOX CRITICS OF APOLLINARIUS

That Apollinarianism should have been condemned by the Oecumenical Council of Constantinople in 381 and restated by the Oecumenical Council of Ephesus fifty years later, and that Cyril who "had got the best of what he had from Apollinarius[1]" should have been canonised for doing so, is an irony not without parallel in Church history[2], but sufficiently unexpected to demand explanation. A study of the circumstances of his condemnation and of the writings of his orthodox opponents will clear up the problem. It is an interesting comment upon the methods by which the doctrine of the infallibility of the Church has been maintained.

As we have seen, Apollinarius was attacked rather as a schismatic than as a heresiarch. Basil, in his formal letter of accusation to the Western Church[3], founded his plea upon the need for unity and the evil resulting from the existence of separate congregations like those of Paulinus and of the Apollinarians. As against the Bishop of Laodicea he brings a charge of Chiliasm, not of unorthodox Christology; for on this subject he merely notes that Apollinarius has indulged in obscure speculations which have caused much perturbation and led

[1] Harnack, *H.D.* iv. p. 178, note.

[2] The case of Nestorius is even more paradoxical. Condemned, deposed and exiled in 431, he lived to see his own belief restated in Leo's Tome and accepted by the very Church which still anathematised him for holding it.

[3] *Ep.* 263.

to profitless disputes about technicalities. At Rome, where speculation was taboo and Tertullian's formula "one person, two natures" was received as ultimate, Apollinarius was condemned for denying the perfect manhood of Christ—for heresy not for schism.

It is unnecessary to emphasise the fact that this difference is typical of the whole quality of Western in contrast to Eastern Christianity, that it represents the essential divergence between the Latin and the Greek. Rome, pagan or Christian, stood first and foremost for an ordered corporate life. Her primal religion reflected her belief in the divinity of the organised society: her gods and goddesses had been the personifications and tutelary deities of the various aspects of man's social and civic duty—Jupiter of the majesty of the state and of the father's place in the home, Vesta of the sacred flame around which commonwealth and family gathered together, Juno of the sanctity of mutual obligation and of the marriage-bed as symbolic of man's loyalties, Janus of adventure and of home-coming[1]. Every citizen had his function as a member of the body politic, owing implicit obedience to constituted authority, and subordinating his every thought and action to the common weal. When Christ came to Rome, His coming gave occasion for the development of a compact and disciplined corporation. Such a body must have its rules of thought and practice. Its solidarity must not be imperilled by private inquisitiveness or the vagaries of temperament. Conformity was natural to the Roman: liberty was anti-social: uniformity was identified with unity. The Carthaginians, with the blood of the veterans

[1] An illuminating account is to be found in Augustine, *De Civ. Dei*, vi. 5–10, where he discusses the *theologia civilis*.

of Junonia in their veins, gave the lead in the promotion of ordered efficiency: to them even Rome seemed lax and undisciplined[1]: Christianity meant the creed, the canons and the constitution of the Church. Tertullian the Montanist was "the master."

To the Greek, as perhaps to St Paul, this simply appeared to be a reversion to Judaism, to the Mosaic Law and the Tradition of the Elders, to the very system and outlook which had crucified Christ. But the Greek, with his creative genius, his versatility and curiosity, his restless activity of spirit, and his passion for the ideal, was always an individualist; and even in his golden age had never succeeded in building up a society larger or more coherent than the faction-ridden city-state. Apollinarius' conviction that two complete personalities cannot coexist without feud is typical of his race; for *στάσις* was the glory and the ruin of Hellenism. Christ came to the Greek as beauty and truth and goodness personified[2]; One in whom each could find and explore new worlds of aesthetic and intellectual and moral life. To crystallise the infinity of His revelation into a formula might be practical wisdom: it was none the less spiritual apostasy. Wide liberty must be allowed to speculation: authority must depend upon enlightenment: the Church must educate but not dictate: unity is of the spirit and compatible with myriad varieties of interpretation and of organisation: faction is an inevitable concomitant of vitality and of growth: what is

[1] Cf. Tertullian's virulent satires upon the Roman pontiff for his readiness to pardon sinners in the *De Pudicitia*.

[2] In contrast to those of Rome the gods of Greece were personifications of aspects of nature or qualities of man—Zeus the clear sky, Poseidon the sea, Athene wisdom and skill, Apollo the creative sun and creative art, Herakles strength.

false will perish, what is true will be gathered into a synthesis only when all truth has been attained.

In the fourth century when Christianity became the established religion of the empire this contrast forced itself upon the notice of churchmen. Hitherto there had been little contact between Latins and Greeks: the genius of each had been free to develop along its own lines. But at Nicea Constantine had infected the East with a new desire for ecclesiastical uniformity, and with a new conception of formulated dogma as a means for attaining it. And in the dreary years of the Arian controversy the longing for Western efficiency grew apace. Disputes on matters of doctrine were interesting and valuable while conducted in the relative privacy of the school of theology: when they affected public policy and became the property not of the learned but of the ambitious, their peril was manifest. In a pagan world disagreement in opinion was counteracted by the unifying forces of common danger from persecution and common enthusiasm for evangelism. After the Edict of Milan ecclesiasticism became a topic of absorbing interest: statesmen looked for solidarity and practical efficiency in the churches: churchmen saw that if they were to influence policy they must stand united and definite. Basil was not alone in comparing the order and strength of the West with the chaos and disputings of the East. To reduce Christian morality to the observance of a code of rules was the business of the organisers of monasticism: to translate the speculations of Christian philosophy into a series of precise definitions was an equally desirable task: in all departments there must be systematic organisation and a recognised authority. Greece had been conquered by Rome before: confronted by the alternative, Rome or chaos, she would again make her submission.

The representative of this passion for uniformity was Epiphanius of Salamis, a pioneer of the monastic movement and the only Eastern rival to Jerome in his claim to be the first of the mediaevals. Epiphanius has about him much of the quality of Tertullian, though he lacks the African's clear-cut mentality and power of phrase. Brought up in a monastery, he has all the small man's love of tidiness and precision. Untroubled by any sense of the largeness of truth, he is happy if he can find a plausible formula and illustrate it with a collection of platitudes. Scholarship is to be used for the cataloguing of heresies and the enunciation of paradoxes. Speculation, however honest, is proof of moral corruption: its difficulties are food for the scoffer; its arguments must be overwhelmed by abuse; its authors are vipers and basilisks. It is in this spirit that he confronts Apollinarius. "Why do persons of this kind play the busybody with God, fabricating their shameful speculations about matters that no prophet nor evangelist nor apostle nor writer has thought it necessary to discuss?[1]" "What value has this innovation for the world? What profit for the Church? Infinite harm, in the creation of hatred and faction. For when once argument arises it produces panic. It does not advance our salvation, nay it is the denial of it, when a man refuses to conform, not in this respect alone, but in the very smallest matter. Not even in the tiniest detail must we swerve from the way of truth. Therefore will we argue against this theory because of our desire not to stir away from our own manner of life, nor to leave the standard of the holy

[1] *Haer.* lxxvii. 18.

Church and Creed of God[1]." It is the voice of mediaeval Catholicism, a voice new to the Eastern Church.

In this spirit his orthodox attack upon Apollinarius was begun. In the *Ancoratus* he is occupied with the exegesis of a few texts and knows only that certain people unnamed[2] have conjectured from them that Christ did not possess a human mind. In the *Panarion* he develops his argument at length, starting with an account of varieties of Christological error, citing in full the letter to Epictetus, detailing his discussion with Vitalis, and attributing the heresy to the teaching of Apollinarius. In neither case is his criticism of much value. He has his formula: Christ is the hypostasis in the Incarnate, and His minds, divine and human, are faculties, whose interaction need not be discussed. He has his proof-texts, and uses them to hurl at the heads of his opponents. And he has his paradox: "We preach and believe that Christ suffered: yet He did not suffer in Himself; nor was the sufferer different from the Lord; nor did the Godhead suffer: but nevertheless our Lord Jesus Christ suffered, His Godhead remaining changeless and impassible, but suffering in the flesh while remaining impassible[3]." To suggest that this needs explanation is blasphemy. Epiphanius does not know what it means and he does not care: if others are curious let them be anathema. It never occurs to him that he and his opponent mean exactly the same thing, so far as he means anything at all, and that νοῦς signifies to Apollinarius what he calls ὑπόστασις. Yet from his multitude of words and flow of repetition the under-

[1] *L.c.* 24.
[2] The list of heretics in *Ancor.* 13 which mentions Dimoeritae or Apollinarians is obviously copied and introduced later from the *Haer*.
[3] *Haer.* lxxvii. 32.

lying agreement is plain enough. Their formulae differ: their faith is the same. Epiphanius is too much an Eastern to doubt that Christ is the Logos in flesh. He is too muddle-headed to see that certain human elements in the record of the Gospels are hard to reconcile with belief in a wholly impassible deity. And so he flings down his phrases and his vituperation, satisfied to substitute orthodoxy for truth, and proud to have added another to his list of heresies.

The work of Epiphanius is a symptom and a portent. Among the wars of history there are few more significant than the miserable campaign which the Bishop of Salamis, and under his instigation his illustrious admirer Jerome, waged against the memory of Origen. With its virility sapped by monasticism and its honesty corrupted by state patronage, cowed by threats of persecution in this world and hell in the next, seduced by pomps and ceremonies, by ritual and relics, pilgrimages and image-worship, miracle-mongering and the cult of the saints, bewildered by its manifest disunion and betrayed by the lying and intrigue, violence and vanity of its leaders, the glory of Greek Christendom was outraged and destroyed[1]. Apollinarius, Chrysostom,

[1] Yet the new era did not begin without protest—protest in which even the saints joined: cf. Epiphanius' attack upon Mariolatry (*Haer.* lxxix): "No one of the saints is worshipped: for the old error of leaving the living God and worshipping His creatures shall not rule over us." "Let no one worship Mary: worship belongs to no woman nor even man, but to God only": Gregory Naz. on Church Councils (*Ep.* 130): "I dread every assembly of bishops; for I have never yet seen any good result: synods do more for the increase than the suppression of evils": Gregory Nyss. on pilgrimages as immodest, full of temptation and valueless (*De Eunt. Hierosol.*): "The Spirit is given in proportion to our faith, not to our journeys to Jerusalem": and Chrysostom's noble protest against the anathematising of heretics (*De Anath.* 4): "If he is alive you act impiously, for he may yet be changed: if dead, much more so; for to God he stands or falls, and has passed out of the power of men."

Nestorius are the principal victims: but the war was not so much against them as against the free search for truth, the wide horizon and clear vision of God, the hope and faith and love which Christian Hellenism had laid at the feet of Christ. Efficiency triumphed, and the splendour faded. Christ was exiled, and the Church Catholic reigned in His stead.

But in the fourth century Epiphanius stood almost alone. He might rejoice: but Apollinarius' condemnation as a heretic came as a shock to the rest of the East, which, save for the small minority at Antioch, fundamentally agreed with him, and, if regarding his opinions as advanced and perhaps dangerously outspoken, had no desire for their expulsion from the Church. Even Epiphanius, who disagreed with him far more definitely than any other of his orthodox Greek contemporaries, can scarcely believe the news of the sentence upon him, and becomes quite pathetic over the reported fall of so great a pillar of the Church. While consoling himself by reflecting with his usual charity that he who errs even in the smallest detail must be reckoned an utter apostate, he cannot work himself up into his general condition of righteous indignation, and is full of lamentation that one so learned in all branches of study, so reverend in his way of life, and so well beloved by all believers has actually brought such grief upon his friends and such shame upon himself. And the verdict of Constantinople upon him, as Lietzmann has clearly demonstrated, proves that the Easterns, while recognising the Roman sentence and deploring the schism occasioned by the new teaching, were not prepared to exclude those who held it from communion provided they would return to the Church.

Indeed, as our study of his predecessors has shown and as the attitude of his critics will reveal still more plainly, Greek orthodoxy was definitely on his side. His denial of a human spirit to Christ might seem unduly drastic and indiscreet: but his insistence upon the error of believing in a dual personality or an inspired manhood, and upon the perfect union of the two elements in the one Christ, was endorsed by all except the Antiochenes. Least of all were the professed champions of the faith in a position to refute him. The great Cappadocians had inherited the mantle of the Christian philosophers and as heirs of the Origenists had been brought up to approach the Incarnation from its divine side. They had hardly more conception than Apollinarius of the full manhood of Christ, and were too busy with the struggle against Eunomians and Macedonians and with practical ecclesiasticism to devote much time to the subject. And so when from the prominence of their position and their zeal for unity they were constrained to attack Apollinarius they found themselves fighting in the dark. So far as they had an intelligible Christology it was so like his that they could hardly condemn him: yet he had been condemned and they must enforce the sentence. So instead of taking his teaching at its true value, they parodied it on the strength of isolated sayings until it was sufficiently transformed to be open to criticism. The real Apollinarius went almost unscathed: a man of straw created by his opponents and bearing only the most distant resemblance to him was gibbeted in his place.

The arguments of the Cappadocians were doubtless less impressive than their names. But they were sufficient to secure the destruction of the Apollinarian writings and so to make the misrepresentation of him comparatively easy and wholly successful. By the middle of the sixth century the regular catchword against his heresy was *convertibiliter*, and Facundus sums up the orthodox view when he states that "Apollinarius did not believe that the Logos became man by the assumption of human nature, but thought that part of the substance of the Logos was converted into flesh[1]." Under cover of such a delusion Cyril, who had reintroduced the genuine teaching of the heretic into Christian theology, could be pronounced rigidly correct; and the work of Apollinarius could be incorporated in the Church's creed. The Bishop of Laodicea, if he knew the facts, would doubtless be content to have it so. He is human enough and great enough to be more amused than annoyed.

Before we consider the work of the Cappadocians it will be well to consider the two books against Apollinarius which have been traditionally ascribed to Athanasius, although the evidence for their genuineness is of the flimsiest kind. Hardly any recent scholars would defend them: but their true character does not seem to have been yet clearly recognised. Dräseke declares them to be by different hands[2] and assigns one to Didymus, the other to Ambrosius: Voisin to an unknown

[1] *Def. Tri. Cap.* vi. 3 (Migne, *P.L.* LXVII. 666). This caricature already appears in Vincent of Lerins, *Commonit.* 34 and 36.

[2] His opinion on this point has been rejected by most subsequent writers except Hoss, *Schrift. und die Theol. des Athan.* pp. 128 ff. In view of the close similarity of style and thought and the identity of detail (*e.g.* the genealogy of Mary and Joseph, I. 4 and II. 13; the mistaken account of Valentinus, I. 11 and II. 3; the references to Adam as ἀρχέτυπος, I. 4 and II. 5; the use of the name Christ, I. 13 and II. 3, etc.), Dräseke's proposition seems more than usually gratuitous.

disciple of Athanasius in Egypt: Lietzmann to a date certainly before the fifth century. They all reject the conclusion of the Benedictine editor that on the ground of style "no one familiar with the work of Athanasius will fail to recognise that he is speaking in these books[1]." But they point to the resemblance to the *Ad Epictetum* and the *Ad Adelphium*, and especially to the fact that Apollinarius is nowhere mentioned by name, as proofs that the author was a contemporary and acquainted with Athanasius.

The first book, unlike the second, is complete, and is certainly based upon the letter to Epictetus, which was very famous and widely quoted as authoritative[2], and had already by Cyril's time been interpolated or edited so as to alter its doctrinal emphasis. It is indeed little more than an expansion and paraphrase of that work with certain sections against Apollinarianism inserted between the treatment of Gnosticism at the beginning and Ebionism at the close. The arrangement is the same; the same heretical opinions are attacked; there are constant similarities of phrase; and the doctrinal standpoint is not widely different. Very much of the work is occupied with criticism of ideas which cannot by any stretch of imagination be supposed to touch Apollinarius: Manichaeans are mentioned five times, Arians four, Marcion twice, Rhetorius[3], Valentinus and Sabellius once each: and the arguments are a curious medley of miscellaneous and rather threadbare rem-

[1] In Migne, *P.G.* XXVI. 1091.

[2] It is quoted by Epiphanius, Ambrose, Cyril, Theodoret and Leo.

[3] Apparently an Egyptian who maintained that all heresies had truth in them; cf. Philastrius, *Haer.* xcvi. and Augustine, *Haer.* lxxii. Otherwise unknown.

nants, suggesting that the original material of the *Ad Epictetum* has been eked out with patches collected from such works as the two letters to Cledonius and the *Antirrheticus*. But within it are certain sections which unmistakably refer to Apollinarius, and these deserve special attention. In the prelude in which the author sketches the scope of his work is a section which gives a brief but brilliant summary of Apollinarianism[1]. "Then they say 'Instead of the inner man in us there was in Christ a heavenly mind: He used the form which veiled Him as His instrument: He could not have been a complete man, for where there is a complete man, there is sin: two complete entities cannot become one, else there will be in Christ the strife against sin which there is in us: there will be need for Him of purification like ours, if Christ has taken upon Himself the element which thinks and directs the flesh in us when He becomes man: rather He assumed the mindless, that He might be the mind in it and be wholly without taste of sin owing to the godlike and mindless nature of His flesh: for His flesh would not sin if that which guided the flesh or was the spring of His thought had not conceived the purpose of sin beforehand and did not work through the body the fulfilment of sin: whence Christ has displayed the newness of flesh by His likeness to us, and each of us displays in himself the newness of his intellect[2] through imitation and likeness and ceasing to sin[3]: so Christ is conceived to be sinless.'" This

[1] *C. Apoll.* i. 2.

[2] τοῦ φρονοῦντος.

[3] This saying, more clearly than any other, suggests that Apollinarius believed Christ to have assumed and redeemed the flesh and to have left men free to work out for themselves the salvation of the mind (so Harnack, *H.D.* IV. 162, note). Apollinarius' soteriology, great as is his stress upon it, is none too clear: but he certainly left room for our own effort and did not treat the question solely from the supernatural side.

passage is perhaps genuinely Apollinarian. The strong sequence of the logic, the short and lucid sentences, and the doctrine expressed in them are all redolent of the master, and as different from our author as one Greek writer can be from another. If not a quotation, it must certainly be based upon genuine sayings of the Laodicene. So fair a summary raises our hopes high. Here at any rate there will be no travesty. Yet when we turn to the sections[1] in which this passage is criticised, there is a sorry change. Instead of clear understanding we get hesitations and quibbles and incoherencies. The author takes the Apollinarian psychology in which flesh and soul constitute the outer man, and argues that this is absurd since soul being invisible must be the inner man. Then he says that if Christ's body was laid in the grave and His soul preached to those in Hades, what became of His spirit[2]? Then he criticises, legitimately enough, the view that human souls are sinful, urging that this is to accuse God of having engrafted sin in Adam[3]. Having thus hit a weak spot in Apollinarianism he goes on to prove how accidental was his success, by stating that if Christ's humanity was His instrument, His deity is here as in Arianism made passible: grief and distress cannot belong to a mindless flesh nor to a changeless Godhead, but to a soul possessed of intelligence—an objection which demonstrates the superficiality of his knowledge of his victim[4]. Finally, he sums up by protesting that Christ must have had a passible soul, yet one which, like His body, was above

[1] §§ 13–16.

[2] Origen had already employed this same problem as a proof of the divinity of Christ's spirit.

[3] Augustine would hardly have agreed: but nevertheless this section can scarcely be earlier than the Pelagian controversy.

[4] The charge of Arianism is fatal to Athanasian authorship: and proves that he had missed all the kenotic teaching of Apollinarius.

human weakness: Christ should thus be called perfect God and perfect man, not by any change of divine perfection into human, nor by possessing two perfections differentiated, nor by progress in virtue, but "by a flawless existence that the two may be one complete in all respects, God and man the same." He leaves off, in fact, just where Apollinarius commenced.

We have examined these sections in some detail because they illustrate the character of the book very adequately; and leave us in little doubt as to its character. The second treatise reveals the same quality still more plainly. Lietzmann assumes that it is a fragment; and it certainly has no formal beginning nor ending. Dräseke's conjecture of different authorship seems gratuitous: for setting aside the influence of the *Ad Epictetum* on the former treatise, the style and method of the two are practically identical. We believe it to be an appendix and restatement, compiled after new Apollinarian material had come into its author's possession. This material is quoted, and certain sayings are very close to those found in the *Anacephalaeosis*[1] and fairly represent the arguments used by Apollinarius against Diodore and Paul of Samosata. So far, at least, the author had acquaintance with his subject. When we turn to his criticisms his futility becomes apparent, and now

[1] *E.g. C. Apoll.* ii. 4: "They speak of Christ as a deified man: how then do they interpret 'In the beginning was the Logos' and 'He took the form of a servant'? It is said to mean a man who died for the world, or a man who was part of the world, or a man ruling over angels, or a man worshipped by creation..." (cf. *Anac.* 9 and 28); *C. Apoll.* ii. 6: "If He assumed the whole He must have had human thoughts, and these cannot be sinless: how then can Christ be without sin?" (cf. *Anac.* 10); *C. Apoll.* ii. 7: "If Christ is man, He is part of the world: a part of the world cannot save the world" (cf. *Anac.* 2—almost verbally identical).

that he has lost the guidance of the *Ad Epictetum* his arrangement becomes mere chaos. The book opens by charging its victim with destroying the unity, and asking him how he explains "The Logos became flesh." This is sufficiently wide of the mark: for the quotation is Apollinarius' favourite text[1]. But worse is to come in such a question as "Tell us how you imagine that God came into being at Nazareth?": the denial of the pre-existence of the Godhead is a curious charge to bring against one who was regularly if wrongly accused of teaching the pre-existence of the flesh. Finally, we get an even more amazing suggestion, when the author asks whether these new heretics belong to the school of Marcion or Manes or Valentinus or Sabellius or Arius or Paul of Samosata: the introduction of that last name is enough to convict him either of the grossest ignorance of the whole circumstances of Apollinarius, or of a wild and misplaced sense of humour. In either case he is certainly not Athanasius. That any contemporary of the Bishop of Laodicea could have charged him with being a follower of Arius or of Paul is simply unbelievable.

For the second book this last evidence is amply sufficient: and if, as we believe, there is no good reason for assigning them to different hands, the first will also be spurious. But apart from it, no one can suppose that Athanasius, whose mind is charitable and clear, whose style is pleasant and orderly, and whose intimacy with Apollinarius is undisputed, can have written against him works so full of bathos and inexactitude, obscurity and vituperation. The man who against the wishes of Basil could receive the embassy from Marcellus, of whose error all men were aware, could not at the very

[1] It occurs at least ten times in the extant fragments.

same time have penned these ferocious attacks upon one who had been his friend and against whom no breath of criticism had yet been raised. The few who accept his authorship allow that the books are only a series of notes: in the Fourth Oration against the Arians we have a similar incomplete work, and the difference in tone between the real Athanasius and this narrow and unintelligent usurper of his name is decisive.

Internal evidence proves that they are not Athanasian, and indicates, as we shall show, that they are not contemporary. External evidence is even more conclusive. The first mention of them is to be found in Proclus, who, speaking at the Council in 553, declared that Athanasius "had written these books after the death of Apollinarius[1]"—presumably, therefore, from heaven. Leontius appears to quote the first book, but without mentioning its author[2]. The Sixth Oecumenical Council cites the title and a sentence from the second[3]. John Mazentius ascribes them to Athanasius, and other later writers have a few scattered allusions to them. Evidence of such a character is less than worthless: it tells decisively against them. Already in the generation after Apollinarius the collection of texts from the Fathers was as popular as from Holy Writ. The whole Two Natures controversy was fought on the evidence of authority. Athanasius' works were ransacked from cover to cover by controversialists of both parties in their search for suitable passages. Almost every one of his genuine books and several, like the *Sermo Major* and the *De Incarnatione et contra Arianos* which are generally thought spurious, are cited again and again as early as the middle of the fifth

[1] Mansi, *Conc.* v. 459.
[2] *C. Nest. et Eutych.* i.
[3] Mansi, *Conc.* xi. 368.

century. Yet there is not one which would have supplied such a mass of offensive material as the works against Apollinarius. It is absurd to suppose that Epiphanius would have quoted the *Ad Epictetum* which he admits to be irrelevant, or called Apollinarius "the ever-beloved of the blessed pope Athanasius" if he had known that the Bishop of Alexandria had spent his last moments in pouring venom upon him. Cyril, who cites the *Ad Epictetum* as authoritative, never uses it in his work against Apollinarius, and never questions the agreement between the two, or suggests acquaintance with these books. Theodoret, whose *Dialogue* is furnished with a complete armoury of quotations directed against exactly the views attacked in them, cites two passages from the *Ad Epictetum* but never refers to the *Contra Apollinarium*. Facundus, who, in his defence of Theodore, has quoted several disputable or lost works of Athanasius in order to provide parallels to Theodore's attacks upon Apollinarianism, could have found whole sections of these books relevant to his needs. Perhaps most decisive of all is Apollinarius' own letter to the bishops exiled to Diocaesarea written not later than 376 in which he claims that "the blessed Athanasius had always sent us letters of communion and knew that we were in agreement with him in matters of doctrine."

The argument from silence is always dangerous: but if ever it be permissible it is at a time and under circumstances such as these. And here the evidence proves, beyond a doubt, that these two books were not known at all, either as genuine or as pseudepigraphic, until at least the middle of the sixth century. This fact tells not only against their Athanasian authorship but almost equally against any theory which ascribes them to the fourth century. Didymus or Ambrosius would have been quoted almost as eagerly as Athanasius: a disciple would have been hailed with enthusiasm as his master's representative: any contemporary antagonist would certainly have been used if not cited. The books are forgeries. They belong to the large class of compilations based upon the writings of the Fathers in an age when the circumstances of their times had been forgotten, by men who had collected relevant passages from their works and paraphrased them to suit a new day. This author (for they are obviously by the same hand) has got hold of the *Ad Epictetum* and possibly other familiar fourth-century writings, and a fragment or two of Apollinarius. He has studied the time well enough to know something of the prevailing heresies and possibly a few of the mannerisms of Athanasius. And he sets himself to produce a piece of work which shall be passed off as authentic. Close parallels to it can be found in the letter to Caesarius, also supposedly an attack upon Apollinarius, and ascribed to John Chrysostom, which is even more certainly a forgery, though by an abler hand, and in the Pseudo-Athanasian *Sermo contra omnes Haereses*, which has several points in common with these books[1]. As we have seen, the two books are works of small importance and only their traditional authorship makes them worthy of detailed mention.

As regards the date of their composition, when once the Athanasian authorship is abandoned there is not much to guide us: for Lietzmann's argument that the absence of names proves them to be of the fourth

[1] In Migne, *P.G.* XXVIII. pp. 501 ff. § 11 deals with Apollinarius, representing him as teaching that Christ assumed flesh only, quoting against him John xii. 27, and asking if Christ's Godhead preached to the souls in Hades.

century is wholly unconvincing, and would rather indicate that although based upon Apollinarian material they were meant to be read as a criticism of later heretics. The doctrine of the books is not very consistent: it is on a par with the general level of muddled thought and illogical argument. But certain phrases indicate, if they do not prove, an origin not earlier than the middle of the fifth century. In the first place, there is the very curious misunderstanding of the teaching of Valentinus, who is stated to have taught that the Father and the Holy Spirit "wore flesh[1]" and that "the passion was common to the Trinity since the flesh was part of the Godhead[2]." If these passages are intended to refer to the great Gnostic teacher[3], it seems incredible that they should have been written until after the disappearance of Valentinian churches[4]. Secondly, the continued stress upon Adam and the Fall in many passages[5], which remind us of Theodore of Mopsuestia[6], is not likely to have been introduced before the Pelagian controversy which first made the subject popular. Thirdly, the Christology seems obviously influenced by the ideas current in the Nestorian controversy. Metaphors of mingling are almost entirely absent[7], and in their place

[1] i. 11. [2] ii. 3 and ii. 12.

[3] The words Οὐαλ. διὰ πρόφασιν γνώσεως πλανηθέντος in ii. 19 would make this certain, if γνώσεως and not ἑνώσεως be the right reading.

[4] They still existed in 376; cf. Epiphanius, *Haer.* xxxi. 7: but had disappeared when Theodoret wrote his *Haer. Fab.* Athanasius, in his genuine works, refers frequently and accurately to them.

[5] *E.g.* i. 7; i. 15; ii. 6. In i. 4 we have ὁ ἀρχέτυπος Ἀδάμ, and the idea of archetypal relationship is repeated in i. 7 and ii. 4.

[6] Cf. especially ii. 9 and Theodore, *De Pecc. Orig.* (Swete, II. 335–6) and almost identically Theodoret, *Repr. XII Cap.* III. (Schultze, v. 15).

[7] ἄλυτος σύγκρασις and συγκεράσας occur only in ii. 16.

appear ἕνωσις φυσική[1], ταυτότης φύσεως[2], ἐνυπόστατος[3], φυσικὴ γέννησις καὶ ἄλυτος ἕνωσις[4], διαίρεσις προσώπων[5], and even the familiar εὐδοκία[6], and the adjectives hallowed by the Chalcedonian formula[7]. Again, the use of "Christ" to indicate "both characteristics, Godhead and manhood[8]," and of χρίσις[9], used here in the sense regularly employed by the Nestorians[10], point to a late date. Finally and most conclusive is the distinction plainly drawn between hypostatic and physical union: in arguing that the flesh cannot be consubstantial with the Godhead, the author remarks that "what is consubstantial and impassible and incapable of death is capable of union not according to hypostasis but according to nature with what is consubstantial[11]." The technical use of the terms καθ' ὑπόστασιν and κατὰ φύσιν did not become current at all until the time of Cyril, and even he did not differentiate in this way between them[12]. The contrast reflects the language of the later Monophysite controversies, and could hardly have been stated before the end of the

[1] i. 10, but nowhere else.

[2] This he attacks, i. 5; i. 9, substituting for it ταυτότης ὑπάρξεως ii. 11.

[3] Used of the relation of soul to body, i. 20.

[4] ii. 2; ii. 5.

[5] Attacked ii. 10.

[6] *E.g.* i. 3; i. 5.

[7] ἀσύγχυτος i. 10. ἀχώριστος, cf. ii. 14. ἄτρεπτος *e.g.* i. 3; i. 11; ii. 2, etc. ἀδιαίρετος ii. 2; i. 6; i. 12.

[8] i. 13, ἑκατέρων τῶν πραγμάτων σημασία. It is very notable that he carefully avoids both μία φύσις and δύο φύσεις—an indication that his own doctrine was none too clear. For this use of Christ cf. also ii. 2.

[9] ii. 3.

[10] Cf. Nestorius, *Serm.* ix and x (Loofs, *Nestoriana*, pp. 254, 269); Theodoret, *Dial.* ii (ed. Schultze, IV. p. 75), etc.: but not explicitly in Theodore or Chrysostom or earlier.

[11] i. 12.

[12] Cf. *Apol. c. Theod.*, φύσις ἤγουν ὑπόστασις, etc. They were differentiated first at Chalcedon.

fifth or beginning of the sixth century. Taking everything into account, the complete travesty of Apollinarius, the reliance upon Athanasius and perhaps Cyril, the use of terms and ideas common in the later stages of the Two Natures controversy[1], and the general stupidity of the books, as well as the external evidence, it would be reasonable to reckon them a deliberate forgery perpetrated by a supporter of Chalcedon occupying a mediating position but attacking Monophysite exaggerations probably in the early years of the sixth century.

Of the great Cappadocians, we have already seen that Basil was largely responsible for the formal condemnation of Apollinarius at Rome. At the time when he was trying to rally the semi-Arian party in defence of the Nicene faith, he had been sorely distressed by the suggestion, made against him by Eustathius of Sebaste, on the strength of his early letters, that he was in communion with the bishop of Laodicea who was accused as an Old Nicene of Sabellianism. At the close of 376 he heard from Epiphanius of the errors of the Apollinarians, and though he refused to take any action then for fear of causing schism, he decided in the next year to include a charge against the Laodicene in his letter to the West[2]. This change of policy seems to have been due to the discovery that Apollinarius was setting up independent congregations and thwarting his own

[1] *E.g.* in addition to those already mentioned *μένων ὃ ἦν* (ii. 3 and 16); *ἀνυπόστατος* in its later sense of impersonal (i. 21, ii. 16—where, if the reading be correct, the heretic attacked is quoted as saying: *σάρκα τὴν ἀνυπόστατον συγκεράσας ἑαυτῷ ὁ Λόγος*, a phrase certainly not Apollinarian nor earlier than Chalcedon: cf. Harnack, *H.D.* IV. 224); *ἐνυποστάτως* (i. 20).

[2] *Ep.* 263.

efforts after unity. In his letter to the bishops exiled to Diocaesarea[1] he expands the charges made to Damasus, and accuses Apollinarius of schismatical actions in consecrating bishops, of Sabellianism and of Chiliasm. Of his Christology he only repeats what he had said before, "Does he not confuse the doctrine of the Incarnation by his obscure and vague speculations? To collect and refute them all would take much time and long discussion." In his letter to Patrophilus[2] he admits that he had read few of Apollinarius' works and had no time for modern theology. And it is evident that he had never any acquaintance with the peculiar views which the Roman Council had anathematised, beyond what he had learnt from Epiphanius, and did not know how to deal with them.

Nevertheless it is constantly stated that he wrote against Apollinarius on the strength of his letters to the men of Sozopolis[3] and to the monk Urbicius[4]. Bright[5], for example, writes: "Basil was very vigilant in opposing Apollinarianism, which he considered to be a revival of the old Valentinian heresy, inasmuch as it denied our Lord's body to be truly of the Virgin's substance. All our interest in the Incarnation, he contended, must depend on the real union of our flesh to the Godhead." This latter sentence is a fair summary of Apollinarius' own position, and, as we have shown, what Bright calls Apollinarianism was never taught by the heresiarch. Nor was it in fact ascribed to him by Basil. The two letters above mentioned are grouped according to

[1] *Ep.* 265.
[2] *Ep.* 244. He is there alluding to Apollinarius' Sabellianism.
[3] *Ep.* 261. [4] *Ep.* 262.
[5] *Hist. of the Church from* 313 *to* 451, I. 158.

Maran's[1] arrangement next before that to the Westerns, no doubt because the learned Benedictine thought that they referred to the same subject. But there is not the slightest indication that they were written at this time or deal with the same doctrinal issues: in fact quite the contrary is true. The letter to the Sozopolitans deals with two crude and, as Basil points out, Valentinian Gnostic beliefs, that "there has never been a sojourn of the Lord in the flesh" since "it was with a heavenly body that He came among us," and that "human feelings are attached to the actual Godhead" which is thus rendered passible: that to Urbicius refers only to the opinion that "God Himself was changed into flesh, not assuming Adam's clay through the holy Mary, but in His very Godhead being transformed into a material nature." These are plainly views similar to those condemned in the *Ad Epictetum*, and there is not a hint that they have any connection with Apollinarius. In the case of Athanasius this of itself might not be conclusive; for the great bishop always hesitated to attack his friends by name. But Basil showed no such compunction: when Eustathius attacked him he did not scruple to denounce Apollinarius explicitly to Meletius[2], though he admitted that the document might not be his: and in consequence of that accusation he would have welcomed any evidence against the Laodicene. Manifestly he had not the slightest idea that these errors were in any way due to him. Moreover, in his comments upon them he shows himself wholly deficient in knowledge of the subject. In the former letter he falls back upon the old Logos-doctrine, maintaining

[1] In the Paris edition of which volume III, containing the letters, appeared in 1730.

[2] *Ep.* 129.

that the Lord, after manifesting Himself through the patriarchs, Moses, the prophets and righteous men generally, "was Himself revealed in the flesh," and that since sufferings belong to flesh endowed with soul (ψυχή) or to soul using flesh "the Lord assumed the natural affections in order to prove His incarnation to be real, and not by way of semblance." In the second he is himself neither clear nor orthodox; for after declaring that God is changeless he adds "how could the benefits of the Incarnation be bestowed on us unless our body was joined to the Godhead and made superior to death? For not being changed[1] He constituted a body of His own, which subsisted because the divine nature was condensed into it." Basil was certainly in no position to criticise Apollinarius.

Gregory Nazianzen stands in a different category; for, owing to the intrusion of the Apollinarians into his native place at a time when he was responsible for its control, he was called upon to deal explicitly with the heresy. Apparently he had come into contact with it first at the time of his journey to Constantinople in 379 and gives a brief description of its main doctrine and of the stir which the holding of an Apollinarian synod had made in the East[2]. But during his episcopate in the imperial city he had to devote his whole attention to the Arians, only dealing cursorily with the problem of the Incarnation in his Theological Orations and sermons.

[1] *οὐ τραπείς* is the reading of all the MSS. except one which has *ὁ τραπείς*. The Benedictine edition gets over the difficulty by substituting *εἰ* for *οὐ*, which saves Basil's orthodoxy at the expense of his grammar. As rendered above, Basil's doctrine is not far from certain phases of Hilary's of Poitier, cf. *De Trin*. x. 16–18: "Though Mary contributed all that is natural to her sex, His body did not owe its origin to her....He is the origin of His own body."

[2] *Carmen de Vita sua* 609–51.

It was in 382, when he had retired in disappointment and ill-health from his high place, and was visiting the medicinal baths of Xanxaris, that the subject was thrust upon him. Nazianzus was without a bishop. Cledonius, a priest, was put in charge, and Gregory undertook to supervise him, so far as his illness allowed. The Apollinarians took advantage of the absence of a bishop to set up a congregation of their own, and finally to appoint and consecrate one of their number to the vacant see. Cledonius wrote in great perplexity to Gregory, and the two letters[1] on Apollinarianism are his reply. These were among the documents adopted by the Councils of Ephesus and Chalcedon, and may claim to be the most important of the strictly orthodox criticisms of Apollinarius. Both in their strength and their weakness they are typical of Greek thought on Christology.

In the first of them Gregory bases his condemnation upon the anathemas of the Roman Council of 377, repeating a long series of propositions against various Gnostic and Adoptianist catchwords, most of them more relevant to the Antiochenes than to their opponent. Then he quotes certain texts favoured by the Bishop of Laodicea, which he connects with the belief in a heavenly flesh. These he explains as "uttered on account of the union with the heavenly, the names being mingled like the natures and flowing into one another according to the conditions of their intimate union"—a saying to which Apollinarius would have given whole-hearted agreement. So he turns to the denial of a human mind with which the central paragraphs of his letter are concerned. Here his first and most famous clause is "What He did not assume, He did not redeem," a saying which

[1] *Eps.* 101, 102.

has been praised by Tixeront[1] as "the fundamental argument against Apollinarius," but which seems to reflect a mechanical notion of salvation, like Irenaeus' phrase "He gave His soul for our souls and His body for our bodies[2]." Yet if taken in connection with the later sections, in which Gregory combats the notion that the human mind is necessarily evil and therefore cannot have belonged to Christ, it touches the weakest point in the heresiarch's doctrine. Apollinarius denied the perfect manhood of Christ: that at least was clear; and Gregory was right in arguing that the mind is not more inevitably sinful than the body and that if so "there is an excuse at hand for those who sin with the mind." Next, after the frivolous objection that if Christ's soul was without mind then it was the soul of a horse or an ox, he fastens upon another sound criticism, and one which applies to almost the whole of Greek theology. Apollinarius had argued that two perfect natures could not become one. "Quite so," says Gregory, "if you are looking at the question materially. Two bushels cannot be put into a one-bushel measure. One body cannot hold two bodies. You are dealing with what is mental and incorporeal: my one personality contains soul and reason and mind and the Holy Spirit." Gregory has laid his finger upon the gravest defect of Hellenic and indeed of most early theology, its subservience to chemical and physical metaphors. All through the literature of the patristic age it is constantly evident how seriously its authors are handicapped by their lack of abstract terms and their habit of concrete and materialistic thinking. Instead of conceiving of God in

[1] *Hist. des Dogmes*, II. 115.
[2] *Haer.* V. I. I.; cf. Clement of Rome, *Ep.* i. 49.

terms of love, in terms appropriate to personality, they are concerned with substances, with images borrowed from the fusion of metals or the mixing of liquids or the hybridising of animals, images too crude to do justice to the subtleties of living relationships, and often making their whole treatment of the experiences of religion seem artificial. The human intelligence, especially in the male sex, is always prone to think of problems rather than of persons; and if to-day the habit still besets us, it was deeply ingrained in the mentality of the Greek.

After these very pertinent objections to the psychology and to the metaphysics of Apollinarius, Gregory's own Christology comes as something of a disappointment. Having protested against the dictum that two perfect natures cannot become one, he goes on to show how fully he agrees with what he has rejected, by arguing that relatively to the divine the human mind is of such infinite smallness that "the greater prevails over it" and it is virtually absorbed. Like his adversary, he cannot escape from the physical. Though his language was more capable of an orthodox interpretation than that of Apollinarius, he had not in fact devoted any great attention to the question of Christ's nature. As the Fourth Theological Oration shows, he hesitates between opinions which seem almost to allow a dual person in the Incarnate[1] and others which suggest agreement with the Laodicene[2]. It is clear that whereas

[1] These are collected by Mason, *Five Orations of Greg. Naz.*, Introd. pp. xvi–xix.

[2] *E.g.* iii. 18, where the human sayings and acts of Christ are ascribed to "the composite Being, who emptied Himself and became flesh"; and iv. 3, where the word μίξις is used of the Incarnation, as is σύγκρασις in iv. 8: cf. also *Or.* xxxviii. 13, and xxxix. 13.

Apollinarius, conceiving that a human mind involved freedom of will and the liberty to choose evil, refused explicitly to admit its presence in Christ, Gregory accepted belief in it by emptying it of that very quality which was to his opponent fundamental. Both were agreed that Christ was physically incapable of sin: the heretic maintained that His human mind was replaced by the Logos, the saint that it was absorbed in Him. Dialectically the advantage was with the latter: actually there was little difference between them. To both the centre of Christ's personality was divine.

The first letter concludes with an attack upon the Chiliasm of Apollinarius, and with an interesting accusation that he introduced grades into the divine Trinity, teaching that "it consists of Great, Greater, and Greatest." This charge, which is difficult to reconcile with Basil's complaint against his Sabellianism, is derived from a common source with it. Apollinarius was an Old Nicene: in speaking of the Godhead he used the familiar metaphor of the sun, its ray and its light[1] in preference to that of three human beings like the Paul, Silvanus and Timothy of Basil's famous letter[2]. This at once offended the New Nicenes because it seemed to

[1] This is the regular illustration of Athanasius, cf. *e.g. De Decr.* 23 and 24; *C. Ar.* i. 27; iv. 2 and 10, etc. The analogy from human beings was used so emphatically by the Arians, to prove that the Father existed before His Son, that Athanasius avoids it, and when using it corrects it by other images—fire and its radiance, a fountain and its water.

[2] *Ep.* 38. The attempt of Harnack, *H.D.* IV. p. 155, note, to associate this charge with the phrases in which Apollinarius speaks of Christ as a μεσότης between God and man seems due to his failure to appreciate Apollinarius' doctrine of kenosis. But so far as Apollinarius recognised the eternal potentiality of Incarnation in the Son, he must have admitted that this differentiated the Second Person of the Trinity from the First and the Third.

underestimate the difference between the Persons, and also as appearing to imply a distinction in dignity, "a ladder of Godhead" as Gregory calls it. It is solely upon the use of this metaphor that he bases his case; and if the accusation is valid against Apollinarius, most of the earlier champions of the Nicene faith must stand in the dock with him. The last lines of the letter refer to the psalter and hymns of the Apollinarians and have been already cited.

This reply to the heretics failed to assist Cledonius against them, and a second was consequently despatched soon after. This is less important, since it deals principally with Gregory's former acceptance of Vitalis on the strength of his confession to Damasus. After discussing the Apollinarian use of the text "We have the mind of Christ[1]" and the sense in which they speak of Him as having been made man, he points out that the heretics divide the sayings and acts of the Incarnate just as the orthodox do, ascribing some to His manhood and others to His Godhead: "and yet they accuse us of teaching two natures and of dividing the union." Evidently he had not understood Apollinarius' doctrine of kenosis or the very real meaning which it enabled him to give to the earthly experiences of Jesus.

Two other letters on the same subject are preserved, that to Olympius[2], the Governor of Cappadocia Secunda, and that to Nectarius[3], Gregory's successor in the see of Constantinople. The doctrinal clauses of the latter and its quotation from a pamphlet by Apollinarius have been already discussed. Both letters have a common

[1] This quotation figures largely in Epiphanius' attacks (*Ancor.* 76; *Haer.* lxxvii. 31): but only occurs in one fragment of Apollinarius (Lietzmann, Fr. 155).

[2] *Ep.* 125.

[3] *Ep.* 202.

purpose. The Cappadocians never hesitated to reinforce the arm of the spirit by a timely appeal to the arm of the flesh. Gregory invites Olympius to repress what his letters to Cledonius had failed to avert, and upbraids Nectarius for his slackness in not insisting that the emperor "will gain nothing by his zeal for the Church in other respects, if he allows such an evil to gain strength by freedom of speech."

It is to Gregory of Nyssa, the youngest and in many ways the most attractive of the Cappadocians, that we owe the single surviving treatise in which the Bishop of Laodicea is attacked. Hitherto it has been uncertain how far his critics had actually read and studied the work of Apollinarius. Epiphanius and Basil admittedly had not done so: Gregory Nazianzen quotes only a sentence: but the Bishop of Nyssa took the most important of the heresiarch's Christological books and set himself to answer it. And to his reply we owe much of our most valuable knowledge of the Laodicene. For Gregory follows the plan hallowed by Origen in his defence of Christianity against Celsus, and takes the *Apodeixis* by paragraphs, citing a sentence and commenting upon it. The *Antirrheticus* is a very bad book: but before we examine it, we must in fairness admit that the critical method adopted is largely to blame for its faults, and if the attempt has proved too much for Gregory it has at least preserved for us priceless material from his victim. Even Origen's massive learning, unrivalled gift of synthesis, and firm grasp of the course of an argument were severely tested by the effort to follow sentence by sentence his very able adversary: and between him and Celsus there was a world of difference. Gregory has much less learning, little power of systematic thought, and a fatal tendency to substitute rhetoric for logic: and, in addition, he is so near Apollinarius in his main beliefs that he cannot possibly produce an honest criticism upon much of the heretic's masterpiece. When he attempts to pour scorn upon every passage that he quotes, the result is a pathetic display of incompetence. He takes isolated phrases, sometimes only a few words long, sometimes even questions, treats them as if they were the clauses of a test creed, and then does his best to devise a reply. The mental gymnastics by which he manipulates the clear-cut language of the *Apodeixis* into a shape in which he can get a grip upon it indicate a mastery of the less reputable tricks of sophistry which is by no means edifying in a saint. He tries hard to prove that Apollinarius is self-contradictory, and in so doing falls himself into strange contradictions[1]. He charges him with quibbling, and supports it by a series of quibbles. He endeavours to cover him with ridicule, at the cost of making himself doubly ridiculous. Even when he is dealing with heresy he does not always succeed in avoiding it. Verbal criticism, a bad thing at its best, has not found a good exponent in him. Special pleading to be successful needs a certain hardness and precision of outlook, a legal mind and a power of pungent phrase. And Gregory, who possessed something of the mystic's sense of spaciousness and wonder and is at his best in his touches of poetry when he is describing the manifold splendour of creation and its God, has neither the mind of the dogmatist nor the tongue of the advocate. Here

[1] *E.g.* §§ 7 and 8, where he first argues that Apollinarius gives Christ a full humanity because he allows Him a soul and a body; and then admits that Apollinarius taught that man consisted of three elements, body, soul and spirit.

and there he displays a depth of insight and an earnestness of conviction which lift the whole enquiry on to a high level[1]: but he has never sufficient clarity of intellect or mastery of logic to seize upon the essentials of the matter in dispute or to present his opinions without confusion. No doubt Apollinarius' strained syllogisms and seeming recklessness of phrase invited piecemeal criticism. But the Laodicene had a consistent position, knew what he wanted to say and had the ability to say it plainly: and the contrast between the lucidity and steadfastness of the heretic and the incoherence and captiousness of his critic pitilessly reveals Gregory's utter failure.

Both in temperament and belief he was wholly unsuited to the task. A dreamer who had been forced into practical life by the statecraft of his brother and the fame of his friend; a lover of wife[2] and home whose sister was a strong-willed nun; an artist who chose rhetoric as a profession and was spoiled by it; a coward born of a fighting stock and in an age of conflict[3]; a peacemaker not wise enough to be honest and too simple to escape being found out[4]; Gregory was ill-served by circumstance. There is in him a spirituality which is lacking in the hard and heroic Basil and in the

[1] *E.g.* in §§ 20, 21, where he states his own view of the Incarnation—and incidentally reveals his resemblance to Apollinarius.

[2] The evidence of Gregory Nyss., *De Virgin.* 3, of Gregory Naz., *Ep.* 95, and of tradition whose prejudice was all in favour of representing a saint as celibate is questioned but hardly shaken by Rupp, *Greg. Nyss. Leben und Mein.* But the marriage under the circumstances must have had its happiness marred.

[3] Cf. *Eps.* 18, 22, etc., where he wails over the hardships of travel and unpopularity, and Gregory Nazianzen's condolence, *Eps.* 72, 73, 74.

[4] Basil, *Eps.* 58 and 60, deals with Gregory's forgeries and untruthfulness.

eloquent and amiable Nazianzen. If he had been left to follow his bent, he would probably have died in happy obscurity: with sufficient encouragement he might have produced work worthy to be compared with that of Clement of Alexandria. As it was, his interest in speculation was cramped by the necessities of polemics and his vision of God distracted by a multitude of dogmas. His temper originally placid and contemplative was embittered by hardship and uncongenial activities and speedily degenerated into a febrile petulance. By the time at which his books were written, he can only show his higher quality in occasional sayings of real insight and grandeur: for the rest, it is all verbosity and violence; he is either turgid or shrill. And in the *Antirrheticus* he is at his worst. Apollinarius is at least large and dignified. Gregory is noisy and self-satisfied, pettifogging and vulgar. It is not surprising that the Church has never regarded his work with much favour; for the superiority of the heretic both in ability and in taste shines out on every page.

And if Gregory is handicapped by his character, he is disqualified by his doctrinal position. Amid the welter of arguments produced in the *Antirrheticus*, it is difficult to discover what his own beliefs are: he is too busy refuting Apollinarius to have much thought for consistency or the definition of his own Christology. But in his other writings he manifests, in general and in particular, a very striking resemblance to the heresy. From the fifth and sixth books of his ponderous work against Eunomius, where the doctrine of the Incarnation is under discussion, there can be collected a pretty complete Apollinarian system, a system in some respects more Apollinarian than Apollinarius himself would accept. "We maintain," he writes[1], "that the body whereby He underwent the passion, when commingled with the divine nature was made by the admixture what the nature is which assumed it." He speaks of this union as "a conjunction and a growing-together[2]," regards it as culminating in a complete transformation of the flesh ("The flesh was not identical with the Godhead, until it was transformed into the Godhead[3]") and illustrates the result by his favourite simile of the drop of vinegar mingled with the sea and losing all its qualities "in the infinity of that which surrounds it." The whole argument is summed up in words that might be a quotation from the Laodicene, "Thus came about that unspeakable mixture and concurrence of human littleness mingled with divine grandeur, whereby even the names which are great and godly are rightly attached to the human, and in return the Godhead is called by the human names[4]." We have in fact in these books all the cardinal points of Apollinarianism, the complete union, involving a self-limitation of the Godhead and a mutual interchange of attributes[5], and, in addition, a definitely Monophysite tendency towards the confusion of human and divine from which the Bishop of Laodicea would have shrunk. Only the explicit denial of the human mind is absent, although there is not the slightest sign of the recognition of its importance except as a centre for the human weakness of the Incarnate[6]. Indeed,

[1] *C. Eunom.* v. 3.

[2] *L.c.* v. 5: *διὰ τὴν συνάφειάν τε καὶ σύμφυίαν*. A few lines earlier *ἕνωσις* is used.

[3] *L.c.* v. 5.

[4] *L.c.* vi. 4: *μίξις καὶ σύνοδος τῆς ἀνθρωπίνης βραχύτητος πρὸς τὸ θεῖον μέγεθος ἀνακραθείσης*. Cf. Apollinarius, *De Inc.* (Lietzmann, Fr. 10).

[5] *L.c.* v. 5.

[6] The strongest assertion of the assumption by Christ of a complete humanity is in *l.c.* ii. 13, where he combats Eunomius' denial of a *ψυχή* to Christ.

though his defenders have generally tried to represent that in Gregory's thought the transformation of humanity into Godhead comes only after the passion of Christ, there is much evidence which makes this postponement seem unjustifiable. "The Light of this darkened world," he writes in a letter which shows definite knowledge of Apollinarius' Chiliasm[1], "flashes the ray of His divinity through the whole mixture of our nature, both soul and body, and so appropriated the whole manhood by His own light and assumed it and made it exactly what He is Himself....Let no one misinterpret the words of the Gospel and suppose that in Christ our human nature was transformed to something more divine by gradual progress; for the increase in stature and wisdom and favour is recorded in Holy Scripture only in order to prove that Christ was actually present in the human mixture, and so to leave no room for the conjecture of those who maintain that a phantom or form in human outline and not a real manifestation of the divine was present." And still more significant is the passage in his letter to Theophilus of Alexandria in which, replying to Apollinarius and again quoting the simile of vinegar, he concludes with the words "They might justly suppose that we taught a belief in two Sons if we recognised any nature different in kind and distinguished by peculiar properties alongside the ineffable deity of the Son, or taught that one was weak or petty or corruptible or ephemeral, the other powerful, majestic, incorruptible, eternal. But all these accompaniments of mortality are transformed into the attributes of Godhead: in nothing is distinction perceptible: what one sees in the Son is Godhead, wisdom, power, sanctity, impassibility[2]." Apollinarius, with his repeated insistence that the union

[1] *Ep.* 17. [2] *Ap.* Migne *P.G.* XLV. 1276.

does not effect a change in the body or destroy its peculiar attributes, would have repudiated such barefaced Monophysitism.

Such being its author's outlook, it is quite unnecessary, and would be very wearisome, to review the *Antirrheticus* in detail: a sample or two to justify our condemnation will suffice. The long section[1] in which Gregory attacks Apollinarius' teaching of the heavenly manhood, to which allusion has been already made, is fairly typical. The Bishop of Laodicea had stated that "the man Christ has pre-existence," explaining this by the following words: "The Lord is the divine spirit in the nature of the God-man," words which safeguard the idea against misinterpretation in a materialistic sense. Apollinarius meant, as we have shown, that the Incarnation was an eternal part of the divine plan, a condition of the very nature of the Son of God. Such an idea must have been congenial to Gregory the Platonist, even if he rejected it. But in Apollinarius he will have none of it. The Son of God incarnate before Abraham! Then the flesh of Christ, the flesh born of Mary, existed before Abraham, and Mary herself must be older than Abraham, older perhaps than Nahor. And the pre-existent Christ, was He babe or boy or youth? If He was adult, how came He to be born a baby? If the Incarnation did not begin from the Virgin, God must have eternally consisted of flesh, bones, hair, sinews and fat—a blasphemy worse than anything in Arius or Eunomius. If Christ has flesh eternally and yet is co-essential with the Father, then the Father too has flesh. How can Christ be united to flesh before the ages, when flesh was not yet created? "To show how

[1] §§ 12–19.

absurd is the notion let us but contrast the man who spat and made clay, who touched the ears of the deaf, who slumbered, wept, sorrowed, thirsted and craved water, with God who is ever acknowledged to be incorporeal, invisible, uncompounded, always unlimited and uncircumscribed, omnipresent, permeating all creation, and who as regards His manifestation was made visible in a human circumscription."

Yet amid all the hair-splitting, amid the mass of physical metaphors in which the fusion of minds is treated as analogous to the fusion of metals, of mathematical conundrums as to whether two units added together make one or two, of unflattering comparisons wherein the unfortunate Bishop of Laodicea becomes now an Arian, now a Manichee, now a wolf and now a serpent, and of mere nonsense and vulgarity, there shines out one gleam of gold from the mire. For a moment and apparently at haphazard Gregory utters a doubt which takes us straight back to Paul of Samosata and the book to Sabinus. It is when he is dealing with the question of Christ's growth and development and of the difficulties of Apollinarianism in view of the crucial text in St Luke. The *Apodeixis*, although its author was enabled by his kenotic theory to allow natural increase to the Christ, had limited this to physical stature and human powers: there was for Apollinarius no room for gradual training, for practice and progress in perfection, since such would imply at least the possibility of failure. Epiphanius had already objected that Christ could not be said to increase in wisdom if He had not a human mind, though he had done nothing to solve, or even to show that he realised, the difficulty. Gregory himself, as we have seen, expressly denied the whole possibility of development in the Incarnate. Yet here in criticising a heretic he dares to raise a question which orthodoxy had evaded for a hundred years, and to ask whether virtue is not inevitably bound up with the power of free choice. "Everyone knows," he writes, "that virtue is the right exercise of free-will." "That which is without sin, if this is not the result of free-will, is not at all to be praised: else shall we be praising those who are restrained from evil-doing by imprisonment[1]."

Thus for an instant he propounds an issue which is quite foreign to the general tendency of Greek thought and is indeed the fundamental objection not merely to Apollinarianism but to all other Hellenic theories of Christology, whether ancient or modern. It goes far beyond the difficulty about the sinfulness of humanity which Gregory of Nazianzus had shown to be largely responsible for Apollinarius' error. We have already observed that if the Bishop of Laodicea had lived to see the Pelagian controversy, he would have been able to abandon his belief that a human mind must necessarily be tainted and vicious and so to allow to Christ a manhood which, while physically complete, yet differed from ours as the sinless from the sinful. The work of Augustine destroyed the validity of the Apollinarian axiom that if a human mind was present alongside the divine there would necessarily be discord and antagonism. When it was seen that perfect humanity involved not merely the presence but the sinlessness of a mind, and that sinlessness meant unbroken communion with God, Apollinarius' dilemma became superfluous. But this further criticism of Gregory's is not so

[1] § 41.

easily dismissed. For it raises objection to the whole conception of Christ as necessarily and by nature sinless, to the doctrine of impersonal humanity as much as to Apollinarianism. Apollinarius argued that Christ if sinless could not be perfectly human, since humanity implied the possibility of sin. The orthodox reply to this is to urge that perfect humanity is sinless and that therefore Christ can be sinless without ceasing to be man. Gregory makes the further point that if Christ is necessarily sinless then His nature is not like ours and His virtue of no value to us, and that therefore the Incarnation is actually a mere theophany. The only answer to this is to abandon even the amount of distinction between Christ and ourselves expressed in the attribute of physical sinlessness, and to admit that His humanity was, like ours, capable of sin, but that in fact He resisted temptation and preserved His relationship with God unbroken: and in this case it is difficult to reconcile the conception of such a hard-won, struggling virtue with the changelessness of His Godhead, and to combine the two, the man and the God in Him, in any vital unity. The Antiochenes, who had always recognised the need of true human progress and human virtue in Christ, alone give us any answer to Gregory; and they, despite Theodore's efforts, are involved in the difficulty that we have noted of establishing an organic union between the eternal opposites which formed the basis of the Greek concept of the relation between God and man. The controversies of the next fifty years did little to clear up the position. The lesson which they enforce is simply this, that the physical conception of God, admirably suited to the purposes of early apologetic and to the formulation of clear-cut dogmatic, is fundamentally defective. Only by a return to the Johannine definition of deity as Life and Light and Love can we find escape from the dilemmas of metaphysics. But it was only after many centuries of toil and conflict that any such return was attempted: and the fulness of it has not yet been reached.

CHAPTER VII

THE ANSWER TO APOLLINARIUS

FROM the whole course of our survey we have seen that Apollinarianism grew naturally and inevitably from the parent stock of Christian Hellenism. Apollinarius was simply the boldest and most logical exponent of a doctrine that can be traced back at least to Justin Martyr and is characteristic of the greatest saints and thinkers of the early Church. If his error was merely technical, if his only fault was that he used the terms νοῦς and φύσις in a sense unfamiliar to the Latins, and subsequently under pressure from the emperor repudiated by a moiety of the Greeks, his condemnation was manifestly unjust: to mispronounce Shibboleth when one has never heard the word before is not to be guilty of heresy. If, on the other hand, his fundamental belief was erroneous, then all that is most honoured in the annals of the patristic age is implicated in his guilt and should share his sentence. For the attempt to represent him as an instance of rebellion or perversity, or his doctrine as essentially different from the traditional faith of his fellow-countrymen, can only be supported by ignoring or distorting the work of his predecessors, Justin, Clement, the Origenists and Athanasius, of his contemporaries, the Cappadocians, and his successors, Cyril, Leontius and John of Damascus. The precise formulation of their belief, whether in terms of the Logos veiled in flesh, or of the denial of a human mind, or of the enhypostasia, the divine Person with His two

Natures and two Wills, does not greatly matter. The result is still docetic: there has been no real union of God and man.

That the cause of this failure is due to the fundamental weakness of the concept of God from which Greek Christendom started its theological thought, has been indicated throughout our study of the subject. It will be made still more plain if we consider the work of those Antiochene thinkers who have been so constantly before us, as it appears in their greatest representative Theodore of Mopsuestia[1]. For Theodore took up the conflict which Apollinarius had opened by his attack upon Diodore, and developed against the Laodicene a Christology which is at once strikingly modern in its general presuppositions and yet is too thoroughly Hellenic to be entirely satisfactory.

In order to get a true approach for our consideration of Apollinarianism we have already quoted the work in which Diodore himself criticised his opponents, the book against the Synusiasts[2]. Living to a great age in full communion with the Church, he was able to give his own reply to the charges brought against him: and enough of this has been preserved to prove how close was his thought to that of his pupil and successor. The Antiochene position is so important and its objections to Apollinarianism so illuminating that we cannot close the subject without a detailed examination of it. And sufficient remains of Theodore's writings to provide a

[1] For Theodore, besides the histories of doctrine, there is not much literature. O. F. Fritzsche, *De Theod. Mops. Vita et Scriptis*, Halle, 1836, is still valuable. H. B. Swete, *Theod. Mops. on the Minor Epistles of St Paul*, Cambridge, 1880, gives a collection of the fragments of the doctrinal works as well as a full introduction. Swete's article on Theodore in *Dict. of Christian Biogr.* is particularly full and important.

[2] Cf. above, p. 123.

clear outline of his system. His own orthodoxy, though often criticised, was not definitely condemned until the Fifth Oecumenical Council in 553 A.D., and from the literature of the "Three Chapters" controversy most of the fragments of his Christological work are collected.

As is the case with most scholars, the life of Theodore is little known. Of his youth our only information is derived from two letters[1] of John Chrysostom, the second of which is addressed to a Theodore who may be our man[2]. Both were apparently taken as referring to him in early times[3], and though Tillemont and Montfaucon take different views of the evidence[4], we may safely follow the latter and accept them both as referring to the future bishop of Mopsuestia. The first is a formal composition stereotyped and bombastic, a specimen of the rhetorical exercises in favour at the time, and perhaps intended for wider publication as a warning against worldliness. The second states the facts much more clearly and its tone is personal and affectionate. They tell us that Theodore was a man of noble birth and the heir of large estates; that while being trained by Libanius, the famous professor of rhetoric and friend of Julian, he had been induced to join a brotherhood under Diodore and Carterius, and to take vows involving perpetual celibacy and poverty; that he had shown exceptional fervour in the ascetic life, "giving his days to study and his nights to prayer"; that he had been recalled to the management of his patrimony, had fallen

[1] *Ad Theod. Laps.* i. and ii.—Chrysostom's earliest writings.

[2] They were contemporaries and lifelong friends; cf. Theodoret, *H.E.* v. 39.

[3] Sozomen, *H.E.* viii. 2, refers to the facts and mentions one letter. Both letters are mentioned in *Adv. Nest. et Eutych.* iii. 7.

[4] Both accept the second: but Tillemont argues that the first is to someone else.

in love with the beautiful Hermione and intended to marry her, thus violating his vows and committing adultery against Christ. Considering that Theodore was only twenty at the time, we can scarcely join Chrysostom in the severity of his condemnation. But that severity prevailed. Theodore returned to his obedience, and henceforward the record of his devotion is unstained. What happened to Hermione is not recorded. If these letters were written after Chrysostom's return to Antioch in 369, as certain allusions in them indicate, Theodore must have been born in 349–50. The Commentary on the Psalms which afterwards incurred bitter criticism and for which he apologised as an early writing that needed revision[1], may perhaps have been composed before his fall and in his eighteenth year[2].

The remainder of his life-story can only be pieced together from fragmentary notices. After the lapse he seems to have returned to Diodore, and shortly after Diodore's elevation to the see of Tarsus became one of Flavian's presbyters at Antioch. In or about 393[3] he was consecrated Bishop of Mopsuestia, an important place in Cilicia, where he spent the rest of his days. On Diodore's death an attempt was made to secure his transference to Tarsus, but this was frustrated by Theophilus of Alexandria, who insisted upon the observance of the law forbidding the translation of bishops[4]. He started writing in earnest about the age of thirty-five, attacked sundry heresies including Apollinarianism,

[1] In a letter to Cerdo quoted by Facundus, *Def. Tri. Cap*. iii. 6.

[2] So Leontius, *Adv. Nest. et Eutych*. iii. 8.

[3] Theodoret, *H.E.* v. 39, says that he spent 36 years in his bishopric.

[4] Leontius, *l.c.* iii. 9.

and produced his great work on the Incarnation during the time of his work as a priest at Antioch. In his later years, probably in 423, he was visited by Julian of Eclanum[1] and other Pelagians, and, as was inevitable, found himself in complete sympathy with them in their defence of human freedom and personal responsibility. Their presence gave occasion for his book *Against the Defenders of Original Sin*, from which Marius Mercator has preserved sundry fragments. He died while Theodotus was Bishop of Antioch[2] and apparently in 428, a few months before the outbreak of the Nestorian controversy.

During his lifetime and indeed until the question of his orthodoxy became a notorious subject of party-strife, his fame chiefly rested upon his work as an interpreter of Scripture. Although the Commentaries on the Minor Prophets and the Minor Epistles alone remain entire, fragments of those on the Gospels and the Epistles to the Romans and Hebrews, as well as on Genesis and several other books of the Old Testament are preserved in the Catenists, and he probably covered almost the whole field of Holy Writ. In so doing he was in a sense only following the footsteps of Diodore and the traditional method of the Antiochenes to whom careful study of the Word was the supreme preparation for ministerial life and the supreme object of ascetic retirement. But whereas, alike to Lucian his predecessor and to Chrysostom his friend, the moral and homiletic value of the Bible was predominant, in his case the task was dictated by another motive. During

[1] So Marius Mercator, *In Symb. Theod. Mops.* (Migne, *P.L.* XLVIII. 213).

[2] So Theodoret, *l.c.* Theodotus died in 429.

the later years of the fourth century much attention was being paid to the influence of Origenism. On the one hand the crude and materialistic notions of God and of the future state which came to a head among the Anthropomorphite monks had already led to bitter controversy: on the other, Epiphanius and Jerome were waging ceaseless war upon any attempt to spiritualise belief in the resurrection of the flesh. The Antiochenes, like Apollinarius, had always disliked the allegorical method of Alexandrian exegesis, and Eustathius had attacked Origen by name on this account. But so long as Origen's commentaries remained the standard exposition of Scripture, his influence was inevitable. Even Jerome, fiercely as he renounced his allegiance and abused Rufinus for his translation of the *De Principiis*, could not but admit the unrivalled value of his enemy's scholarship and his own indebtedness to him. The desire to free the Church from this obligation and to supply an independent and less dangerous interpretation influenced Theodore even more certainly than it had done Apollinarius. The lost five books "Against the Allegorists[1]" no doubt explained the character of his commentaries; and their composition accounts for the comparatively slight allusions to Origenism in the existing works. Facundus' statement that opposition to Origen was responsible for the literal and moral interpretations which were afterwards so vigorously criticised is amply substantiated by Theodore's own repudiation of allegory in his commentary on the Epistle to the Galatians[2]; and it is noticeable that in almost every case

[1] Mentioned by Ebedjesu (Assemani, *Bibl. Orient.* III. I. 34) and Facundus, *Def. Tri. Cap.* iii. 6.

[2] *Comm. in Gal.* iv. 24 (Swete, *l.c.* I. pp. 73–6).

in which Origen's exegesis can be compared with his the two are totally different.

But the assault upon symbolism and speculative mysticism was not an end in itself. Theodore was striving for something larger than a method of biblical study. He wished, above all, so to explain Scripture as to justify by its authority the doctrinal position to which he and his colleagues were committed. Swete points out that "Origen approaches the sacred text as a seeker after truth; Theodore as one who has already found the key of knowledge and who, thus furnished, proceeds to unlock the treasures of St Paul's teaching with almost entire confidence in the result[1]." He is, above all, the champion of Antiochene theology. His interpretation is always coloured by his views on the nature of God and man. His labours earned him the title of "the Exegete": he would himself have preferred to be known as "the Theologian." For it is in doctrine that his real interest is centred; and by doctrinal motives his whole work, including his attack upon Apollinarius and his defence of the Pelagians, is inspired. Early in life he received his cardinal belief from Diodore, and for five and forty years he maintained it with a fearless consistency, even when it led him into conflict with the main body of Catholic opinion.

This great principle, of which all Theodore's works are an application, is the conviction that the human element in religion is vitally important and must not be overshadowed or forgotten. To him, as to all the Antiochenes, the efforts of Christian Platonists to see life in all its manifestations as one great act of divine self-revelation seemed alike false to history, unworthy

[1] *L.c.* I. p. lxxvii.

of the dignity of man, and subversive of all sense of the reality of the moral struggle. If the universe were simply a theatre on which a single author spoke his plot through the mouths of puppets, what a mockery it all was! What was the value of prayer, of the fight against sin, of holy purpose and high endeavour, if all men were alike empty masks speaking a prearranged part, unable to swerve a hair's-breadth from their allotted places in the play? If the fall of a soul into sin is merely an incident giving variety to the drama, if it is not an outrage in the sight of God and an act of rebellion against His will, then saints have toiled and martyrs perished in vain. Rather than run the risk of weakening the incentive to moral effort we must insist upon the independence of man, upon his power to promote or to thwart God's purpose, upon his full control of his own destiny, his full responsibility for his every action. We must do so even if it be impossible to reconcile such belief with the supremacy and foreknowledge of God. Theodore was not a sufficiently clear thinker to follow out his convictions to their conclusion or to emancipate himself from the Greek concept of Deity. But holding tenaciously to the divine impassibility and omnipotence, he had the courage to sacrifice his logic by an equal insistence upon human freedom. God and man are still antithetical to one another: but Theodore at least abandons the attempt to reconcile them, and looks for a union along moral rather than metaphysical lines.

This desire to give full weight to the human element underlies his objection to the allegorisers and his treatment of Scripture. He saw that Origen and his school found in the records of the Old Testament only a dark enigma whose meaning was wholly independent alike of the characters of its authors and of the events which they professed to narrate. As "spiritually" interpreted there was in the story of the Fall no Adam, no paradise and no serpent[1]: every detail of the law, every verse of the Psalms, every incident of Jewish history, every utterance of the prophets was torn from its setting and twisted into a cabbalistic revelation of the divine purpose. The accuracy of the records was sacrificed: they were mere fictions embodying moral or mystical teaching. The Bible lost all its objective value. Men can no longer learn from it the knowledge of God and His dealings with them, the development of the religious consciousness, or the value of the struggle for virtue. Instead there is a book of riddles, to be read according to preconceived ideas of what is befitting, as fancy and prejudice dictate. Scholarship disappears: ingenuity in the manipulation of symbolism is all that the student requires. The rival treatment of the Song of Songs is a case in point. To Origen it is "wholly compact of mystic utterances[2]": not only is the general meaning an allegory, but each least epithet is a cryptogram. To Theodore it is a human love-poem, celebrating the joys of wedlock and the beauty of Pharaoh's daughter[3]: if such a view led him to reject it from the Canon we must blame the asceticism of his training. Similarly, when he refers most of the Psalter to the times of Ezekiel or Zerubbabel, or condemns the book of Job as Edomite, or repudiates the accuracy of Chronicles, Leontius may call it "his shameless denial of inspiration, and his love of debased and historical interpreta-

[1] Theodore, *Comm. in Gal.* v. 24. Swete (*l.c.* I. 75) aptly compares Origen, *In Gen.* ii. 9 and 15, and *De Princ.* iv. 16.

[2] *Prol. in Cant. Cantic.*

[3] So Leontius, *Adv. Nest. et Eutych.* iii. 16.

tion[1]": we at least can see that he recognised the importance of authentic historical records and was taking the necessary first steps to secure them. And in the New Testament his method is the same. However much his explanations are influenced by doctrinal considerations, he makes a genuine effort to interpret even down to the slightest word the writer's own meaning. Preconceived ideas undoubtedly prevent him from doing full justice to the thought of St Paul; yet he never deliberately overrides the Apostle's language. His analyses of the argument, his examination of every clause, his enquiry into each allusion, prove that he placed the discovery of the author's intention before all other interests, and sincerely believed that the resulting theology was not his own. If the Alogi are the first Christian critics, Theodore is the first exponent of the historical method of study.

His work as a commentator is governed by the belief that the human factor, the author's particular circumstances and knowledge and spirituality, condition the fulness of the revelation contained in his writings. Man must co-operate with God if he is to be inspired by Him. The same conviction appears in the book on the Incarnation, which was the first, and his book on Original Sin, which was the last[2] of his theological writings, in his attack upon Apollinarius and in his attack upon Augustine. Of the latter, only two out of the five volumes[3] are represented in the fragments, and these are preserved by Marius Mercator, an unintelligent and bigoted opponent. But enough remains if taken along

[1] *L.c.* iii. 11.
[2] Swete, *l.c.* I. pp. lxii and 208, conjectures that the Commentary on the Epistles is later.
[3] So Photius, *Bibl.* cod. 177.

with the commentaries on St Paul to illustrate his position and to explain much of his Christology. In each case Theodore was opposing a ruthlessly logical system, a system which had gained its consistency and completeness by eliminating human freedom. Apollinarius, striving for the divinity and changelessness of Christ, had secured it by denying to Him the possibility of moral struggle: Augustine, in his desire to vindicate the omnipotence of God, had formulated a theory which tended to destroy the meaning of conduct. Theodore's criticism of them both follows the same general lines.

Briefly recapitulated, the steps of the determinist argument are these. Adam, created immortal, disobeyed God and his sin was punished by sentence of death: to prevent the undoing of God's creative work God gave man the power of procreation, sex being thus the consequence of sin: sexuality is itself sinful as involving concupiscence: by the act of begetting children are physically tainted, being literally born in sin: mankind is a mass of corruption in whom dwells no good thing: Christ alone has brought a remedy: baptism into His body the Church washes out our guilt, and His resurrection restores immortality, though sinners and the unbaptised will spend this immortality in hell: God knows who will be saved, and only those predestined to receive His grace can escape damnation. Marius, who was an unpleasant product of this unpleasant belief, naturally cites only those passages which specially shocked his own sensibilities, passages in which Theodore deals flippantly and wittily with the theme. "Surely God knew that Adam would sin: yet He gave him six hours of immortality and after his first meal turned him out of paradise, changing His own plan and punishing man not Satan with death[1]": "Christ gave us the blessing of resurrection, a mixed blessing if we are to spend eternity in torment[2]": "God lost his temper, and for one man's fault sentenced the unborn to death: Enoch, like Satan, was let off; he must have been better than Abraham or Moses or Christ: yet Abel the first righteous man was also the first to die....We are mortal because sinful; Christ was mortal; on this showing He must also have been sinful[3]." But these extracts hardly do justice to the seriousness of his conviction. Theodore argues alike from the wording of Genesis[4] and from the fact of sex[5] that death was no angry afterthought but part of God's original purpose. "God made this present life mortal in order to train us in the pursuit of virtue and to educate us in all things needful[6]." Mortality involves the possibility of change and progress and the exercise of free choice. "God has made us masters of our will so that we can choose what we like[7]." But improvement implies temptation and the likelihood of sin: risk is inevitable if freedom is to be used and trained. Mortality fills us with yearnings after worldy things, the greed of gain, the passion for renown, the lust of pleasure, so that no mortal in this life can be wholly sinless[8].

[1] *De Pecc. Orig.* iii. Fr. 1. Swete, *l.c.* II. 332.

[2] *L.c.* Fr. 2. No doubt sayings of this kind underlie the charge that he mocked at the terrors of the hereafter: cf. *Adv. Nest. et Eutych.* iii. 20, where the author adds grimly that no doubt he knows better now!

[3] *L.c.* Fr. 3.

[4] *De Pecc. Orig.* iv. Fr. 1. Swete, *l.c.* II. 336, quoting Gen. ii. 17.

[5] So Theodore, *In Gen.*, ap. *Catena Niceph.* (Fritzsche, *l.c.* pp. 44–5).

[6] *Comm. in Gal.* ii. 15; Swete, *l.c.* I. 26.

[7] *Comm. in Gal.* ii. 16, Swete, *l.c.* I. 28.

[8] *Comm. in Eph.* i. 7, 8, Swete, *l.c.* I. 126.

Nevertheless, such a state is eminently favourable for the cultivation of character, and God has given us sufficient guidance by warning and precept. "His warnings are enough to bestow full knowledge of goodness if we use our wills[1]." "God's grace summons us to make the effort and promises us a reward: that we abide consistently in the life of faith is not His business but our own[2]." "The man who keeps himself from the influence of evil is a vessel of profit and this is within the power of our own free choice[3]." Sin, unlike death, is "a matter not of nature but of volition"; for Christ, in assuming humanity, did not assume sin[4]. It is perfectly true that "our zeal finds God's grace co-operating with it, and such co-operation is necessary if we are to think and do what is well-pleasing to Him[5]"; yet by giving thought to good works we can earn a rich reward in the future life for a small effort in the present[6]. Any stronger exercise of God's determining power would overthrow human responsibility, would make our perseverance an irrational acquiescence, and reduce us to the level of the brutes[7].

Thus Theodore makes a real attempt to give due weight to each side, although, like all the semi-Pelagians, he finds it a hard task. It is when he tries to analyse and explain the source of our impulses towards good that his thought reaches its highest level. He has allowed that man cannot in this life remain virtuous unaided, but has rejected Augustine's claim that in every case the choice of virtue is originated by God's

[1] *In Gal. l.c.* [2] *In Gal.* v. 9, Swete, *l.c.* I. 91.
[3] *In 2 Tim.* ii. 22, Swete, *l.c.* II. 211.
[4] *De Pecc. Orig.* iii. Fr. 3, Swete, *l.c.* II. 335.
[5] *In Phil.* ii. 13, Swete, *l.c.* I. 225.
[6] *In 1 Tim.* vi. 20, Swete, *l.c.* II. 187. [7] *In Gal. l.c.*

Holy Spirit. It is left for him to apportion the parts played respectively by divine grace and man's free will, or at least to justify his belief that each has its proper function. In doing so he avoided the difficulty into which some of his Pelagian friends fell of treating the divine and human agents as if they were wholly independent and of asking which of them takes the first step. Instead he declared that every good action can be considered from two points of view; on one side it is a manifestation of God's power, on the other, it is an expression of man's will: the process which results in a good action can be rightly interpreted as either divine or human. There must be co-operation between the two: it is because God reveals Himself in man that goodness is possible; it is when man voluntarily enters into relationship with God that it is achieved. Between them there is the link of love. In putting his thought into words Theodore has recourse to language almost identical with that of Paul of Samosata[1]. Man is drawn to God and God bestows Himself upon man, in proportion to man's devotion to virtue. Between God and His saints there is a mutual goodwill, an affection to which Theodore gives the characteristic word εὐδοκία[2]. And this is in one sense the result and in the other the cause of all human holiness. The fixed disposition of God is such that wherever there is good we can recognise a manifestation of His goodwill: yet such goodwill is only revealed where there is a real effort after good on the part of man. In one aspect it is the right exercise of human choice which earns as its reward the indwelling

[1] Theodore expressly condemns Paul in *C. Apoll.* iii. Fr. 12, Swete, *l.c.* II. 318, and *De Myster.* xiii. *l.c.* 332.

[2] For its meaning, cf. below, p. 302.

of the divine εὐδοκία: in another this indwelling is a divine gift bestowed by God's foreknowledge in anticipation of and to inspire human merit. The analysis may not be very logical, and the statement of it is often exaggerated and one-sided. Sometimes his language seems sheer Pelagianism: sometimes the stress laid upon providence seems to leave no escape from determinism. But, in general, he refuses to resolve the paradox, and is content to insist that each set of facts is true and necessary. Considering his own strongly intellectual outlook and the desire of every controversialist to construct a complete system as inevitable as a proposition of Euclid it is remarkable that he is so successful. A satisfactory synthesis may be beyond his power. Contrasted with the clear-cut logic of Augustine the conflicting aspects of his belief make him appear muddle-headed and obscure. At least he has the courage to prefer truth to consistency; and although after his death opponents arose who demonstrated the instability of his work and by exaggerating one side of his paradox convicted him of heresy, Catholicism has rejected Augustine's doctrine much more decisively than Theodore's. The heretic was less in error than the saint.

With these preliminaries we can turn to the central phase of his life and consider his doctrine of the Incarnation; for the general position which we have been sketching underlies his criticism of Apollinarius. Unfortunately, our knowledge both of the fifteen volumes of his great treatise and of his various books against Apollinarianism is derived almost entirely from fragments, and the sources are wholly biased in their quotations. The propagandists and pamphleteers of the sixth century, Facundus on one side, Justinian and the various authors whose works are traditionally ascribed to Leontius on the other, and the Acts of the Fifth Council have between them preserved a number of his utterances and these naturally the most heretical. It is not their fault if posterity judges Theodore leniently. Facundus, his sole apologist, is well-meaning but not too intelligent; in spite of the length of his Defence he has quoted singularly little and omitted almost everything of importance: he gives us his opening speech as counsel for the accused in full, but has not thought it necessary to preserve the evidence to which it is the introduction. The commentaries on the Epistles furnish some assistance, but cannot take the place of a considered statement of doctrine. If justice is to be done to the great Antiochene, we shall have to correct the incompleteness of our picture of him by reference to the newly discovered writings of Nestorius. If Theodore was justly condemned as responsible for his fall, he must be allowed to benefit by his vindication. But for our present purpose, the discovery of his objections to Apollinarianism, his own works are sufficient: a one-sided presentation of his Christology, though it may do him an injustice, will bring out all the more clearly his criticism of the Bishop of Laodicea.

Apollinarius had based his belief upon the contention that Christ in order to conquer Satan and redeem mankind must be free not only from actual sin but from all possibility of yielding to temptation. He must be perfect by nature not by practice or effort, good without possibility of change: only so could He be truly divine. Believing that the highest human mind must inevitably fall short of this, Apollinarius had denied the complete manhood of the Incarnate. The Cappadocians only differed from him in representing the human mind as assumed but absorbed by the divine: they had not the least doubt that the centre of His personality was the Godhead and that He was physically incapable of sin. We have seen that Gregory of Nyssa[1] alone and for a moment raised the question whether the possession of changeless and automatic virtue would not render Christ's temptations a mockery and empty His sinlessness of all meaning. It was left to Theodore to develop this criticism and base upon it a general attack upon Apollinarianism and the Hellenic Christology akin to it. "If Christ did not receive a soul[2] and if it was His Godhead that conquered sin, then there is no possible advantage to us in His achievements; for what is there in common between the Godhead and a human soul when the attainment of a perfect way of life is in question? Our Lord's struggles would seem to have been merely the gratification of a love of display[3]." He adds that this is obviously incredible and that the effort to overcome temptation was a fierce struggle on our behalf. Like ourselves, He was assailed "by the passions of the soul and those of the flesh." "In assuming flesh and soul He strove through each to win each, alike by mortifying sin in the flesh, taming its lusts and making it readily subject to the direction of His soul, and by educating His soul and training it to subdue its passions and to restrain the lusts of the flesh. It was the indwelling Godhead that effected these conquests, the indwelling

[1] Above, p. 270.
[2] *Anima*—the Latin version may be responsible for the inexactitude, which is here unimportant. Theodore uses generally a twofold division, though there are passages in which spirit is treated as a separate and controlling element.
[3] *De Inc.* XV. Fr. 3, Swete, *l.c.* II. 311.

Godhead that healed the ills of each[1]." This plain declaration that alongside of the divine in Christ there must be a true manhood, a manhood whose conflicts and temptations are no stage play, can be paralleled in a famous extract from the books against Apollinarius[2]: "If the Godhead, as you declare, took the place of the sense[3] in Him who was assumed how did Christ experience terror in His Passion." That His fear was real is proved by His cries to the Father, by the drops of sweat and the need of ministering angels. Yet such manifestations, though quite consistent with a theory of close co-operation between human and divine, are impossible if His Person was wholly divine. Later from the same book a passage is quoted in which an additional proof is drawn from Christ's rebuke to St Peter: the words "Get thee behind me Satan" show that Christ's mind was capable of being scandalised by Peter's criticism and must therefore have felt the possibility of another course of action[4]. Finally, in other sayings, he argues "If as they say Godhead took the place of sense in the Lord Christ incarnate, why did Christ need the co-operation of the Holy Spirit? For on their view the Godhead of the Only-begotten would not have needed the Spirit for justification, for conquering the devil, for working miracles, for learning what course He had to pursue, for remaining stainless. Had Godhead taken the place of sense, its virtue had sufficed for all this; nay, all His actions must have been accomplished from

[1] *L.c.*

[2] *C. Apoll.* iii. Fr. 4, Swete, *l.c.* II. 315.

[3] *Sensus*. This probably translates *αἴσθησις* and may be used in reference to the wording of the *Tom. ad Antioch.*: or it may be used for *νοῦς* which would be more accurate as against Apollinarius.

[4] *C. Apoll.* iii. Fr. 5, Swete, *l.c.* II. 315; cf. also *l.c.* Fr. 10, p. 317.

that source, so that the indwelling of the Holy Spirit would have been superfluous[1]": and this is to contradict the whole tenour of Scripture. The facts of His guidance and inspiration prove that there was in Christ a nature which required to be guided and inspired. It is evident from the fragments that this particular book dealt chiefly with this aspect of his criticism of Apollinarius, and as we find the arguments recapitulated in the last volume of the *De Incarnatione* it is probable that Fritzsche's[2] conjecture is correct, and that though quoted as from the third volume "against Apollinarius" both this and the fourth volume are in reality part of the longer work.

This insistence on the manhood of Christ is the real basis of Theodore's Christology. His second criticism of Apollinarius is equally radical, and is contained in the fragments of his fourth volume. In this he attacks the theory of the transference of attributes which he regards as a bewildering subterfuge whereby the heretics are enabled to escape the just consequences of their denial of a true humanity and to quibble with the meanings and implications of the words God and man. Certainly they had used this device in order to apply to the Godhead qualities and experiences which could only belong to humanity, and which can have no proper place in the constitution of one who had no human centre of personality. Theodore suspects that they are

[1] *C. Apoll.* iii. Fr. 7, Swete, *l.c.* II. 316; cf. also *l.c.* Frs. 6 and 11, pp. 315, 318.

[2] *L.c.* pp. 91 ff. Swete, *l.c.* II. p. 312, regards this as not proven. Theodore certainly wrote against Apollinarius several works (so Facundus, *Def. Tri. Cap.* viii. 4), one of them thirty years after the *De Inc.* (so fragment *ap.* Facundus, *l.c.* x. 1). The *De Inc.* was itself directed against Apollinarians and Eunomians (Gennadius, *De Vir. Illustr.* 12).

really making Christ's divinity passible when they represent the sufferings of the body as transferred by the fact of union to the Deity and that a body to which divine attributes can be attached is no human body at all. To talk of God the Word as having been made man as a result of such a process is absurd for anyone who has not been infected with Apollinarianism. The use of such language involves a confusion of the two elements. "We should never allow it to be said that He was made man in your sense of the words, though we quite admit that He assumed man[1]." The first case cited by Theodore to disprove the principle of *Communicatio* is drawn from the analogy of soul and body which, though admittedly separate natures, combine to form a single man. Apollinarius[2] had employed this same illustration in his own argument against the confusion of the elements, pointing out that though the two are perfectly united their properties remain distinct, the soul continuing invisible and the body mortal. Theodore developed this contention and asked: "Are we to preserve the distinction which you allow by confusing the two natures and saying on the principle of transference that the soul is flesh and the flesh soul? The soul is, you admit, immortal and rational: the flesh is mortal and irrational. Are we to transfer the attributes and say that the mortal is the immortal and the irrational rational?...So it is in the case of the Lord Christ, although the unity of the nature assuming and the nature assumed is inseparable and cannot be in any way dissolved, that which assumes is not that which is assumed, nor is the assumed the assuming[3]." In a

[1] *C. Apoll.* iv. Fr. 2, Swete, *l.c.* II. 319.
[2] *C. Diod.* Lietzmann, Frs. 134, 135.
[3] *C. Apoll.* iv. Fr. 1, Swete, *l.c.* II. 318–9.

similar way he protests against Apollinarius' dictum[1] that "He who was before the ages has become Him who is in these last times," declaring that if this is allowed then we must be prepared to turn everything upside down to the great distraction of the faithful. "If we follow your principle let us abolish all distinction between the form of God and the form of a servant, between the temple and the dweller in the temple, and between all such familiar antitheses[2]." Such criticism, if directed solely against Apollinarius, may be exaggerated and unfair; for the heresiarch was always careful to say that such transference does not involve change or confusion, and is only to be regarded as language legitimated by the completeness of the union. Even Theodore does not always refuse to employ the principle of transference to justify certain expressions provided there are adequate safeguards against confusion[3]. But certain of the Apollinarians and still more their Monophysite successors did in fact fall into the errors which Theodore denounced and had tried to prove that in doing so they had the authority of the Bishop of Laodicea behind them. It was certainly important in the interests of clear thinking that the two natures if they were to be considered as opposites should be kept separate; and the suggestion that the *Communicatio Idiomatum* is a piece of sophistry which means nothing unless it means that God and man are identical was a valuable contribution to theology.

In consequence of this insistence that the attributes of Christ's manhood are real in themselves and must not be confused with or transferred to His Godhead,

[1] Cf. *Ad Jov.* I, Lietzmann, p. 250.

[2] *C. Apoll.* iv. Fr. 3, Swete, *l.c.* II. 320. Cf. *De Inc.* x. Fr. 3, Swete, p. 302.

[3] Cf. *Ad Baptiz.* Fr. viii, Swete, *l.c.* II. 325.

Theodore raises against the Apollinarians an issue which soon after his death became painfully notorious. We have seen that Apollinarius appealed to the title of Mother of God applied to the Virgin as a corroboration of his Christology. From his words it is probable that the term θεοτόκος was at that time popular but not universally accepted. The first, longest and most famous of the fragments from Theodore's third book against Apollinarius challenges the statement that "He who was born of the Virgin is God and of God, being consubstantial with the Father." Theodore asks how this can be, unless the child is, materially speaking, the creation of the Holy Spirit, and goes on to express his own opinion. This is, that the Son of God was indeed present in that which was formed in the womb: "from the first moment of its formation it received the privilege of being the temple of God": "but we must not on that account suppose that God was born of the Virgin, unless indeed we suppose the temple and the Logos, the God in the temple, to be the same....For if, as you say, He who was born of the Virgin was not man assumed but God made flesh, how could He who was born be called God of God and consubstantial with the Father, since flesh cannot be given this title? It is ridiculous to say that God was born of the Virgin....If so, the flesh must be called God of God....It was not the divine nature that was born of the Virgin: He was born of the Virgin who consists of her substance. It was not the Logos of God that was born of Mary: He was born of Mary who was of the seed of David. It was not the Logos of God that was born of a woman: He was born of a woman who was formed in her by the power of the Holy Spirit. He who is consubstantial with the Father has not issued from the womb, for according to St Paul's words He is 'without mother,' but He was born who was formed in these latter days by the power of the Holy Spirit in His mother's body, and is therefore called 'without Father[1].'" Obviously, if this passage stood alone we should infer from it that Theodore would have repudiated the title θεοτόκος altogether, and that whatever may be said of his unfortunate successor he at least was a Nestorian. But when he recapitulates his argument in the last volume on the Incarnation, he uses much more guarded language. He protests against the use of antitheses, warning his readers that they may easily be driven into a false position if they answer such questions as "Was it God or man that was crucified?" and saying "When they ask us 'Was Mary mother of man or mother of God,' let us say 'Both: the first by the nature of the fact, the second by association[2].' For she was mother of man by nature since He who was in Mary's womb and issued from it was man; she was mother of God since God was in the man who was born, not circumscribed in His nature within man"—a hit at the Apollinarian doctrine of kenosis—"but being in him according to the disposition of His will[3]." In controversy he might utter phrases which exposed him to the charge of dissolving the true union of Godhead and manhood in Christ, but in his own Christology he strove to give due weight to each. "Men would fain make a case against us," he writes, "on the ground that

[1] *C. Apoll.* iii. Fr. 1, Swete, *l.c.* II. 313–4.

[2] ἀναφορᾷ, which the Latin renders as *relatione*. In Theodore's Creed (Hahn, *Biblioth. der Symb.* pp. 302–4; Swete, *l.c.* II. 327–31) ἀναφορά, in the only place where its Latin rendering is intelligible, appears as *societas*; and this is probably its meaning here.

[3] *De Inc.* xv. Fr. 2, Swete, *l.c.* II. 310.

if we speak of two perfect entities[1] we must necessarily speak of two Sons. We do not speak of two Sons, but rightly confess one Son, since the distinction of the natures ought necessarily to remain, and the unity of the person to be preserved inseparably[2]." And again, "Each is rightly called Son since there is but one person constituted by a union of natures[3]." And an excellent summary of his position is contained in the Creed which despite the protests of Facundus is certainly his composition[4]: "God the Logos assumed a perfect man of the seed of Abraham and David and of the same nature as they, a man perfect in nature, of a reasonable soul and human flesh subsisting. This man in nature like ourselves and formed in His mother's womb by the power of the Holy Spirit He conjoined in fashion indescribable to Himself. He prepared Him for the trial of death, raised Him from the dead, uplifted Him to heaven and set Him at God's right hand, whence He receives worship from all creation as possessing an inseparable conjunction with the divine nature by association with God and sharing in His mind[5]. We do not speak of

[1] The famous δύο τέλεια of the Apollinarian aphorism.

[2] *De Inc.* xii. Fr. 2, Swete, *l.c.* II. 303–4.

[3] *De Inc.* xv. Fr. 1, Swete, *l.c.* II. 309.

[4] Facundus, *Def. Tri. Cap.* iii. 2, believing that this Creed had been condemned by the Council of Ephesus, where it was quoted *Act.* VI. (Mansi, *Conc.* IV. pp. 1347 ff.) and possibly condemned, along with all others except the Nicene, implicitly by Canon VII (a view maintained by the Fifth Oecumenical Council *Act.* IV), and finding its condemnation a stumbling-block, represents it as the work of two presbyters otherwise unknown. Fritzsche, *l.c.* pp. 119–122, is certainly right in arguing that style, content and scriptural quotations prove it to be by Theodore.

[5] ἀναφορᾷ θεοῦ καὶ ἐννοίᾳ: the meaning is very obscure and Marius Mercator's Latin version, *supra omnem cogitationem et intellectum*, seems to have no relation to it. For ἀναφορά cf. above, p. 295, note.

two Sons or two Lords, since there is but one Son by nature, God the Logos, with whom He shares the title and honour of Son by conjunction and participation in the Godhead....We speak of one as Lord, even the Lord Jesus Christ by whom all things were made: primarily we mean God the Logos who is in essence Son of God and Lord, but with Him we mean also that which was assumed, Jesus of Nazareth, whom God anointed with spirit and power, as sharing Sonship and Lordship in conjunction with God the Logos[1]."

From this summary of his belief it is clear that Theodore's opposition to Apollinarius is not confined to an attack upon certain phases of his thought or upon the particular denial of a human mind which brought the Bishop of Laodicea into conflict with the orthodox Alexandrian and Cappadocian doctrine. Gregory of Nyssa and even Cyril could criticise Apollinarius' definition of the mode of the Incarnation, though fundamentally they are thoroughly Apollinarian. Theodore represents a wholly different method of approach to the problem. Between him and them there is the same divergence as between the moderns and the traditionalists of to-day. It is this which gives his work its present significance. The Church has decided that Apollinarianism is a heresy. Apollinarius can only be condemned by those who are prepared to allow that the whole Greek school from Justin to Leontius and John of Damascus is similarly at fault, since the divergences between them and the heresiarch are merely verbal and superficial. Theodore is the greatest representative in patristic times of a tradition earlier than the Hellenic, a tradition which insisted that instead of

[1] Hahn, *Biblioth. der Symb.* pp. 303–4; Swete, *l.c.* II. 329–30.

starting from the belief that Jesus is the Logos incarnate, we must start from the facts of the Gospels, from the manhood not the Godhead of the Master. Like the Apostles we must begin our discipleship at the feet of the Man of Nazareth, learning by patient study of the records to know Him in the days of His flesh, absorbing His teaching and letting His personality make its impact upon us. When we have been convinced by contact with Him and by experience of His power to save, we shall be led as they were led to confess Him Lord and God; and our knowledge of Him will fill our thought of His Father with a new content. Thus and thus only can we reach a Christ-centred theology. But this is not the method of the Greeks. They began at the other end, with Christ as the incarnate Word. Their interest was in His relation to the Father rather than in the facts of His earthly life, in the problem of His descent from heaven and the difficulty of reconciling a life of service and suffering with preconceived notions of deity. Such a line of approach involved them in constant difficulties, as they strove to adapt the evidence of the New Testament to their theories of what incarnate Godhead would say or do. The Jews were not the only people who found the Cross a stumbling-block: Greek orthodoxy was always tempted to minimise or make apology for the remnants of humanity in Christ which its exegesis was unable to expunge from His portrait: at heart it was as incurably docetic as is much of our traditional religion to-day. Theodore draws his importance not so much from his own greatness: he is an uninspiring writer, full of repetition, obscure and unattractive in style and often crude and exaggerative in his presentation. But he is the outstanding member of a school in which we can recognise a type of theology not far removed in method or result from that to which the scientific movement has constrained us. He at least starts from history not from dogma, sifts the evidence of the New Testament, accepts its obvious emphasis upon the manhood of Christ, and only then asks himself in what sense the Nazarene is God. We may well conclude our study with a survey of his general position.

Of the manhood of Jesus, Theodore has no doubt: albeit enshrining the Logos Jesus was a man of the very substance of our race. It is interesting to compare his exegesis of the crucial text in St Luke's Gospel[1] with that of Athanasius. The Alexandrian writes: "Progress is of the body: as it progresses there progresses in it the manifestation of the Godhead to those who saw it[2]." The Antiochene is less obscure, "Jesus progresses in age as time passes; in wisdom by acquiring understanding in accordance with the passage of time; in favour by following the virtue which accompanies understanding and knowledge; from this virtue favour with God takes its increase for Him[3]." Athanasius is thinking in terms of Godhead revealing itself more fully as the envelope of flesh in which it is contained expands: Theodore sees the development of a human being perfectly correlated with the development of the relationship between that human being and God. There is in Jesus the normal growth from infancy to childhood, though naturally the union between Him and the Logos makes His advance steady and rapid. "Before He reached the age at which other men properly make a distinction between good and evil in their actions[4], He

[1] ii. 52.

[2] *Or. c. Arian.* iii. 52.

[3] *De Inc.* vii., Swete, *l.c.* II. p. 297.

[4] The reference is to Isaiah vii. 16, a verse regularly interpreted by the Fathers as Messianic.

had an advantage and pre-eminence over the rest of mankind. If even among ourselves there are often found infants who give proof of such understanding as to surprise an onlooker by an intelligence beyond their years, it was of course inevitable that this man should far surpass those of His own age[1]." This period of development Theodore regards as continuing until the Baptism, an event to which, in common with the New Testament and the Antiochene school, he attached the greatest importance. "The glory of adoption" (that is, of conscious Sonship) "so far as His manhood is concerned He first received when He was baptised in the Jordan[2]." "Before His baptism He observed the law with due care, after it by the Spirit's co-operation He fulfilled with as great care the life of grace[3]." From it springs the power to overcome Satan, work miracles, and undertake His active ministry[4]. Yet His humanity is still real and to some extent still developing. He suffers fear, is exposed to temptation, and is strengthened by external support. The triumph is guaranteed by the fulness of His conscious union with the Logos: it is not yet consummated; and only after the resurrection is a complete and manifested unity achieved. "He received at the first a human soul immortal and endowed with sense: He raised it to immutability by the resurrection....He sits at the right hand of God as judge of the whole world since the divine nature exercises judgment in Him[5]."

[1] *De Inc.* vii., Swete, *l.c.* p. 297. Cf. also *De Inc.* xii. Frs. 2 and 7, Swete, *l.c.* pp. 303, 306.

[2] *De Inc.* viii., Swete, *l.c.* p. 298.

[3] *De Inc.* xiii. Fr. 1, Swete, *l.c.* pp. 306–7: cf. *De Inc.* vii. p. 296.

[4] Cf. *C. Apoll.* iii. Fr. 7, Swete, *l.c.* p. 316.

[5] *C. Apoll.* iii. Fr. 10, Swete, *l.c.* p. 317.

Accepting as he does the attribute of changelessness as characteristic of God, Theodore recognises that the facts of the Gospels, the facts of growth and struggle and suffering in Jesus, are incompatible with the idea of an essential indwelling of the divine in Him. Greek thought had insisted that the Godhead of the Incarnate was an *οὐσία οὐσιωμένη*, and whether this means that the inmost stuff of the nature of Jesus was deity, or, as we believe, that the centre of His personality was not human but divine, Theodore will have none of it. If Godhead is united with manhood in this fashion then no sophistries can conceal the fact that Godhead is capable of growth, struggle and suffering. Subtleties like the theory of kenosis or the principle of *Communicatio* only obscure the issue: they cannot alter the conclusion. Moreover, such a union of essence is not only false to the New Testament, it is false to the whole nature and method of God. "If we say that His indwelling is in essence, we must either confine His essence to those alone in whom He is said to dwell, in which case He will be outside all else—a monstrous idea to apply to a nature unlimited, omnipresent, uncircumscribed—or we must suppose that because He is everywhere present in essence, that this omnipresence bestows His indwelling upon all, upon men, upon beasts, upon stocks and stones. Both of these are absurd, and it is ridiculous to speak of the divine indwelling as effected essentially[1]." Theodore has revolted against the materialistic and chemical analogies from iron and fire, from gold, silver and electrum, from the drop of vinegar and the ocean, which had made Greek thought so painfully artificial. He turns from the category of the

[1] *De Inc.* vii., Swete, *l.c.* p. 294.

physical to that of the personal, from the relationships of substances to those of personalities. "As we cannot suppose the divine indwelling to be effected by essence or energy, what remains? Obviously we ought to say that such indwelling is effected by goodwill (εὐδοκία): for goodwill signifies that best and highest desire of God which He exercises when He takes pleasure in those who are eager to cling to Him[1]."

This is the greatness of Theodore as it had been of his predecessors, that he breaks away from the characteristic emphasis upon the metaphysical and substitutes for it a stress upon the moral and personal: εὐδοκία takes the place of οὐσία. And here the current translation of the word has done him injustice. "Complacency" has a chilly and formal sound: it suggests a distant alliance between partners ill-matched and loosely connected: it sounds Nestorian. Theodore wished to express a link far closer and more vital: εὐδοκία to him rather means "love"; and "love in action" or "love expressed by will" would render it adequately. We must remember that ἀγαπή, in spite of its scriptural usage, was never quite dissociated from implications inconsistent with Divine impassibility and had seldom commended itself to Greek Christians as an appropriate description of the relation between God and man[2]. To express an affection free from sentimentality, a yearning undisturbed by spasms of emotion, a love serene and pure and holy, εὐδοκία, sanctioned as it was by the song of the Angels, was the least unsatisfactory word. And as we realise that Theodore meant by it what we are not afraid to call love, much of his dullness disappears. His prosaic and

[1] *De Inc.* vii., Swete, *l.c.* p. 294.
[2] In patristic theology its use is exceedingly rare.

redundant paragraphs reflect something of the glory of the Fourth Gospel.

This definition of the method of God's indwelling brings the special relationship between God and man in Jesus into line with the whole attitude of the Father to His children. Wherever men seek righteousness there is manifested the loving presence of Him who is its source. "He draws near to some and shrinks away from others, determining His relation in every case in accordance with the quality of His disposition.... Though present everywhere in essence, He is separated from the unworthy by the quality of His disposition[1]." God cannot deny His own nature: He cannot force His love upon those who say "evil be thou my good": only as men respond by the exercise of their prerogative of choice, can God reveal Himself in them. Theodore has already developed this thought in his treatment of inspiration and of man's free will: he applies it fearlessly to his interpretation of the Incarnation. God's presence in Jesus must be analogous to and in harmony with His whole dealings with mankind. The communion between God and man in Jesus, if it is to be intelligible, must be stated in terms similar to those which describe His communion with ourselves.

Is not this to reduce Jesus to the level of a prophet? Was not Apollinarius right when he said that such a Christ could not be the Saviour of the world? Orthodoxy has rejected the belief that the Incarnate differs only in degree from His human brethren, and the instinct which demands a divine Redeemer is too strong and elemental to be overlooked. Theodore saw this plainly enough; and in the next paragraph to that quoted

[1] *De Inc.* vii., Swete, *l.c.* p. 295.

above sets himself to discuss it. "When we speak of an indwelling in the apostles or the righteous, this is effected by God's love to them, by His characteristic pleasure in their virtue. But we do not admit that the indwelling in Jesus took place on this wise: to do so were sheer madness. In Him it was as in a Son. Thus by an act of love accomplished once for all[1] He dwelt in Him. That is to say, by the act of indwelling He united to Himself wholly the man whom He assumed, and prepared Him to receive a share in every privilege which He, the Indweller, the Son by nature, already possessed. In consequence, according to this union, He constitutes with Him a single person, He makes Him His partner in all authority, He accomplishes all things in Him, He completes the judgment of the world in Him and in His presence[2]." "The Logos was present in Him not merely at the Ascension, but at the Resurrection,...not merely at the Resurrection but at the Crucifixion and the Baptism. It was present alike during the Gospel-life which followed baptism, and in the period of obedience to the Law which preceded it; at the Presentation, at the Circumcision, at the Swaddling of the Newly-born, and from the first moment of Conception[3]." "This indwelling differs wholly from the ordinary indwelling of God and from the gifts of grace which we see in so many. It is peculiar inasmuch as we speak of the two natures as united, and of one person as constituted by their union[4]." "This union of natures

[1] Note the aorist participles εὐδοκήσας and ἐνοικήσας and contrast it with the εὐδοκῶν which he uses of God's relationship with the righteous.

[2] *De Inc.* vii., Swete, *l.c.* pp. 295–6.

[3] *C. Apoll.* iii. Fr. 2, Swete, *l.c.* p. 314: cf Eustathius, *Sermo in Prov.* viii. 24, *ap.* Theodoret, *Dial.* ii. 135–6.

[4] *De Inc.* xiii. Fr. 3, Swete, *l.c.* pp. 307–8. Cf. *l.c.* viii. p. 299, xii. 7, p. 306.

effected by the principle of love effects homonymously a union of title, will, energy, authority, majesty, lordship, dignity, power between them which nothing can divorce[1]." "The person constituted by the union is one, yet the natures remain separate; and when we wish to emphasise their separation we can call that of the man or that of the Godhead a perfect whole[2]." "The expression 'union according to essence' is only rightly applied to things coessential: applied to things essentially different it is quite inaccurate for it cannot then escape the sense of confusion. The method of union according to love while preserving the natures unconfused allows an indivisible oneness of person[3]."

We have strung together a number of typical passages so as to present Theodore's Christology in his own words, though his style does not do justice to his thought. The distinction which he means to draw between Jesus and the rest of mankind is certainly none too clear. From his criticism of the belief in essential unity it is plain that the words "as in a Son," which are his formula for the contrast, are not to be taken as implying a physical bond like that which constitutes paternity. Rather he maintains that whereas the indwelling in the saints is a condition dependent at each moment upon their continuance in virtue and so highly precarious and at best, since all men are sinful, imperfect, it is in Jesus a definite and permanent relationship continuous from the very first and establishing a union of the most

[1] *Ep. ad Dommum*, Swete, *l.c.* p. 338. This language is only paralleled in the fragments in that on the Miracles (Swete, *l.c.* p. 339). But the Nestorians afterwards were willing to allow, as Theodore does here, μία θέλησις and μία ἐνέργεια: cf. *Patrol. Orient.* VII. 84.

[2] *De Inc.* viii. Swete, *l.c.* p. 300.

[3] *Ep. ad Dommum*, Swete, *l.c.* p. 339.

intimate kind. Like many modern thinkers, he would seem to believe that it is the sinlessness of Jesus which constitutes His uniqueness and proves Him to be in a union with the Logos distinct from that which other men can reach. We have sinned and thereby through our own rejection have destroyed the completeness of our communion with God: in the Incarnate there has been no break: from the first His conscious life has been spent in open and flawless harmony with His Father. United in perfect love with the Logos the one person of Jesus Christ never does or says or thinks anything at variance with the divine. He reproduces in the fullest measure consistent with life upon earth the whole quality of Godhead. His nature is not human only but divine. He is perfect God; for He is perfectly united with the Logos in the only way in which such union is possible, by perfect love expressed in perfect unity of thought and feeling and will. He is perfect man, having in its fulness that unbroken communion with the Logos which is the crown and glory of humanity. To that extent at least Theodore may claim to be the father of Chalcedon rather than of Nestorianism[1].

No doubt logically, and if the Godhead and manhood in Christ are separated, there is the same dilemma in his thought on the Incarnation as there is in his answer to the determinists. If the Logos dwells in Jesus from the first, the manhood was never unaided and the free choice of virtue is illusory: conversely, if Jesus is free,

[1] The treatment of Theodore by Catholic scholars is interesting. Tixeront, *H.D.* III. pp. 15–22, after a very unbiased examination of his position admits his orthodoxy, and then states that his language is often one-sided and ill-advised and that "he deserved to be condemned if only for his use of expressions liable to heretical interpretation."

there is at least the possibility of a separation between His human will and the Logos, and His divinity is conditional and inspirational. Theodore, hampered as he is by his refusal to challenge the traditional antithesis[1] between God and man as Changeless and changeable, still refuses to surrender either to the Adoptianists or to the Apollinarians. No doubt in the fragments that now represent him, selected from works against Apollinarius by men who wished to convict him of Nestorianism, the emphasis of his teaching is on the human more often than the divine. As a result his work seems one-sided, and in an age when physical metaphors were universal and "impersonal humanity" was an accepted formula he was condemned. But even among the extracts chosen to vindicate the verdict there is evidence of a consistent stress upon the necessity of both aspects. "The union with God the Logos of which He was deemed worthy according to the foreknowledge of the Logos, conferred on Him no ordinary inclination towards good. As soon as ever He could decide between good and evil, He conceived a great hatred for evil and joined Himself with an irresistible affection to goodness; and by receiving the co-operation of the Logos correspondingly with His own determination He was secured continuously without change or deviation towards evil: in the one sense it is because of the bent of His own will, in the other it is because His purpose was secured by the co-operation of the Logos[2]." Here, as elsewhere, he

[1] This is the chief weakness of his theology; for it compels him to separate Godhead and manhood more widely than a modern student would do. Yet his emphasis on the divine love is a long step in the right direction.

[2] *De Inc.* vii., Swete, *l.c.* p. 296. Cf. for an equally clear statement of the correlation between human and divine, *De Inc.* xiv. Fr. 2, Swete, *l.c.* pp. 308–9.

has the courage to refuse an answer to the questions which would drive him to accept one or other alternative. He simply points to the fact that in ordinary men there is the same problem. Logically divine foreknowledge and human freedom may be irreconcilable. Experience tells us that in fact the dilemma is due to our own intellects not to the nature of things.

Jesus is Very Man; Apollinarianism, whether in its technical or its orthodox shape, is false alike to the facts of His life and to the records of the apostolic impression of Him. Brilliant as was the work of the great Laodicene, and ingenious as are the devices by which he substantiated his error, we cannot but admit that the postulates upon which his Hellenic theology was based were mistaken, and that the method of deduction by which it proceeded is no longer possible for us. History not mythology must be our starting-point: we must begin with what we know, rising from the recognition of the Very Man to the acknowledgment and interpretation of the Very God. And Theodore, like his rival dishonoured and condemned by lesser men, may help to show us the way.

INDEX